IN THE
COMPANY
OF
CHAMPIONS

WHAT PEOPLE ARE SAYING ABOUT FRANK LODATO

"Doc was very instrumental in helping me win five Grey Cup Championships, to become the winningest Head Coach in CFL, and to help build many CFL Hall of Famers into Players, Coaches, and Builders. I spoke to Doc once a week until he passed away. Doc was family—a great friend, a great physician/psychologist, a great husband, and he loved his family. He cared for people and was always willing and able to help. He received five Championship Rings and a lot of love and gratitude for his work. He was one of a kind."

— Wally Buono, Head Coach, CFL

"Doc's ace in the hole was that, in addition to possessing a brilliant knowledge of what I call 'the human condition,' he was 100 percent egoless and 100 percent trustworthy. Players and staff could feel it, sense it, and believe in it. As I progressed in my own career, I tried to take Doc everywhere I went . . . Doc's victories far outpaced mine, but I was fortunate to be a part of three championships with him riding shotgun. Nonetheless, I value the man far more than I value the rings. He was a second father to me."

— John Weisbrod, NHL/NBA Executive

"Over the years I saw time and again the fruits of Frank's labor and belief in what he was teaching. It was amazing how it crossed into all types of sports, and while results were never 'guaranteed,' Doc was always pushing, pulling, and prodding to keep the athletes focused. If they were willing to put in the effort, then he was there for them. There were highlights and downturns over our nearly 40-year collaboration. But the one constant was 'the measure of the man': his strength in the face of adversity and pure joy in winning, but enjoying it with grace, unwavering loyalty and friendship, love of family, and tremendous religious belief. I know that his memoir will be a reminder of the true power in [sports] psychology when applied by a conscientious and caring person."

— Nick Beverley, Head Coach, NHL

"I use task analysis in everything I do now. When I talk with younger players, I talk with them about task analysis: `Younger players, if you want to be the best of the best, you need to visualize and understand what the other team is doing and going to do. You need to be able to play the game in your mind.' Doctor Frank made me a better player. We had fun in the times we shared together. He was a very good friend."

— Harry Carson, Linebacker, New York Giants, NFL

"Frank was the best at getting the best out of everyone. Everyone wanted a piece of him to get better. Frank helped the young players who had no direction, even if they were in a slump. I can't thank him enough. It wasn't by accident that the Solar Bears won the championship. He was a big part of it. I wish every sports psychologist could have learned from Frank."

— Curt Fraser, Head Coach, Orlando Solar Bears, AHL

"Doc Frank advised me how to work with the players. He was able to disarm, make everyone comfortable, and have a few words to prompt us to make a change or think about things differently. His idea was your idea. He would compliment me about things I did not expect him to compliment me on, and it lifted me up. He brought out the best in the players. He helped them focus. 'Turn it off when you leave the rink, and then turn it back on when you come back to the rink.' It helped the players show up in a positive and energetic way and to be the best version of themselves. He showed them how to get there. The best teams are those that practice well, and he helped the players do so. He never asked for any credit or a pat on the back. It was always, 'We did it.'"

— Peter Horachek, Head Coach, NHL

"Frank was very important when navigating situations with the Bruins. He taught us a lot about life, how to communicate, and how to respect each other more. He was such a good human being. It is a privilege to have good friends. In Chicago, I met his family in his hotel room, and it was great. He was a tremendous friend and so helpful to us. Loved Frank and it was such an honor. He taught us a lot about sports, leadership, and about life."

— Zee Chára, Boston Bruins, NHL

IN THE
COMPANY
OF
CHAMPIONS

A Pro Sports Psychologist's Adventures in the Halls of Athletic Greatness

Francis J. Lodato, Ph.D.
with **Janice E. Lodato, M.A.**

Publishing support provided by
Ignite Press
55 Shaw Ave. Suite 204
Clovis, CA 93612
www.IgnitePress.us

ISBN: 979-8-9917113-0-2
ISBN: 979-8-9917113-1-9 (E-book)

For bulk purchases and for booking, contact:

Janice Lodato
info@janicelodato.com
www.janicelodato.com

Library of Congress Control Number: 2024922764

Cover design by MotivatedDesign | 99Designs
Edited by Cindy Tschosik and Cathy Cruise
Interior design by Eswari Kamireddy

FIRST EDITION

For my mom, Patricia A. Lodato,
and to all those who selflessly support others in living their dreams.

—Janice E. Lodato

ACKNOWLEDGMENTS

If you knew my father, then you knew it all began with family. His devotion to his family was limitless. So that's where I'll start.

First, I'd like to express heartfelt gratitude to my mother, Patricia Lodato, for her support and encouragement of this project. She made it possible to complete this book that my dad and I started so many years ago. She was also the person who kept everything together at home while my dad chased his dream of becoming a sports psychologist. I know in my heart that he loved her, was eternally grateful to her, and is smiling down from heaven upon her.

Second, I'd like to thank my brother, Ray, and sister, Denise, who supported this project in multiple ways. Ray provided insights into Miami Dolphins' history that was missing from Dad's original manuscript. Denise provided photos of our dad with the Stanley Cup, and I relied on her incredible memory for many details. Thanks, also, to you two for being the best siblings!

Third, my gratitude extends to my husband, Chris Hopper, and our kid. They supported me through the emotional rollercoaster that this manuscript took me on after my father's death and helped me move from emotions to actions that took the book to completion. You both are truly the wind beneath my wings.

As with any book of this size there are many who made it come together. I'd like to thank my editor, Cindy Tschosik. Together, we rode the highs and lows of life, parenthood, and technical glitches to bring this all together in honor of my dad. Cindy, your vision and creativity were exactly what this manuscript needed. A million thanks.

I'd also like to thank Everett O'Keefe and his team at Ignite Press. Your immediate enthusiasm for this book, your professionalism, and your know-how throughout the publishing process provided me with the confidence and drive to finish it.

Thank you to all the athletes and coaches who agreed to be interviewed for this book either over the phone or through email. Your time and stories make this story so special and provide a 360-degree view into how the application of psychology in sports transforms players and teams to win. Thanks also for being willing to give the various psychological techniques a try, even in the early days of my dad's career . . . and thank you for your friendship and kindness. You all meant the world to him.

~Janice E. Lodato, M.A.

CONTENTS

A LETTER FROM DR. FRANCIS J. LODATO

"DOC FRANK"

Dear Reader,

During the years, as I built my sports psychology consulting practice, I was surrounded by winners and was in the "company of champions." Becoming a sports psychologist for winners and champions was a long and windy road fraught with roadblocks that I had to tackle; rules, skills, and vocabulary I had to learn; boundaries I had to maneuver; short-term and long-term relationships I was honored to build; and pure joy at watching the growth of humans and mindsets as players reached their goals, became winners, and, for select players and teams, became champions.

With every goal we set out to achieve, it took hard work, stamina, determination, passion, and will. All in all, despite the hardship and in light of the incredible opportunities and relationships, it was a path worth traveling. As you read my life's work, I hope you learn something you didn't know. Each season, as you are entertained by athletes, I hope that you learn to appreciate their talent and sacrifices; you find compassion and delight in the surprises; you strengthen your own mindset and skill set; you honor the people you love and who love you; and you grow into an even better person, athlete, professional, or sports psychologist than you ever thought possible. Because with a dream, a plan, hard work, determination, and resilience, like the people I worked with, you too will be a winner!

– Doc Frank

PART 1

THE LONG DRIVE TO BECOME A SPORTS PSYCHOLOGIST

CHAPTER 1

IT'S A ROUGH TURF – HUDDLES, HAIL MARYS, AND LONG DRIVES

DOC FRANK'S LESSON
5 DISTINCTIVE CHARACTERISTICS TO BECOME A WINNER

Many individual characteristics separate winners from losers. When one enters a room, one can almost instinctively separate the winners from the losers. Clothes have little or nothing to do with it. Winners exude an aura. Does it come from confidence? Is it a type of smugness? It's hard to say.

One thing is for sure: there is a type of attitude that follows one who is a winner. Winning can become a habit, almost an expectation. Losing can also be contagious, kind of like an infectious disease, one which permeates a team. Through my work with numerous professional athletes, I've recognized five of the most distinct characteristics of those who can be classified as "Winners":

1. Winners know themselves.
2. Winners eliminate self-doubt.
3. Winners are action-oriented.
4. Winners do things effortlessly.
5. Winners are self-sufficient.

PRINCIPLE ONE: WINNERS KNOW THEMSELVES

Winners have insight, set goals, and know the means to attain those goals. Winners have dreams. Winners achieve. Winners can function independently. So if we were to break down the characteristics of winners, we would find the following:

- Winners understand their inner workings.
- Winners understand their needs.
- Winners know the meaning of the goals they set for themselves.
- Winners know the direction they would like to see their life go.
- Winners understand limits.
- Winners always have their eye on the goal.
- Winners understand the concept of effort.
- Winners understand the importance of talent.
- Winners understand the value of work to achieve a goal.

PRINCIPLE TWO: WINNERS ELIMINATE SELF-DOUBT

Those who achieve, those called "winners," exude self-confidence, and that self-confidence is well placed. Knowing themselves and being emotionally secure enough to recognize their shortcomings, they know what they can do to produce. What winners must avoid is incorporating negativity into their makeup, and when that occurs, it produces self-doubt. The temptation to question oneself and one's ability is ever present in the environment. This is particularly true when one experiences failure on any level. The temptation to self-doubt comes from a lack of trust in oneself and in one's abilities. Winners reduce self-doubt when they learn the meaning of the task and possess the means to execute the task. Giving oneself positive and truthful messages is one way to help contribute to success.

PRINCIPLE THREE: WINNERS ARE ACTION ORIENTED— THEY DO THINGS EFFORTLESSLY

Winners work willingly. They appear to do things effortlessly, although in fact, it is not effortless at all. One Sunday, in the sweltering heat of a south Florida autumn, the Miami Dolphins' offensive team noticed how fatigued and depleted their opponents had become. They decided to run the length of the field at the change of sides prior to the start of the fourth quarter. The purpose was to demoralize the opposing unit. It did. It led to another victory. The Dolphins remained undefeated.

Perhaps the cliché that applies here is: "Quitters never win. Winners never quit." When one looks at the accomplishments of successful people, one is amazed at how versatile they are and how diversified their skills and interests. There are many reasons for their successes. The one important factor is the ability to see a task as it is. They neither exaggerate the task nor make a simple task a monumental stumbling block. They don't waffle over the task; they simply do it. While others are trying to decide the next move, winners have already successfully acted.

PRINCIPLE FOUR: WINNERS ARE SELF-SUFFICIENT

Not enough can be said for the need of character in the makeup of a winner. Winners admire good in all its forms. True winners are principled, moral, and ethical. They see more than immediate goals.

Winners are self-sufficient. Winners are integrated whole people, emotionally stable, ethically committed to time-proven ideals, have insight, see the demands of a task, and execute them with efficiency. They are mature, appropriately assertive, and have confidence in their ability once they have realistically appraised it.

INDIVIDUAL CHARACTERISTICS OF WINNERS

- Winners never quit.
- Winners improvise.
- Winners know their limits.
- Winners eliminate self-doubt.
- Winners accept challenges.
- Winners are self-sufficient.

STEP 1
PICK A DREAM, MAKE A PLAN

The year was 1955, 35 years after Coleman Griffith established the first sports psychology lab at the University of Illinois. I had just earned my Ph.D. The ink had hardly dried on my diploma when, almost immediately, I began to wonder if there would ever come a day when psychology would impact sports. At the time, few, if any, sports psychologists existed in the United States.

Griffith's attempts to influence the sports world about the benefits of applying psychology to sports were met with derision among his clients, the Chicago Cubs players. However, iconic Notre Dame football coach Knute Rockne expressed great curiosity. Rockne and Griffith exchanged many letters in hopes of bringing psychology to the Fighting Irish. Little research was available. The sports world was not yet ready for what was to follow.

I, for one, was interested and determined to examine the possibility of applying psychology to sports performance. I had no idea where I was going with this thought or even if it made any sense. Talking with other psychologists, most notably Drs. Ben Alimena and Anthony Summo of Manhattan College, I was pleasantly surprised that they also harbored the same questions. Talking with them made it clear that, once one graduated with a psychology degree in those days, entry into the sports world was not a given.

Many issues blocked the way. First and foremost was the thought harbored by many laypeople that the need for psychological intervention meant you were insane or on the road to insanity.

The mere idea that coaches required someone outside of the organization to help a player's performance might indicate that the coach had failed in his calling. The fact that the sports world was closed to anyone who was seen as an "outsider" did not offer any consolation. In addition, few people knew that each sport had its own culture, traditions, and rituals. All these obstacles, and many others, had to be hurdled before a psychologist was eligible to present himself and was worthy of being interviewed by the sports world. The first steps were apparent for a new doctor of psychology:

1. Learn about the sports environments.
2. Pick one.
3. Hope for the best.

This was the starting point of the journey that led me to assist other practitioners in bringing psychology to the sports world. The trip was far more complicated than I envisioned it to be.

COMMENTARY FROM WALLY BUONO, HEAD COACH, CALGARY STAMPEDERS (CFL)

I met Doc the summer of 1983 at the Olympic Stadium, the Big O, in Montreal. He was on the turf visiting with Joe Galat, who was the GM and head coach on the Montreal Concordes of the CFL. I was the linebacker coach for the Concordes. My first impression of Frank was not favourable! Doc was unshaved, wearing a red flannel lumberjack shirt, and quite gruff in his induction. I left the encounter with not a very positive impression. We joked about that many times because Doc wasn't at all like my first impression.

I really hadn't given any thought to his discipline because I believed psychology and psychologists were not part of a football organization. We had coaches, support staff, players, and medical doctors who took care of the injured and their medical issues. Mental health, as far as I can remember. was a non-issue.

I left Montreal in 1987 and went to Calgary Stampeders to coach linebackers. I became the defensive coordinator in 1988. In 1990 I became director of football operations and head coach. I don't remember the exact date or year, but very early in my tenure in Calgary, Doc became a fixture! He worked very closely with the coaches, players, and our medical staff in dealing with programs and helping everyone to be the best they could be. Doc was with me from the early 1990s to 2018, which was my last season as the VP, GM, and head coach.

Doc was very instrumental in helping me win five Grey Cup Championships, to become the winningest head coach in CFL, and to help build many CFL Hall of Famers in players, coaches, and builders. I spoke to Doc once a week until he passed away. Doc was family, a great friend, a great physician/psychologist, and great husband, and he loved his family. He cared for people and was always willing and able to help. He received five championship rings and a lot of love and gratitude for his work. He was one of a kind. He loved to eat Italian food, pasta, and have a glass of red wine. Grazie!

CHAPTER 2

THE GAME PLAN – ALWAYS ADD VALUE AND MORE VALUE

DOC FRANK'S LESSON
6 PRINCIPLES FOR A STRONG WORK ETHIC

Success can be measured in many different ways. To some people, achieving success is defined as possessing the wherewithal to live in an expensive neighborhood, sending children to private school, taking vacations every spring with frequent interludes to Europe, and always traveling business or first class. Others see success as involving power over other people, control of a company's destiny, invitations to the White House, and never missing an opportunity to pose for an open lens. And still others believe success is the result of hard work that is truly satisfying.

This work ethic is exemplified in the athletic careers of many men and women. This group is our focus. Their type of success can be seen in athletes who play even what can be mistakenly considered a minor role, but still contribute to the success of the team. In football, offensive linemen exemplify those who do an outstanding and important job, and who receive little praise or recognition. They are the straws that stir the drink. Many fans do not even know their names. Nevertheless, without them, little if any success is possible.

In hockey, the athletes are role players. They may be in a game for only a few shifts or may be called upon to take face-offs in a particular zone. Their on-ice minutes are few. Their contributions are monumental.

These people would be as content in leading a junior high school team as they would be coaching a sport in a major college program. They bring to this team the same zest, enthusiasm, and fervor day in and day out. They cherish a victory.

In loss, they search for answers. One thing these athletes have in common is their work ethic.

Let's look at Geordie Kinnear. He played most of his career in Albany, New York, and worked as an assistant coach there with the Albany River Rats. He exemplifies the ideal work ethic. As a player he brought the same intensity to practice as he did to games. As a coach he does the same. He is fiercely competitive, aware of the complexity of his role on the team, and capable of being an outstanding leader—loyal and honest.

Gordon Chiesa, a former assistant coach with the Utah Jazz, has said it clearly: "Practice doesn't make perfect; good practice makes perfect." At first this statement may strike one as silly, but experience will lead us to its underlying truth.

Some amateur athletes and even some professionals practice what they can do well and avoid the tedium of what requires adjustment, concentration, and change. This is not good practice. Young players balk at coaches who want to work on players' shortcomings. Others repeat the same errors each time they practice, like high handicap golfers who are satisfied with swinging poorly time after time in the hopes of accidentally hitting a drive well.

The following components make for a good work ethic:

- A good work ethic has a goal to improve performance.
- A good work ethic focuses on the goal to be achieved.
- A good work ethic can be developed.
- Make room for mental preparation in developing a work ethic.
- Consistency helps develop a work ethic.
- A work ethic can be evaluated.

PRINCIPLE ONE: A GOOD WORK ETHIC HAS A GOAL TO IMPROVE PERFORMANCE

Tiger Woods exemplifies this desire to excel. After an excellent round of golf, he retreats to the practice area to continue to improve. A good work ethic requires the ability to remain focused on the goals at hand. If the goal of a practice session is to correct a slice, then a good session can be measured by the degree to which that slice has been corrected. Positive results must flow from a good practice session. One ethic determines the value of the session. The length of a practice session is less important than the quality of that session.

PRINCIPLE TWO: A GOOD WORK ETHIC FOCUSES ON THE GOAL TO BE ATTAINED

Since one of the goals in applying psychology to sport is to make what is a conscious activity into an unconscious one, repetition of the activity to be improved is essential. However, what is repeated must be as close as possible to perfect execution. Since the neural pathways are also enhanced by perfect visualizations, this activity is an important adjunct to physical practice. Suppose, for example, that it was definitively decided that all sports activity is 20 percent mental. It follows that the person who does no mental preparation is only 80 percent ready to play. One may conclude that the work ethic, properly employed, would find room for mental as well as physical preparation.

PRINCIPLE THREE: A GOOD WORK ETHIC CAN BE DEVELOPED

Obviously, a good work ethic is one that produces the necessary and desired results. The question is, "How does one get to that point?" Analysis of the task to be accomplished helps develop a work ethic:

1. Know what you are trying to achieve.
2. Know what is required in order for you to achieve the stated goal.
3. Budget your time.
4. Evaluate your work ethic daily.
5. Assess your progress honestly.

Work ethics, like personality characteristics, are unique to an individual. If a pattern works for you, produces the desired results, and doesn't hurt anyone else, then it's a good one. If you have improved your performance in fact, not merely in your fantasy, and if others see the improvement you claim, then the work ethic is good for you.

PRINCIPLE FOUR: MAKE ROOM FOR MENTAL PREPARATION IN DEVELOPING A WORK ETHIC

For a work ethic to be effective, it must be consistent. Progress does not come simply from a day in and day out routine. Daily routines that are engaged in with intensity, sweat, and passion bring results. Not only is the required repetition taking place, but the opportunity to think about perfect execution is reinforced.

Some athletes have innate abilities and instincts for some sports. Most have to learn the proper mechanics from square one. Even gifted athletes have to develop a sound work ethic. Wayne Gretzky, Bill Bradley, and Michael Jordan all enhanced their natural abilities by developing a regimen that was productive in helping them improve on their basic skills. Working from the back of the net, the place Gretzky called his office, required peripheral vision and the ability to see the ice. Bradley learned to dribble and shoot while he was blindfolded. Jordan's late game heroics were occasioned by being in excellent physical condition. These were not haphazard occurrences.

PRINCIPLE FIVE: CONSISTENCY HELPS DEVELOP A WORK ETHIC

A good work ethic can be developed. A schedule, a desire, consistency, goals, and determination are all that is required. If something is worth doing, it is worth doing well. Doing an activity well requires a dedication to continue to improve in the execution of the activity, discovering the means that will help one accomplish the task, and employing those means to the full extent of one's abilities. The measure of a person's success can be found in the individual's growth and maturation. The person who continues to make the same mistakes, who shows no ability to improve over yesterday's errors, and who has no track record will never find himself in the winner's circle.

PRINCIPLE SIX: A WORK ETHIC CAN BE EVALUATED

Those whose work ethic is valuable is defined by those who work efficiently, consistently, purposefully, intelligently, and honestly. These are the criteria for evaluating a work ethic. It's easier to develop a work ethic when one understands the task at hand, one's limitations, and one's abilities.

When athletes or others lose sight of their abilities, their performance suffers. They are now asking themselves to do what they are incapable of doing. They may be deceiving themselves. If they are, little evaluation is possible; objective evaluation demands honesty. An effective work ethic produces results because it shows evidence of hard work, goal orientation, and a clear understanding of what one can accomplish and what one expects from the deed being perfected. This is not success that comes from effectively executing a plan that will guarantee personal satisfaction because it comes from the exertion of one's energies toward the achievement of a desired goal. People who position themselves for success are more apt to achieve it than people who are passive viewers of the current scene. A 10th-round draft choice who makes it big might be a rarity. However, the person who marshals all his abilities (mental, physical, and spiritual) stands a better chance at succeeding than the self-important braggart who commits himself to nothing.

If you want to succeed, develop a work ethic that makes sense. Challenge yourself to improve. Look for progress in the viewfinder of an imaginary camera that is focused on your performance. If this is corroborated by someone capable of evaluating your performance, you have succeeded.

STEP 2
A SOLID FOUNDATION BREEDS CAREER LONGEVITY

It has often been said that "all roads lead to Rome." But few roads lead to a career in the National Hockey League, the National Football League, the Women's National Basketball Association, Major League Baseball, the Ladies Professional Golf Association, the Professional Golf Association, the National Basketball Association, the Olympic Teams, or the Premier Soccer leagues. The roads that do are often strewn with the unmarked bodies and broken dreams of those who simply ran out of talent, money, motivation, determination, and stamina. Most of the "wannabes" never get to that road; for them, the door slammed shut early. Those few who make it are either destined for a shining career in a never-ending spotlight or positioned as an "also ran." I was one of those wannabes.

For me, some success on the sandlots of Brooklyn and Queens fanned the flame, but that was not nearly enough. My line drive singles were great, but being small of stature and lacking power at bat resulted in a lack of home runs, which was not great. In the 1930s, it wasn't uncommon to see Major League Baseball scouts at sandlots. They all looked past me after they saw my weak and inaccurate throwing arm. I made a play, snared a ball, then flung it so far off target that even the greatest first baseman could not come up with it. The dream was slowly fading away.

The sports world still called. My second home became Ebbets Field, the home of the Brooklyn Dodgers, even though I experienced my first Major League Baseball game at the "Old House that Ruth Built." It was a doubleheader between the New York Yankees and the Washington Senators.

After that game, I swore I would be a Yankees fan for life. That oath died after I saw my first game played by the boys in Dodger Blue. My loyal promise to the Brooklyn Dodgers also died, partly due to the nefarious actions of the Dodgers' owner, Walter O'Malley. In my opinion, moving a team from Brooklyn to the West

Coast of the United States just for money had to be a sin that cried to heaven for vengeance. My love for baseball died for many years. I not only gave up on the Yankees and the Dodgers; I gave up on baseball.

After many years, my interest returned, but without the passion that had colored my youth. Although I was an avid baseball fan, it didn't overshadow the fact that all competition excited me. I was hooked on the sports milieu; my interest in football, basketball, and hockey started as a series of small fires within me that grew into a roaring, uncontrolled forest fire.

Nevertheless, life goes on, with or without a sports career. College, graduate school, and college teaching took up most of my time. Other than following the men's basketball teams of Manhattan College, St. John's University, and Seton Hall College (women athletes had not yet been recognized nor respected), I spent little time going to sporting events. That didn't mean, in any way, that my infatuation with the sports world had been dampened. It was just hung out to dry.

During graduate studies at Fordham University, and later at St. John's, my curiosity intensified to find a link between psychology and sports performance. I didn't have a clue as to the connection. I knew something was there. What that something was remained a mystery. Once the Ph.D. was earned, I could take a deep breath, exhale, and look toward the future. The second semester after graduating from St. John's, I was offered the opportunity to return to Manhattan College to teach a course in adolescent psychology. I spent my freshman year at Manhattan College, and the opportunity to teach at the college I attended was a dream come true.

There were other benefits for me. Before class, I spent time in the psychology office with fellow professors, Drs. Ben Alimena and Tony Summo. Each day, the world became a better place because we solved all the world's problems before teaching our respective classes. We also broached other topics. The most fascinating to me was psychology in sports. In the late 1940s and throughout the 1950s, psychology in sports was reawakened by forward-looking coaches, including Coach Don Shula of the Miami Dolphins and Coach Tom Landry of the Dallas Cowboys. Both coaches already worked with psychologists: Thomas Tutko, who was also a fellow professor, and Bruce Ogilvie, who was known as the Father of North American Applied Sport Psychology.

Coleman Griffith was also the sports psychologist to the Chicago Cubs, a venture that contributed to driving Griffith away from sports. Some circles consider him to be the Father of Sports Psychology in the US.

In the Psychology Department office at Manhattan College, Summo, Alimena, and I, along with Dr. Fabian Rouke, chair of the Psychology Department at Manhattan College, talked, dreamt, and imagined being contacted by major sports teams for psychological advice. Little did we know that the field of sports psychology would become as important and as competitive as it is today. We didn't only talk. We acted. Summo, Rouke, and I independently did some work with the college's athletes. We didn't know what we were doing, but it was a start. Unfortunately, both Summo and Rouke died early, their dreams unfulfilled. With the help and encouragement of Alimena, I persisted. My first venture with Manhattan basketball players went nowhere. The track men also showed little progress, leading me to step back, move slowly, and try to overcome my ignorance.

Summo and Alimena are owed a deep-felt expression of gratitude from those of us who try to follow in their footsteps. They opened the door for me to enter the sports environment, and I hoped it wouldn't close on me.

THREE KEY MODALITIES

In 1959 Rouke, Summo, Alimena, and I took a workshop in clinical hypnosis provided by the American Society of Clinical Hypnosis (ASCH). There we were fortunate to have been instructed by Milton Ericksen, M.D., who rebirthed the interest of hypnosis in the US. With each workshop my skills improved, along with my confidence. The unlimited potential for the use of hypnosis became obvious to me. How subjects reacted to hypnosis was extremely gratifying, and the results exceeded expectations. Despite the fact that hypnosis was my treatment of choice, I still sought other modalities. I found the Holy Grail in techniques that were newly incorporated in the training of special education teachers. The following three modalities were extremely useful tools and helped round out the picture of how I would build my practice in sports psychology:

1. Task analysis
2. Behavioral rehearsal
3. Hypnosis

Look out, sports world! I was armed for bear. College student athletes were extremely cooperative in offering their time to me as subjects. I worked using whichever psychological tool was available, including:

- Concentration
- Goal setting
- Relaxation
- Visualization

I was at ease with my clinical skills, and now I was also at ease with the tools I amassed to improve athletic performance. Short case studies and book reviews of mine appeared in the *American Journal of Clinical Hypnosis,* for which Milton Erickson served as editor. I began to think that the only thing that limited the use of hypnosis was lack of creativity. I was willing to explore new techniques. I tweaked old ones, researched to the best of my ability, and followed the directions I was given.

INTEGRATING HYPNOSIS

Once again, the ASCH came to the fore. Drs. Alimena, Irv Sector, and Leo Wollman offered criticism of my work, as did Milton Erickson. Not only was this shaping up, but it was also becoming fun. I later served as chair of the ASCH publicity committee for an annual meeting in Miami. Also, I contributed a few book reviews and some case studies in the *American Journal of Clinical Hypnosis.* Attendance at annual meetings was a must for me. Delivering papers on hypnosis and sports during each meeting left me invigorated, motivated, and optimistic. I was becoming part of a movement in two areas: hypnosis and the application of psychology to sports.

After many years of probing, observing, and communicating with people of similar interests, it was all coming together. I realized that the goals were different in each circumstance and complicated. The dimly burning flame began to shed more light. I was beginning to get it. Hallelujah!

Now we were at a crucial next step, and this one was a doozy. Having ideas, skills, and encouragement was great. But if it could not be sold, it was all in vain. Where were the takers?

I remember when the Dodgers were still in Brooklyn they had a pitcher, Rex Barney, who had an incredible but unpredictable fastball. His bases on balls were becoming too common. Someone in the Dodger organization suggested he see a hypnotist. Whether this person was a clinician or not I have no idea. I think the intervention failed to produce the desired results.

Naively, I began to write letters to sports organizations explaining what I had learned and how it would help their respective teams achieve better results. No one answered. My confidence and optimism, which had both reached a pinnacle, slowly eroded. Sometimes being stubborn pays off. I am not sure whether I was being stubborn or doggedly determined, but I was confident I was not turning back now.

At Manhattan College, the coaching staff had changed, along with the administration of the Athletic Department. As fate would have it, I still had my foot in the door; I had many of the athletes in class. They were the keys I needed to open a locked door. My students would tell other athletes that we were trying to emphasize the relationship between psychology and sports performance.

I was at first surprised at the interest level of these athletes. Later I realized athletes are always looking for an edge, and psychology could well be that edge. The basketball players began to recruit track and field athletes. Although not all of them persevered, the few that did helped me learn tons of information about the field I hoped to enter. Alimena kept pushing me; he wouldn't accept my discouragement because he wanted to see applied psychology make a difference. For that and many other things, I am eternally indebted to him.

Progress was slow. Though I could sell the attributes and talents of another person, I was not a good self-promoter. Through a series of unexpected events, I was on leave from Manhattan College and teaching at Barry College. While at Barry, Sister Ann Thomas, the chair of the Education Department, mentioned my name to the president of neighboring Biscayne College, which needed a part-time counselor for their students. Father John Farrell, an Augustinian Priest, hired me. Though I was only on that campus two days a week, those two days were golden. First, I enjoyed working with the Biscayne students. Second, Don Shula became the head coach of the Miami Dolphins. Practices were held at Biscayne College. It was at that time that I met many of the Miami Dolphins players: Mike Kolen, Tim Foley, Earl Morrall, Larry Little (who attended a workshop I ran at Barry College), Curtis Johnson, Dick Anderson, and Nick Buoniconti. Some of these men and their coaches—Bill Arnsparger, Monte Clark, and Mike Scarry—were instrumental in my development.

Years later, after the Miami Dolphins completed their undefeated season, Arnsparger became the head coach of The New York Giants' football team. Foley pled my case and Bill permitted me to be a consultant to the New York Giants. Imagine that a great organization, run by one of the grandest men in sports—Wellington Mara—was going on my resume, which opened other doors for me. A career is more than one consultancy. Being a one-trick pony just doesn't cut it. Anyway, this was a grand beginning. These stories will be enlarged upon. Hang in there. Buckle up. There is much more to follow.

LESSONS LEARNED: WHAT I DIDN'T KNOW

I thought I could just enter the sports world and be welcomed. I would navigate it easily and ultimately be successful. Right! For the most part, this ain't it, kid.

Especially in sports. Fans fantasize about working in sports, but the jobs are the same as they would be on the outside. If you are an accountant, a physician, or a lawyer, you are still doing the same things you would be doing outside of sports. If you are planning a career in sports, you must know that each sport has its own culture, idioms, rituals, and entrance requirements. Visitors are grudgingly permitted.

IF YOU ARE PLANNING ON A CAREER IN SPORTS, YOU MUST KNOW THAT EACH SPORT HAS ITS OWN CULTURE, IDIOMS, RITUALS, AND ENTRANCE REQUIREMENTS. VISITORS ARE GRUDGINGLY PERMITTED.

One seeking a career in the sports world is not welcome until they have completed a circuit, which includes jumping through hoops held loosely together by red tape. And even then, they might not make it. Each sport has its own entrance requirements, whether it be for players, general managers (GMs), or whatever. Once identified with a certain sport, one is immediately identified as a "basketball gal," a "hockey guy," or whoever.

The Orlando Solar Bears, a hockey team in the now defunct International Hockey League, hired a young, bright, hardworking Harvard graduate, John Weisbrod. His hockey experience included winning a championship as a player at Harvard and with the American Hockey League, as well as working as a GM with the Albany River Rats (an affiliate of the New Jersey Devils of the National Hockey League [NHL]).

After a short time, the team's owner, Richard Devos, recognized the leadership qualities of his new hire and put him in charge of the entire sports operation, which included the National Basketball Association (NBA) team the Orlando Magic.

Despite making a daring trade and improving the basketball team with that trade and the subsequent draft, Weisbrod was always referred to as "the hockey guy." He was never fully accepted into the basketball community. His success didn't help change their attitude.

I didn't anticipate that each sport was a world unto itself. Early in my professional life, I was invited by the daughter of a friend of mine to address her soccer team. Being more familiar with basketball at the time, I didn't realize that the action that causes the ball to be put back into play has one expression in basketball and a different one in soccer. I repeatedly mentioned "inbounding the ball." My audience looked at me blankly and, in a few cases, giggled. Inbounding in basketball is known as a "throw-in" in soccer.

While I was adept at testing, interviewing, and counseling, I lacked other techniques, modalities, and disciplines that I needed to be successful in sports. So back to the classroom I went. Under the tutelage of Dr. Samuel Beck at the University of Chicago and Dr. Florence Halpern at Yeshiva University, I honed my Rorschach skills. Numerous conferences with people who were studying learning styles led me back to rereading educational psychology literature. Special education was becoming espoused by educational leaders, and I explored that research as well.

I was invited to attend a workshop conducted primarily by Dr. Milton Erickson in the practice of hypnosis, which proved to be one of the most informative sessions I attended.

Hypnosis became one of my best tools because it was so adaptable. You can tweak it and take ideas from all sources to fit into the circumstances. Fortunately, the newly formed ASCH offered numerous workshops intended to assist practitioners in improving their skills. I attended several of these. Those added years of preparation were time well spent.

From the special education professionals, I was introduced to the topic of "learning styles." If an issue arose and was brought to the attention of the coach involved, the coach would say, "I told them what they should do." That was the way coaches were taught. But teaching methods moved into more sophisticated grounds. When I was with the New York Giants, we drafted a running back who was underperforming in training camp. After working with the player, I suggested a protocol to his coach, Alan Webb:

1. Meet with the player after each practice.
2. Review the practice tape in slow motion.
3. Visually show him what had to be done.
4. Ask him to do it.
5. Monitor his progress.

The coach was successful using this protocol; his running back had a productive season. The chemistry between player and coach was remarkable. Coaches still use the walk-through in their coaching. It seemed to me that those coaches who demanded perfection and repeated the walk-through until it was executed perfectly made more efficient use of the drill than those who were less demanding.

TASK ANALYSIS

Over the years, I began to appreciate the importance of task analysis—breaking a task down into its component parts. Nowhere was this more important than in working with kickers. For instance, the field goal kicker: A successful field goal is a marvel to behold—the precision, the rhythm, the cohesiveness of all the parts, and the execution of the task makes it something special. Fans credit or blame the kicker for the execution. But he is only one part of the equation, which begins with the offensive line being disciplined enough not to draw a penalty.

The following process begins long before the kicker steps onto the field. Hundreds of hours are spent practicing with the intent to kick the football between those two goal posts. There are essentially three people responsible for the nail-biting drama:

1. The long snapper delivers the ball to the holder.
2. The holder must then position laces as he places the ball on the designated spot.
3. The kicker sends the ball through the uprights as the concluding act.

From the stands and through the screen, it looks like a relatively easy assignment. It is anything but. The struggles of the holder to make a bad snap kickable are often overlooked. Yet the satisfactory execution of a field goal is a prime example of the interdependence of one position on the others. If the kick is good, everyone loves the kicker. If the kick is bad, everyone blames the kicker, but there are three players who can be held responsible at any time.

I don't recall exactly how many kickers I have worked with; my guess is about two dozen. Each had his own set of issues. One was obsessed with getting the right holder; he repeatedly asked the special team's coach to change his holder. Another was so intent on punting the ball that he would drop the snap. Kicking the shorter field goal was an adventure to a CFL kicker in contrast to "money-in-the-bank" on longer ones. Kickers use many little gimmicks to build their confidence. Paul McFadden of the Philadelphia Eagles told me of a mind game he used. He would, whenever possible, approach the ball positioned for a field goal from many yards away. He would then fixate on the goalpost as he walked toward it. This produced the illusion that the posts were opening, and he would have a greater area to kick through.

Two areas of utmost importance to me were using hypnotic techniques to enhance visualizations, and a treatment modality that was referred to as "glove anesthesia."

RELAXATION AND VISUALIZATION

During a training camp, I emphasized the importance of relaxation exercises to the team. I made a careless guarantee to them that by using this technique they would resume a healthful sleep, only to find out later that I had omitted one of the most important components of the task. What I had categorically stated would work only succeeded when the subject concentrated on breathing and was not distracted by other thoughts. This affected my credibility with some players, and it taught me to be more precise and inclusive in my subsequent presentations.

Consider visualization. Most people have some idea of what it means to visualize. You may attempt to visualize what the hotel may look like at the resort on your next vacation. Or you may recall, through visualization, the last restaurant you visited. True, this is a type of visualization, but it is not what we are talking about here. The kind of visualization I am referring to is a more complicated, structured entity that includes all the components that lead to the successful completion of a task. Before I suggest visualization to a client, I review with them the steps they must go through in completing a task. Each part of the task analysis must be committed to memory. Then they are ready to begin the visualization process.

When I meet a new group of athletes, I ask them what kind of mental preparation they employ. Many of them reply that they go over the mistakes they made in their last game. In my opinion, this is unequivocally the wrong thing to do. What that does is reinforces the errors and permits them to go deeper into one's unconscious mind. The mistakes will more likely be made again.

I am a believer that visualization is clearer and that the images come to life easier after the client has relaxed through a series of deep breaths. It is important that the images are not a replay of what went wrong or what might go wrong.

In an experiment I did with hockey players, published in the Swedish journal *Hypnos*, I found that players who did prolonged deep breathing before their visualizations found the images to be sharper and more effective. I think the reason for this is, when properly done, the relaxation exercises help them focus and limit the number of distractions that may interfere with producing an effective image. In my opinion, the sharper the image the more effective the visualization. The visualization must always be perfect. No flaws or slipups can be tolerated. In my estimation, a successful visualization always permits the client to see themselves in perfect execution: they always throw the completed pass, or score the winning basket, or make the perfect putt. This approach not only builds confidence, but it is another attempt at making the action repetitive.

The great basketball point guard, Oscar Robertson, claimed that in one year he took thousands of shots in practice. Reps are important in sports. Visualization is another rep. Breathing also has a role to play apart from visualization. Taking a series of deep breaths and releasing them slowly produces a relaxed state of mind when one learns to concentrate on the breathing while avoiding all outside interference. This is a valuable tool in itself. Athletes function in a world replete with distractions: the noise of the crowd, coaches shouting instructions, opposing play-ers trash talking, and the inherent pressure to perform at a high level, all tend to compete with the players' attention. Taking a series of deep breaths during a game, when the opportunity presents itself, permits the competitor to refocus.

BREATHING AND GLOVE ANESTHESIA

Using breathing exercises prior to the employment of the glove anesthesia modal-ity also proved effective. I am reluctant to describe this procedure in detail for fear that persons who have no clinical training may try to employ this technique to the detriment of others. In brief, the technique is used to relieve clients of symptoms they are experiencing physically. I have *never* used this technique without receiving a go-ahead from medical staff, who assured me there was no actual physical basis for the players' symptoms. Here are some examples of successful interventions:

- A hockey player who had recovered from a groin injury but was still re-luctant to return to the lineup was referred to me by the trainer with the blessing of the medical staff. The coaches were becoming impatient and frustrated with the player, and the player agreed to try the treatment pro-posed to him. He returned to the ice after one session of glove anesthesia.
- A player had developed a serious twitch—so serious that he was doing dam-age to his neck muscles. On a road trip on the last day of the regular season, I was asked to intervene. The player was eager to try anything at that point. That night after the game, the coach permitted the players to celebrate the end of the season for an hour before the bus was to leave. During our cele-bration, many players approached me and asked what I had done for their teammate, commenting that he no longer twitched.

This technique, when used professionally under medical supervision, is a valu-able asset for a practitioner to master. After all the extra study and practicing the different modalities, I was now confident and ready to take my place among psy-chologists who chose to work in sports.

As the years passed, and the role of a psychologist working in sports became more accepted, many of the techniques that were foreign to the sports environment became acknowledged as standard practice:

- Coaches now attend seminars on the role that psychology can play in sports.
- Universities have recognized this field by offering graduate programs.

- The stigma requiring a mentally ill diagnosis to engage a psychologist has lessened.

Unfortunately, the progress that has been made over the past 50 years is not as comprehensive as I, for one, had hoped. There are still segments of the sports world that give psychology more lip service than actual respect. Is it a better environment today than when I entered sports? Of course it is. For instance, Olympic committees all over the world now show respect for what their sports psychologists have done, which makes the sports environment less hostile and more congenial for psychologists.

COMMENTARY FROM DAN DORAZIO, OFFENSIVE LINE COACH, BC LIONS (CFL)

I first met Frank during training camp in June 1998. I was the Calgary Stampeders offensive line coach. It was my first job in professional football after previously coaching for 25 years in US college football. My first impression of Frank was one of respect and admiration. He gave you his full attention and carried himself with humility. He had a great ability to listen, seize, and hold firm what he learned about football, and used it for the betterment of those he dealt with.

I always have had a high regard for psychology in sports. Games are won and lost not just by talent and skills of the performers, but more so by what is in their hearts, souls, and minds. There is a very high value placed on being able to psychologically reach your players so as to get them to play at a high level. Over the years we stayed in touch and developed a lasting personal and professional relationship. In the book Thank You Coach written by Angus Reid, a perspective written by Frank went a long way to describe what we shared.

We had many times together, which have made lasting memories. I can remember him standing at practice near my drills, just watching and listening with an intent of introspection. I can remember him getting in front of our team or in front of my group giving them his wisdom. I can remember him on gameday on the bench and what his presence meant to me and others. The significant memories that I cherished most were the following:

- *My wife, Lisa, and I hosted a barbeque at each training camp for our guest coaches and staff. Frank was always there.*

- *We spent many hours sitting around the table or on the deck just talking things over. Listening to Frank was a priceless moment we all enjoyed.*
- *While Lisa and I were in Florida, Frank and Pat invited us to their home for lunch. The afternoon we shared together was the highlight of our trip because of Pat and Frank's hospitality and graciousness.*

Finally, I add, going to Holy Mass together on road trips brought out Frank's spirituality as a big influence on me to allow my faith to grow. We will always miss his influence and presence, along with Frank being the man he was.

COMMENTARY FROM JIM PAEK
ASSISTANT COACH, GRAND RAPIDS GRIFFINS (NHL)

I first met Doc when I was assistant coach with the Grand Rapids Griffins, a farm team for the Detroit Red Wings. It seems like many years ago. We had a mixture of old and impressionable young players to develop for the NHL. When I was a player, I used visualization and relaxation techniques to help me with my game. I truly believed in the positive mindset to help in my preparation and to build confidence. So when I heard Doc was going to come and help our players, I was very interested. When I first shook his hand, he had my instant respect for all of his accomplishments. I was honored to meet him. The more we met and had conversations, my respect for him grew. I understood why he was a champion.

We lost touch for a few years until I had a job with the Korean National Team to prepare them for the 2018 Winter Olympics. I reached out to Doc for some advice. He was always willing to help, even though I was halfway around the world. I still have his email reply:

About Mental Toughness: this is the hard part. It is difficult to teach and hard to change. But I have had some success, though limited, by trying this method.

1. **Learn from the Best.** Get tapes—audio or video—of mentally tough players. Here are three examples from Boston:

    a. Tim Thomas challenged shooters after they scored on him.

    b. Patrice Bergeron played with broken ribs.

    c. Gregory Campbell finished a shift with multiple fractures of his leg.

    Play these bits over and over for the players. Elicit comments and comparisons from them. Then put it to bed for a time. And then play it again. Repeat the sessions periodically.

- **Breathing.** Breathing exercises should begin immediately. Tell the players to get comfortable, close their eyes, and get relaxed. Have them repeat this daily for two weeks.
- **Documenting.** Have them keep a log for each session: how long it takes to get relaxed, time, and number of breaths.
- **Individual Goal Setting.** Give them the material I sent you. Have each player set goals for each shift. Most of their goals will be too complex. One shot, one good pass, or one hit. And one off the ice, even.
- **Position Goal Setting.** Then have your forwards set goals for their line each shift. Defense ice pairings also. Evaluate practice and games. A shift where the goals are met is a plus–where they are not, a minus. These are good starting points for you.

I still use the material he sent me with my teams. Putting all the mental stuff aside, my fondest memory of Dr. Lodato was sharing a dinner of Mexican mole–friends who were having casual conversation. I think that was his secret: trust. I was very fond of Dr. Frank Lodato, and I hope his works will continue. I know they will continue with me.

CHAPTER 3

IF YOU CAN'T "BE" THEM, BUILD THEM – IT'S ALL ABOUT RELATIONSHIPS

DOC FRANK'S LESSON
5 PRINCIPLES OF BUILDING AND NURTURING RELATIONSHIPS

Many adults who participate in some form of counseling do so because of difficulty in establishing and maintaining relationships. Often, we are forced to enter into relationships that we would not freely choose. For example, college freshmen have little choice as to who their roommates will be. Workers rarely can choose their workmates, and players cannot choose their teammates. There are six principles that will help establish relationships:

1. Know the level of relationship you are seeking.
2. Be loyal in relationships.
3. Know what you are willing to give.
4. Know what you expect in return.
5. Know the limits that exist in establishing a relationship.
6. Avoid permitting relations to distract you from achieving your goals.

PRINCIPLE ONE: KNOW THE LEVEL OF RELATIONSHIP YOU ARE SEEKING

Three days after Doug Flutie arrived in Calgary for the Stampeders training camp, he was the undisputed leader of the team. Traded from the British Columbia Lions,

Flutie was to replace the ever-popular Danny Barrett. Danny not only had been a team leader but also had been voted by his teammates as the MVP of the Stamps. Barrett had all the attributes required of a starting quarterback in the CFL. He brought with it not only a sense of belonging, but a type of pride in participation. Each unit was made to feel that it had something to contribute.

Stepping in for him would be no mean feat. But Flutie did it and did it well.

One way he did it was by demonstrating to his fellow Stampeders that he was in excellent shape, running with the fastest of them. After that, his football savvy came through immediately. Flutie possessed a better-than-average arm, but his real assets were to be found in his head, his heart, and his feet.

The talk of training camp soon turned to Flutie, his competitiveness, and his instincts for the game. Victories and dramatic finishes have characterized Flutie's career. His tenure in Calgary would be no different. The first few days in camp helped establish Flutie as not only the starting quarterback (QB), but also the emotional team leader. Not only did Flutie have to overcome the problem of replacing the popular Danny Barrett, but he was also a marquee player, a distinction created to enable star players to earn considerably more than the rest of the players so that they would stay in the CFL.

Many people around the Stamps organization, including several players, felt that they were never out of the game as long as Flutie had one more chance to score. This confidence in their offensive leader, and the strong defense that characterizes Wally Buono-coached teams, made the Stamps a power to be reckoned with, and one that would amass many winning seasons.

Many teams have tried to promote the concept of family to establish a feeling of camaraderie and closeness. The Pittsburgh Pirates, during their World Series-winning season, pushed the concept of family. Camaraderie extended beyond the playing field. Players were made to feel that they had a role in each victory.

Fans may often overlook the closeness that athletes are forced to adopt with one another over the course of a season. Long road trips, half the season on the road, practicing, playing, eating, traveling, recreating, and resting—all are done in an almost lock-step fashion. Athletes, like so many other people, are forced to spend time with people they might ordinarily avoid. Competition, jealousy, envy, or even animosity are not foreign in the world of sports. Ethnic, racial, religious, and cultural differences all play a role in achieving team harmony.

Relationships are difficult on all levels. The majority of adults who seek counseling do so because they have impaired interpersonal relationships. Relationships may go sour for a myriad of reasons: financial differences, feelings of inferiority, romantic interests, stress, and personality clashes. Relationships that go sour may impede an athlete who is on the express lane to success. Unless one withdraws to the hills and chooses to live in a cave, relationships are essential.

One thing a successful athlete must do is learn how to best understand his situation. Since so many different levels of relationships exist, one must distinguish among them. Not every acquaintance needs to become a bosom buddy. Some relationships cease at the end of the workday. Others may continue on. Teenagers confuse these distinctions. Mature adults should recognize them and act accordingly. True, some circumstances bind men and women more closely than others. Winning a championship has that binding effect.

Surviving a battle in war may produce an even stronger bond. In these circumstances, a man's interdependence on his fellow man cannot be denied. Here the main principle still applies. There are many levels of bonding with another person, and these levels are undoubtedly determined by our need at the time. Recognizing what one expects from a friendship, and the limits that are to be imposed on one, is of utmost importance. Ask the following questions: What do I want from this relationship? Do I merely want to bask in another's achievements? Am I manipulating others for my own good? Am I capable of liking this person for who he is rather than what he represents?

PRINCIPLE TWO: BE LOYAL IN RELATIONSHIPS

One may latch onto another player or worker because of the prestige that surrounds the other person. Entry into places otherwise barred to an individual may open through a particular relationship. Rookies may find themselves in the company of their childhood idols and find that the adulation they once had for this person was unwarranted.

Seeing and knowing people in different relationships may change one's attitude toward that person. Some young players eager to make it to the "big time" often spend many hours with trainers, equipment managers, and members of the sports medicine team. Then, once they achieve their goal of advancing to the next step, they quickly forget the support staff. Often these players find functioning difficult on the higher level because they have underestimated the attention they received from minor league support staff.

One notable exception to this scenario is ex-New York Giants linebacker Harry Carson. Almost 20 years later, Carson still acknowledges the help given him by the support staff when he was an insecure rookie. Paul Fenton from the Nashville Predators; Kenny Baumgartner, a former assistant coach with the Boston Bruins; and Allen Pitts, the holder of the most receiving records in the CFL, all remember the many people who helped them on the way to the top. Perhaps the most stunning examples of player loyalty exists in hockey on all levels. A tough player coming to the aid of a weaker player always demonstrates the existence of good personal relationships and of good team chemistry.

PRINCIPLE THREE: KNOW WHAT YOU ARE WILLING TO GIVE; KNOW WHAT YOU EXPECT IN RETURN

Suspicion and lack of trust do more to destroy relationships than any other factors. Consciously or otherwise, one may see in others a threat. An aging athlete may feel that the rookie is slated to replace him and may view this younger prospect as a threat to his job. There may be some truth to this feeling. There also may be some lack of self-confidence. Each situation must be evaluated.

Once the relationship in that particular situation is understood, it becomes less of a distraction or a hindrance to performance. You must try to understand what a relationship means to you and what it means to the other person involved in the relationship. Try to be as astute as possible in judging the person you are attempting to involve in a relationship. Know what you can tolerate. Your need to nurture may confuse the relationship. The person you are leading may become too dependent, causing you to flee from him. The reverse of that is also true. You may enter into a relationship with someone you wish to depend on only to find that you are being smothered.

PRINCIPLE FOUR: KNOW THE LIMITS THAT EXIST IN ESTABLISHING RELATIONSHIPS

When one looks at the many roles one is forced to play in life—daughter, wife, mother, executive, teacher, lawyer, physician, or whatever—it becomes clear that the types of relationships one has may be tempered by one's role. The person who leads must show a degree of maturity, sound judgment, emotional balance, energy, and enthusiasm. The person who follows must show signs of loyalty, trust, and cooperation as well as a respect for authority. For example, in the sports milieu, some malcontents who have the ear of the owner or general manager may cause a coach to be fired. Lower-level employees may also have the same clout in industry. The problem here is that the disgruntled few may be registering their own selfish protests, or the trust in the leader may have eroded. Most likely, the same result will ensue: the person in charge will be replaced. Basically, these illustrate the flaws in interpersonal relationships, which change according to circumstances.

Second-guessing, whether it be done by athletes, coaches, trainers, or psychologists, makes for a poor emotional environment.

PRINCIPLE FIVE: AVOID PERMITTING RELATIONSHIPS FROM DISTRACTING YOU FROM YOUR GOAL

Relationships, when they are going badly, or even if they are going well, may distract from a performance. Athletes cannot permit the behavior of coaches, fans, family, or friends to hinder their performance. Basketball coaches who parade up and down the sidelines shouting instructions to their players would sometimes do better just to sit down. The players should have been prepared before the game began. Coaches who consider themselves motivational gurus find that what works the first year gets old the second, third, fourth, and fifth years. These coaches might be better off on the college level where personnel changes occur more regularly.

Fans immediately assume that a team playing at home automatically has an advantage. This assumption may not be valid. Sometimes practice for the visiting teams are more focused because they don't have the distractions of being at home. They have been playing hockey or baseball and living their sports almost exclusively. When they are home, the ordinary foibles of life occur. These include everything from arguments with a spouse to squabbles with children. Even paying bills or cutting the grass may distract players from having the home court advantage. The greater the ability of a person to focus, the less relationships become a distraction to them.

After all is said about relationships, questions still remain. Obviously, no normal life can be lived without relationships. The secret is to know what you want from them, to know what you are capable of giving to them, and to avoid the pitfalls of suspicion, lack of trust, and the normal conflicts that arise between you and particular personality types.

An experience I had many years ago with the Calgary Stampeders may shed some light on this matter. I was traveling with the team during training camp. When we returned to Calgary, Wally Buono, the winningest coach in Canadian football history, noticed there was some dissension on the defensive team. Three of the veteran players with varying degrees of experience were constantly ragging at one another. What at first appeared to be good-natured ribbing was far more serious than that. Wally asked if there was something that could be done to alleviate the situation since it was becoming a distraction to the other players as well as to the three players involved.

In my bag of tricks, I have a technique I have used over the years—one that many of my coaches have used and continue to use successfully. I don't know if I learned this from someone or whether it is a hybrid of many experiences lumped into one. It really doesn't matter. Buono wanted to be present when we applied the technique. I was extremely happy about his presence.

We sat the defensive players around in a circle, each player choosing his own seat. We made no reference to the fact that we were aware that a relationship problem had emerged. We introduced the notion that each player in the room, if asked, could point out each of the other players' strengths and weaknesses. We were careful that our focus would be positive and that we expected the players to approach their contributions in a positive fashion. After acknowledging the fact that the players were aware of the contributions of the other players, we then asked each player to look at the man next to him and make a statement that would help the player become a better player. There was some initial reluctance.

After a short while the players got into the spirit of the exercise. The meeting lasted over two hours. The three offending players, after listening to some of the younger players comment on how bickering during practice—and especially during games—affected their play, took on a new demeanor. Obviously, the entire problem was not solved, but the air was cleared. The offending players, even though they had never been singled out by us (the coaches), began to understand how their behavior was hurting the team's performance.

After the players left the room, Wally said to me, "I never thought that would work."

I replied, "If I didn't think it would work, I'd have never tried it."

STEP 3
GREAT RELATIONSHIPS ARE TIMELESS

As confident and professionally prepared as I was to consult with a sports team, I was also gripped with feelings of insecurity. I knew I didn't know enough about the sports environment. My experience as an aspiring athlete was limited to pickup games and sandlot baseball where last week's rivals were this week's teammates. There was no coaching, no opportunity to correct errors in techniques. In reality, my athletic experience was zilch. How could I learn about a sport without having been in it?

One way was to pick a sport and try to learn something about the culture, the nuances, and the people who were and are significant to it. As limited as this was, it was a realistic starting point. I also knew that my scope had to be limited to a local area. It was then that I decided on basketball as the sport, and the New York Metropolitan area as the place.

As a college student, I was a rabid fan of the St. John's College men's basketball team. I hung out with the players who were my classmates. I attended practices, and even went to most home games. We discussed the ups and downs of the team whenever I had the opportunity, and stayed in touch with basketball people. But that was not nearly enough. I had never been at a team meeting, traveled on the team bus, or experienced the bumps and the grind of an organized practice. The ire of a coach was never directed at me. The experience of winning a championship, or of losing a deciding game in one, escaped me. I had always been on the outside looking in. But I felt as slim an opportunity as it was, I wanted to think I had a foot in the door.

The angst, the uncertainty, and the unknown would have been unnecessary if I had known I wanted to work in sports. I might have looked for a program in sports psychology, which would have made my career path a little easier. Back then there was not a proliferation of graduate programs in the field as there is today.

RESEARCH = PREPAREDNESS

Research was something I was reluctant to do, but that had become essential. I did not know the depth of learning I had to dive into to establish and achieve a long-lasting career. In my initial research I discovered:

- There were over 300 men's basketball teams in Division One in the NCAA.
- Women's basketball and women's sports, in general, had a small place in the upper tiers of college sports.

At first, this knowledge seemed of little importance, and looking at it more close-ly, it contained information some would say was useless. However, it revealed bits and pieces of trivia that were not only pertinent but applicable to all other sports.

All the teams were classified under one umbrella, while at the same time each was unique to the other. In terms of status and success, all teams were not equal. To me, this meant that what was successful with one group might not be appropriate for another. One size did not fit all. Each team had its own needs. You couldn't, if you were a serious professional, simply reach into the files, pull out last year's team proposal, and apply that to the new team. The effort to pull together the individual proposal would pay off despite the fact that it was not monumental.

THE IMPORTANCE OF TRADITIONS AND HISTORY

I found that no degree of study provided me with the information that only came from experience. Continuing education would never end. Teams changed. Players changed. Environments changed. Even from the outside, it was evident that tra-dition was extremely important to some teams. Because of their dominance over many years, the New York Yankees, Boston Celtics, Montreal Canadians, and Notre Dame football were examples of teams who knew that their history and traditions mattered. If I was to work for those teams, I needed to know that about each team. I was curious to uncover how many other teams also had rich pasts. The traditions of powerhouse programs were easier to uncover. The smaller schools were much more difficult. This is where limiting the search to a small area paid off.

FOLLOWING THE BOUNCING BALL

It was a long and arduous road to land a team consultancy role in basketball. In 1957 I witnessed the relationship of how psychology could and did impact athletic performance, primarily with Manhattan College basketball players.

In 1993 I began a consultancy with the Manhattan College Lady Jaspers. The resume of their head coach was impressive. She had won with every team she coached. The Lady Jaspers were in a rebuilding mode. They had the perfect coach for it. However, off the court, the humanitarian activities of Michele Sharp were also impressive. An article by Vincent M. Mallozzi on March 19, 1995, "Basketball: Far Above and Beyond the Call of Coaching," described her generosity and unself-ishness in detail. Our association resulted in a Metro Atlantic Athletic Conference (MAAC) Championship and a lasting friendship.

A run with a National Association of Intercollegiate Athletics (NAIA) basketball team, Northwood University, led by Hall of Fame Coach Rollie Massimino, resulted in a championship ring. Northwood became Keiser University and Massimino continued coaching until his death, even though his body was rapidly deteriorating due to numerous cancers.

Later, two stints in the NBA with the Orlando Magic permitted me the opportunity to get to know Patrick Ewing at the end of his playing days and NBA legends Steve Francis, Johnny Davis (the master of the fast break), Paul Westhead, Chris Jent, Clifford Ray, and Doc Rivers.

As previously mentioned in 1957, two years after I was awarded a Ph.D. from St John's University, Manhattan College offered me the opportunity to teach an adolescent psychology course to its physical education students, most of whom were either varsity basketball players or track athletes. In that class there was a junior basketball player, Jack Powers, who was destined to become an icon, not only at Manhattan College but in basketball circles throughout the New York Metropolitan area. His enthusiasm for what I was doing encouraged other athletes to get on board.

KNOW YOUR HISTORY

Some bits of the history of college basketball around New York City would certainly prove important, and they were. This was another area where research paid off. There were many changes in the sports world of college basketball from the time I was a student to the time I was seeking employment. In the 1940s, the prestigious college postseason basketball tournament was the National Invitation Tournament (NIT). The National College Athletics Association (NCAA) tournament existed, but in our minds, it was of less importance. As implausible as it sounds today, it was also possible for a college team to play in both tournaments. As students, we felt that our school should only participate in the NIT. City College of New York (CCNY), led by legendary basketball coach Nat Holman, who was a teammate of Joe Lapchick (the St. John's coach), not only took advantage of playing in both tournaments, but won both titles in the same month. The moment of greatness, the limelight shining brightly upon them, would soon be tarnished.

In the early 1950s, seven City College players were accused of shaving points to assist bookies to cover the point spread. This scandal infected other major colleges. It also erased CCNY from Division 1. New York University, Long Island University, and Manhattan College student athletes were also inflicted by the greed of earning some quick cash. The scandal spread to other colleges. The repercussions were great beyond college campuses and impacted the economy of New York

City. The NCAA decided to punish the Metropolitan area of New York for the transgression of some players. No NCAA Final Four Tournament would be held at what was then the "Old Garden." These sanctions lasted many years.

As implausible as it may sound, these facts were of utmost importance to my career. They helped me to understand why teams spent several sessions attending seminars with law enforcement agents, members of the narcotics squads, and the bureaus that oversaw sports betting. I was at first annoyed, then bored, when I first sat in on these sessions. But as the sessions progressed and the ties to the history of betting in that sport became more relevant, I learned that my attendance was essential if I was to be effective in my trade.

NEVER SAY DIE

Though the future of college basketball in New York City seemed bleak at best in the 1950s, there was a moment that would rekindle the flame and help to reinstate basketball to a place of prominence. I, along with other college basketball fans, reveled in the moment in 1958 when Manhattan College was scheduled to compete against West Virginia at Madison Square Garden. No one gave Manhattan College a chance. In fact, many fans of the West Virginia team skipped the game, thinking it would be a laugher.

But the Jaspers of Manhattan College were not to be denied. Jack Powers, of the team from Riverdale, New York, along with his teammates, considered Madison Square Garden to be home court. They played accordingly. Fans were certain that the local team could not contain Jerry West, West Virginia's superstar. To the delight of Jasper fans and the dismay of all other viewers, the game was a squeaker. This was thanks to the efforts of Jack Powers, who scored 29 points and had 15 rebounds. His roommate, Dick Wilbur, held Jerry West to 12 points and a low shooting percentage (5 for 12) from the floor. Manhattan prevailed 89-84.

There was joy in Gotham that night. Jack Powers became a Manhattan College legend that day. His dogged tenacity and his "never say die" attitude all contributed to the culture that, for many years, became the trademark of Jasper basketball. I learned that each sports program had its own icon. He later coached the Jaspers, where he brought with him the fire and thunder necessary to compete. At the end of his coaching career, he became the athletic director at Manhattan College and then the executive director of the NIT. This was one area where pre-information helped again. There were many changes in the sports world of college basketball from the time I was a student to the time I was seeking employment. The making of a psychologist who aspired to ply his trade to sports was far more complicated than I thought it would be. Each day brought with it a new challenge. Remember, in the 1950s this was a budding part of the psychological realm. The knowledge I acquired about basketball was pivotal to my preparation, even though I didn't work in basketball until later in my career.

Something I didn't realize was that the role of a psychologist in sports would raise some serious problems, both ethical and logistical. This fact caused me, with the help of my daughter, Janice (who was teaching ethics at the time), to present an early ethical model for psychologists who practiced in the sports environment. When I was trained, we were taught that the counseling session would be conducted under near-ideal conditions, in a private, relatively soundproof space, offering comfort and anonymity. I was to find out later this was not the case.

When I first started to consult in sports at Manhattan College, I had the privacy of my own office. Students came and left, and no one questioned why they were there. Naively, this is what I expected to find in the bigger sports world. It was quite different. Confidentiality is treated as a serious matter in the training of a psychologist. Team management was the employer, the athlete the patient. Management's expectation in terms of feedback differed from team to team. This issue caused athletes to be reluctant to bare their most intimate feelings to someone who was employed by management. This suspicion causes today's athletes to be cautious as to their involvement with consultants. Some athletes have experienced circumstances that have been painful to them. Understandably, they don't want to be vulnerable.

In my first consultancy, I was at times offered a coach's office; most of the other times my sessions took place seated next to a player on the team bus, in the stands of the arena, on a plane, at a player's locker, or in whatever makeshift space was available. I rationalized it away by thinking that not all surgeons performed operations in sanitary operating rooms; some were required to ply their trade on battlefields and roadsides. I never had a space to call my own in all my years of working with sports teams. But this was not a unique experience; it also happened to me when I was functioning as a school psychologist.

My colleagues and I used to joke about being assigned to either a broom closet or a storage space. Welcome to the real world, which in many ways differs from the ideal one in which we were trained. I had a good idea of how psychologists, in general, were perceived; in my earlier days, they were either deified or demonized. Of how a psychologist working in sports was perceived, I had little knowledge. Additionally, I was unsure about how I wanted to be perceived. Was it as a clinician who did "shrink stuff," or a person who could help a player improve performance? Intuitively, I knew there had to be boundaries. What they were, I was not sure. Do you go in and be the hail-fellow-well-met, or do you go in and deliver an esoteric lecture that was destined to isolate you? Neither option seemed viable.

Over the years, I learned to adapt to a variety of situations. I met some environments in which I and my work were ridiculed. In others, my work thrived on the players' curiosity, some ignoring me and being hostile, and some sincerely interested in what I was selling. There are many things I wish I knew then that I learned later, sometimes too late. After I had blundered into an awkward situation, I got the message.

When I was a consultant to the Orlando Magic, my second tenure, I traveled to New York on the team plane. On previous flights I had been assigned a seat and everything went smoothly. On this flight I was neither given instructions nor information about the changes made concerning team travel. I was completely unaware that an incident had occurred on the plane and that the players had demanded their own space. I boarded the plane in Orlando and took a seat in the section I normally sat in. Before long, I was informed that the section was now reserved for players and that I was to find another seat. There is no training in preparing for this type of situation. The fact that I was not taken too seriously by some players and staff had already been obvious. This did nothing to enhance my image.

Another incident that occurred because I had not been kept up-to-date from visit to visit was even more embarrassing. I met the Calgary Stampeders team of the CFL at the airport in Ottawa two days before our game. One of the team's doctors, Peter McMurtry, had family in Ottawa and he religiously made the trip from Calgary to Ottawa. As I took my seat on the bus, I noticed he was not present, but had been replaced by another doctor. I shouted out, "You must have had to murder Mac in order to make this trip." Suddenly the bus went silent. I laughingly sat down next to one of the coaches who nudged me and said, "We buried McMurtry on Thursday." It took the entire bus ride to get my foot out of my mouth.

AVOID THE PITFALLS

My missteps demonstrated to me that one needed to be brought up-to-date from visit to visit. From then on, I learned to be informed before I met each team. Potential pitfalls began to emerge. One was the team's locker room; the other, the training room. I never thought that the training room would be one of my most popular meeting places. My ignorance about both was unending. The locker room was more than a place where athletes changed from street clothes to uniforms. The training room was more than a place to be taped, treated, and offered Tums.

**IF YOU ASSUME THAT YOU ARE WELCOME IN A TEAM LOCK-
ER ROOM, THINK AGAIN. HAVING SOMEONE AROUND
WHO WAS HIRED BY MANAGEMENT, BUT WHO HAS NOT YET
EARNED THEIR SPURS, IS NOT A GIVEN. YOU HAVE TO TRY
TO EARN THE TRUST OF THE TEAM.**

If you assume that you are welcome in a team locker room, think again. Some coaches and GMs prepare their teams by introducing the psychologist to the group. They may even say that the psychologist has permission to enter the locker room, the exercise room, or wherever. I learned that this did not sit too well with players on some teams. I learned in my later years to ask the team captain to poll the players to determine if my presence in the locker room made them uncomfortable.

Despite the casual way the locker room is treated by management, it is sacrosanct to players. They horse around together, complain about the coaches, and tell stories about their dates, children, plans for the future, anxieties, and hopes. Having someone around who was hired by management, but who has not yet earned their spurs, is not a given. You have to try to earn the trust of the team. On some teams, this was impossible. I was in locker rooms where I was cleared by the players and still noticed that conversations abruptly stopped or changed because I was within earshot of the speaker.

The training room is different. Players sometimes welcome the opportunity to talk while being treated. Conversation sometimes makes the boredom of being attached to a stimulator more tolerable.

THE TRAINING ROOM

Before I began my career in sports, it would have been nice to understand the importance of the trainers' room. Many times, the tone of the day was set there. The tenor of that room often carried over into practice. It often is the first gathering place of the day for players and staff. The gathering of older men, mostly Cuban-born, on Calle Ocho in Little Havana in Miami, reminded me of a trainer's room on any given morning.

Early each day before most personnel arrive, the trainer is either getting ready to work or is already at work. These dedicated men and women play an essential role in bringing about team success. They prepare a well-designed treatment plan for each player who will visit for treatment. They know to expect the revelation of new symptoms. They also understand the need for making cold remedies available, as well as a supply of Tums, with no questions asked.

Trainers are on call 24 hours a day, either at home or on the road. Their work requires a high level of skill and an even higher level of integrity. They handle the subtle pressure of making a player available as soon as possible, which sometimes contrasts with the welfare of the player. The trainers I worked with were equal to the challenge. I regret that I don't remember the names of all of them. Here are but a few:

- Johnny Johnson was a longtime trainer for the New York Giants and the Manhattan College Jaspers who treated more knees and sprains than even he could keep track of. If he is not already in, he belongs in everyone's Hall of Fame.
- Scott Green, with whom I worked on several teams, began a brilliant career in New Haven, Connecticut, and went on to achieve success with many NHL teams.
- Don DelNegro of the Boston Bruins was a pleasure to be around. His professionalism, sense of humor, and dedication to his job made him one of my favorites.
- Pete Demers of the LA Kings helped me respect the work of all trainers.
- Lisa Toscano was exemplary in helping to pave the path for women trainers. One of the assignments I worked at Manhattan College was as a faculty moderator of the Women's Club Basketball Team. Lisa was one of our student stars, scoring the winning points in our victory, which enabled us to claim bragging rights for winning our conference. She went on to be a skillful trainer.
- Dave DeNovi, formerly with the Florida Panthers, was an outstanding practitioner who did not survive the house cleaning.
- Pat Clayton of the Calgary Stampeders was as devoted to his work as a Trappist Monk reciting lauds and matins. Clayton's willingness to help and his sense of humor helped lighten up the sometimes somber tone of the training room.
- Bill Reichelt of the BC Lions was always on hand, as the arthritis in my feet made walking difficult for me. His approach to the players was professional, friendly, and effective. Time spent with him was profitable and fun.

To all the others, thanks! You made my job easier.

In Boston, Calgary, Los Angeles, or British Columbia, a typical day around the training room went something like this: The trainers were set up for work. Each player, as he passed by, either simply said, "Good morning," or informed the trainer that the appointment was not forgotten and would be honored shortly. Some players milled about the room, talking to injured players, passing the time of day. Hangers-on like myself often frequented the room. The patience of these trainers in trying to apply their trade amidst the distractions was remarkable.

Conversations ranged from inquiries about family members to happenings around the league, or trying to discern truth from fiction in the latest gossip. Coaches would pop in to say hello, PR people went in and out, trying to gain information to give to the media during their early briefing. The bonding value of the training room was almost as important as the treatment. The heating pads, stimulation, rubdowns with exotic ointments, encouraging words from the person in charge of the room, and the TLC made rehab more palatable.

Trainers, take a long, profound bow. You and your work merit the praise you receive from grateful players who know the impact you have had on their lives, and set the standards high. Despite being unsung and probably underpaid, we couldn't do it without you. Without you, we are nothing. Your work is hard, the hours long, and your skills are many, which has led to the enormous success each of you has achieved, and has played an integral part in the success of the teams. Thanks, Thanks, Thanks.

NO ROOM FOR FRIENDS

ANOTHER MISTAKE THAT IS EASY TO MAKE IS TO THINK YOU ARE THE PLAYER'S "FRIEND." THEY MAY BE FRIENDLY TO YOU, BUT YOU ARE NOT THEIR FRIEND.

A common mistake that is easy to make is to think you are the player's "friend." They may be friendly to you, but you are not their friend. The differences between consultant and player are significant—age and financial status being the greatest barriers. If by chance a close relationship between consultant and athlete lasts, that is a bonus, not the norm. There are so many things I wish I had known during my period of continuing education that I never even considered.

Not only are we not the players' friends; we are not their teammates. When we overstep our role and consider ourselves a teammate, we are forcing ourselves into an area in which we are not welcome. Players have ridiculed nonplayers who consider themselves teammates. Players can accept the fact that we are all members of the same organization, the same team, but we each have different roles. Players put their bodies on the line at each practice and each game; nonplayers do not. As I matured and understood the sports scene better, I learned to appreciate the magnitude of the effort players make. After each ring ceremony, for which I was happy to participate, I made it a point to congratulate and thank the players for their effort and their achievements. After all, the victory was about them. If they don't execute to the max, there is no championship. Remember, it is about the players, not the consultant.

In one of my early consultancies, I heard a coach tell his players that members of the media were not their friends. I found out later that this attitude was a change from the past. Earlier, players and reporters mingled together, ate together, went to movies, and played cards. Because of this, reporters were more inclined to be protective of players' information than to disseminate it. This gave the players a feeling of trust and comfort.

However, as players' salaries started a trip into orbit while the salary of reporters rose only slightly, the disparities widened. The "we and they" attitude gradually took hold, and the peccadillos of the players became fair grounds for revelation. Hence, the attitude of caution was sounded to the players. The message was loud and clear: "Watch what you say to the press." There were, and are, so many lessons to be learned. My list only scratches the surface. I hope this clarifies some of the pitfalls facing a new consultant. No matter how much I probed or how exhaustive the search was, it could never be complete. I had to be satisfied with what was uncovered and be alert about what might follow.

COMMENTARY FROM JOHN WEISBROD
ASSISTANT GM, VANCOUVER CANUCKS (NHL)

I first met Doc Lodato in 1994, while working as GM of the Albany River Rats, the AHL affiliate of the New Jersey Devils. He came to our team based on his prior relationship with our head coach, Robbie Ftorek. Since his hiring was executed by New Jersey, I was not involved in the process. I was a 24-year-old, inexperienced "punk" (for lack of a better term), but I was wide-eyed and big-eared, looking to learn everything I could about the industry. Robbie suggested that I stay close to Doc, that he was "the best" I could learn from. My first impression of Doc was underwhelming, mainly because he was different than I expected. All of the sport psychologists I had dealt with before were "guru" types—often young, fresh-out-of-school sports enthusiasts who had somehow sold their "system" to management and were in the locker room to teach you how they could make you better, if you followed their steps.

Doc was none of that . . . he was older, humble, and disarming. He had an "aw shucks" type of demeanor, never used any technical terms, and struck me as a fatherly presence . . . a guy who truly cared about people and just wanted to get to know you better.

As I grew in the sports world, I realized that was the key to Doc's effectiveness. In my experience, the top cause of failure for sports psychologists in pro sports environments was an inability to find an entry point . . . to gain genuine trust. Often players were put off by the ego of the psychologist, getting the sense that he was more interested in the advancement of his own career than theirs. Other times, players felt the psychologist wasn't trustworthy with their personal information and worried that he was serving as some type of mole, feeding information upstairs to the front office.

Doc's ace in the hole was that, in addition to possessing a brilliant knowledge of what I call "the human condition," he was 100 percent egoless and 100 percent trustworthy. Players and staff could feel it, sense it, and believe in it. As I progressed in my own career, I tried to take Doc everywhere I went. From Albany, he joined me in Orlando, where I worked for the Solar Bears (IHL), and later the Orlando Magic (NBA). From there, we worked together with the Boston Bruins (NHL). In the end, our relationship spanned 27 years. (Doc went to heaven on my birthday, October 8, 2021.)

I used to joke that the reason I took Doc with me everywhere was because my personal mental health required constant upkeep. That may have been true, but the real reason was that his presence was conducive to winning. He brought out the absolute best in people. He made people comfortable with themselves, which made them comfortable with others. He never tried to squeeze anyone into some "brilliant mental system" that he had concocted. Instead, he met you exactly where you needed to be met, and helped you become the best "you" that you could be. Doc's victories far outpaced mine, but I was fortunate to be a part of three championships with him riding shotgun . . . the 1995 Calder Cup (Albany, AHL), the 2001 Turner Cup (Orlando, IHL), and the 2011 Stanley Cup (Boston, NHL). Nonetheless, I value the man far more than I value the rings. He was a second father to me.

One story that I think sort of encapsulates the key to Doc's success occurred back when I was the general manager of the Orlando Magic, in 2003. Doc was visiting, doing some work with the team, and was scheduled to sit with me at our game that night. Unexpectedly, our team's owner, Rich DeVos, the founder of Amway and a tremendous man in his own right, decided he was going to attend the game. He wanted to sit with me and talk about the team. DeVos was a kind and gentle man, but his visits were rare. He always cut right to the heart of the issue. He wasn't a time waster or a small talker. Before the game, I introduced Rich to Doc, but without identifying what Doc did for us. I just introduced him as "a friend of mine."

After a few hours at the game, discussing various subjects together, Rich stood up and announced that it was time for him to get going. As I walked him back toward the arena exit, he inquired again as to "who that older fella was" that we were sitting with. When I explained he was Frank Lodato, a sports psychologist we had hired to work with our players, Rich immediately said, "Oh, now it makes sense." When I asked what he meant, he said, "The whole time we were talking, I was trying to figure out how Frank was making me feel so comfortable. I'm not always comfortable in those situations. He has such a disarming personality. It was like I was talking to a good friend that I had never met before. You should keep him close to our players and coaches."

Rich DeVos was a great judge of character.

COMMENTARY FROM NICK BEVERLEY
ASSISTANT COACH, LA KINGS AND HEAD COACH, NEW HAVEN NIGHTHAWKS (NHL / AHL)

During my first full season as head coach of the New Haven Nighthawks [1982-83], I had the pleasure of meeting Francis J. Lodato when he arrived unannounced at the office and asked to be introduced. It proved to be a momentous introduction for both of us, and the way it came about was a source of much laughter over the years we spent working together and enjoying a very special friendship. I teased Frank that he "barged into my office," and he would point out that "it was your lucky day." I readily admit that it definitely was just that!

Frank was interested in applying his sport psychology techniques to hockey, but his exposure to the game, as well as to managers, coaches, and players, was minimal. He needed an opening. I happened to have a strong interest in the "people" side of sports, namely how to get the most out of individual talent while dealing with the myriad personalities involved. "The Doc" had an amazing ability to meet people and immediately put them at ease while introducing them to his formula. It paid dividends in getting highly motivated (but often "over-the-top" and troubled athletes) to embrace the visualization and relaxation techniques that brought success to so many. Learning to "see" individual and team achievements while in a controlled state of mind allowed actual performances to come to the fore, even under the most rigorous game conditions.

Over the years I saw time and again the fruits of Frank's labor and belief in what he was teaching. It was amazing how it crossed into all types of sports, and while results were never guaranteed, Doc was always pushing, pulling, and prodding to keep the athletes focused. If they were willing to put in the effort, then he was there for them. There were highlights and downturns over our nearly 40-year collaboration, but the one constant was "the measure of the man": his strength in the face of adversity and pure joy in winning, but enjoying it with grace, unwavering loyalty and friendship, love of family, and tremendous religious belief. I know that his memoir will be a reminder of the true power in [sports] psychology when applied by a conscientious and caring person. I'm so fortunate to have been along for the ride.

THANKS, DOC. LOVE YOU ALWAYS!

PART 2

NATIONAL FOOTBALL LEAGUE (NFL)

CHAPTER 4

MIAMI DOLPHINS (NFL)

STEP 4
NEVER STOP LEARNING

I have never worked in any capacity with or for the Miami Dolphins. Still, my experience with many of their players and coaches provided the jumpstart that gave traction to my stalled career in sports. I was clearly going no place. At the time, I only dabbled in the budding profession. My purpose was to stay engaged, better understand the sports world, and communicate how psychology could enhance sports performance. I took courses, attended workshops, delivered papers at the local and national meetings, and wrote articles on sports-related topics.

None of these activities drew the kind of attention that could produce a consultancy, although years later, because of this elementary step into sports, the relationships I built resulted in appearances on radio and television shows. These included two visits to the NBC show *Major League Baseball: An Inside Look*, and regular appearances on Art Rust's *Sportstalk* show on WABC radio in New York City. I was also quoted in several sports-related articles in the media.

The circumstances that became the turning point for my pursuit of a sports consultancy resulted from a happy accident. Beginning in June 1969, while I was on a one-year leave from Manhattan College, I began teaching at Barry College. The purpose of the leave was to test whether we, as a family, wanted to live in Florida. There were many questions that came up as we pondered the move. Was the move going to be a good one for our children? Did we really want to be so far away from our parents, siblings, and friends? Could we easily leave the house in Katonah, New York—the house my wife helped design and I helped to build? In addition to all of this, we loved Katonah. For us it was conveniently located to family, shopping, schools, and my work.

But move we did. The experiment turned out to be a mistake, except for one circumstance. We had moved from Katonah, where we lived in a large house on six and a half acres, to a high-rise apartment in Miami Beach. This turned out to be the first of many mistakes. The children instantly reminded me that "this is the city and we are country kids." I heard this each morning as I drove the two older children, Denise (10) and Raymond (8), to school. The children found their school lacked a challenging curriculum and, all in all, it was an unpleasant experience. The only rewarding bright spot of the year was teaching at Barry College, where I connected with the Miami Dolphins and gained more experience learning about the sports world.

DON SHULA, HEAD COACH, MIAMI DOLPHINS

In addition to my work at Barry, I also had a part-time consultancy at Biscayne College. Coincidentally, Don Shula had become the head coach of the Miami Dolphins and had chosen Biscayne College as his training facility. The influence of Shula and his staff became immediately evident. Shula inherited several players from his Miami predecessor, head coach George Wilson, 12 of whom contributed to the success of the team.

Their turnaround was due partly to the fact that Shula came to Miami with most of his Baltimore Colts' coaching staff, each bringing with them years of experience. The addition of newly hired rookie coach Monte Clark proved to be a game changer. Each coach and each coordinator were committed to the football philosophy of the new Miami Dolphins' head coach. In a nutshell, the underlying theme was to never ask a player to do more than he was capable of doing; excuses for losses were anathema. The only explanation for a loss that Shula declared acceptable was "The team did not play well enough to win." All Dolphins players were expected to be in shape and stay in shape throughout the entire season, plus the playoffs. Rules were to be obeyed.

With the coaching staff in place, the next item on the agenda was to sign the players who were capable of winning. The draft that year was productive. Players Tim Foley, Curtis Johnson, and Doug Swift signed on. With free agent signings, the team was on its way. From time to time, I ambled over to the playing field where, occasionally, players hung around. Some would talk, others simply nodded as they passed by. From those jaunts, I began to meet some of the Dolphins players.

At that time, I knew only one Dolphins player, Larry Little. He shared with me his desire to become a counselor after his playing days ended. I happened to be organizing a conference at Barry to address the state of school counseling. I obtained Little's phone number and called to ask if he was interested in appearing at the seminar. He accepted immediately. A few days after the phone call, I met Little for lunch at the Miami Playboy Club. He was familiar with Barry College, and his sisters attended graduate courses there. As the weeks passed, we talked on the phone, and on one or two occasions we met in person. Soon we became friends. Later, in turn, he introduced me to lineman Wayne Moore. The offensive line coach, Monte Clark, claimed Moore off the waiver list. I fostered a strong relationship with Moore, and he became a family favorite of ours until his untimely death.

One day when my family was looking for something to pass the time (even spending every day at the pool can get boring), we drove over to the Biscayne campus and watched the players go through the rigors of training camp. When we lived in New York, we attended several Giants training camps. In fact, for a time, we were season ticket holders at the old Yankee Stadium in the Bronx. The children reveled in collecting autographs and having their pictures taken with New York Giants players. We waited for the players after their showers. A few got to know us by sight, some players made small talk with the children, and the coaches would nod or smile when they went by.

TIM FOLEY, CORNERBACK, MIAMI DOLPHINS

Training camps, for our family, were not a new experience. The Dolphins camp was different. First, the Miami players mingled with the fans as they went for their showers. They were generally more accessible than the Giants players. Many days, we hung around after practice, where my children sought autographs from willing players. It was here that I met cornerback (the position now called defensive back) Tim Foley. Each time we visited training camp, we spent time talking to players. Some of these talks led to future lunch or dinner dates with Little, Foley, and Moore.

The time spent with Foley and his roommate, cornerback (defensive back) Curtis Johnson, and later with linebackers Mike Kolen and Bob Matheson, provided opportunities to enhance my skills with relaxation and visualization techniques. These men patiently listened to my spiel, challenged me to be clearer in my discussion of the techniques, and helped me evaluate the effectiveness of the interventions. Some gave me feedback after each game. Since we had season passes for the Dolphins, we saw the players and coaches after home games. Each time I met with individual players I took copious notes. They were not only helpful, but essential to my career.

A year in Florida convinced us that we missed the northeast; we moved to Brookfield, Connecticut. The distance the move created from the Dolphins did not in any way dampen our affection for the "Fins." Occasional phone calls to Little and Foley kept us apprised of happenings at Dolphins' headquarters. Mainly we discussed the hotel they were staying in and the availability of game tickets. If there was an item of interest or humorous occurrence, they shared it with me, and it was often about the new crop of Dolphins.

Our first fall in Connecticut found us catching up with the Dolphins in Massachusetts and New York. During the following seasons, we continued following the Dolphins. We traveled to see them play at Foxboro, Massachusetts, the new home of the New England Patriots, as well as the New York Jets at Shea Stadium; the Giants at their home, Veterans Field; the Washington Redskins at RFK Stadium; and the Buffalo Bills at War Memorial Stadium in New York. We had become fixtures to the Dolphins players and coaches. We stayed in the same hotel, had meals with individual players, and were considered to be loyal fans.

I considered myself to be more than a fan; in my mind, I was doing an internship. On one of those trips, I was invited to speak at the chapel service the morning before the game. The invited speaker canceled at the last moment. Each away game we attended became a source of new connections with players and coaches. The impact of being associated with the Dolphins organization never crossed my mind. I had not even considered the tremendous impact it was having on my professional development. I never thought about where my dormant career was going. I doubt if any of the players had an inkling of what their playing careers would eventually look like.

It turned out that I would be in the "Company of Champions," men who would appear in the Super Bowl game for three successive years, winning two. On the road to the Super Bowl, the Miami team went undefeated during the regular season, dominating through the playoffs and into the Super Bowl. Football, like all sports, is filled with highs and lows. You lose some games you should have won and win some because that day the football gods were smiling on you.

In the 1971-72 season, the Dolphins team, after more than half the season was completed, began to think of possibly going undefeated. It then became an achievable goal. The Miami team expected to win; fortunately for them, so did some of their opponents. Foley shared an incident that occurred as the teams were leaving the field at half-time. The gregarious Foley frequently spoke to opposing players. He commented on how well his opponents were playing, and the opposing player replied, "You guys will come back in the second half." The confidence level, encouraged by the leadership of Coach Shula and of the defeatist attitude taken by some of the Dolphins' rivals, was beginning to soar.

Late in the second half against Minnesota, the Dolphins were behind by two scores. They faced a fourth and long situation, seemingly outside the range of field goal kicker Garo Yepremian. It was evident to the kicker that his number would not be called. To his surprise, Shula decided to roll the dice. Yepremian headed onto the field. Years later he recalled his thoughts: "I knew I had never kicked a field goal that far. I also remembered how important it was for Shula to win this game; if Shula thinks I can do it, maybe he knows something I don't. So here goes." The kick was successful; the Fins were still alive.

Called the "No Name Defense" by Tom Landry of the Dallas Cowboys because the players were all unknown, they held the Vikings to three and out. On the next possession, Jim "Mad Dog" Mandich caught quarterback Earl Morrall's pass in the end zone. The point after was converted, and the streak was kept alive. It seemed each week a different player came up with a play that helped keep the goal of being undefeated in reach.

This feat of 17 straight victories placed them in the rarified air of "elite teams." To this day, the record has not been broken. Many of these players achieved the ultimate validation of their playing days by being elected to the NFL Hall of Fame. Most were successful in their post-football careers.

Let's turn the clock back to the mid-1960s. Pro football was experiencing growing pains. Several rival leagues attempted to challenge the NFL. None succeeded. The AFL was different. First, it survived thanks in part to a strong TV contract. It presented the public with a good product and reached fans in cities that had been passed over by the NFL.

Some teams were more financially able to compete. The proof of this was the signing of Joe Namath by the New York Jets for what was an astronomical amount of money at that time. The NFL had not yet captured the sports market, but was on its way. A great marketing plan and an even greater hyping of the league had the NFL on the path to being considered on the level with Major League Baseball. Adding the AFL would speed up the climb to the top of the sports ladder for the league.

The first event that brought the leagues together was a championship game between the two leagues. It was to become the Super Bowl. It is hard to accept the fact that the first Super Bowl did not sell out. There were over 30,000 unsold seats. The multibillion-dollar business that the NFL would become was years away. Even though the New York Jets made headlines with the blockbuster deal they entered into with Joe Namath, the organization was only a few years removed from when the New York Titans passed the hat around, seeking money to pay the players and to meet other expenses.

New ownership changed all of that. As an aside, the experiences I had were all new to me. I had my foot in the door of the sports world, but I was still on the outside looking in. I was learning some things about the sports world I never suspected. Specifically, I was surprised to learn:

- How much politics was involved in each decision
- How many factors, like image and public relations, affected every move
- That some coaches and coordinators were more respected than others
- That some assistant coaches were always on the griddle
- That mistakes were not tolerated
- That excuses were unacceptable
- That "Do your job" was the credo for each player and coach
- That some players were permanent residents in their coach's doghouse; this usually was a sure bet that a ticket to another team or home was the next step
- How important support staff, trainers, equipment guys, PR people, travel secretaries, and office workers are
- How much effort was expended before the Sunday Spectacle
- All about travel, charters, and the intricacies of playing on the road
- How little time players had for themselves and the varied ways players chose to use that time

The evolving role of the players' association and how they became a strong force in negotiations was becoming more evident. I can't help but repeat the fact that, although I was on the outside and barely able to see, this was the closest I had ever been to a pro sports team.

Each day revealed some fact that I never even knew existed. There were many obstacles that helped me understand the emotional states athletes and coaches live in every day, which I saw as fertile ground for a psychologist to explore.

STRESS-INDUCING OBSTACLES FOR PLAYERS AND COACHES, AND LESSONS FOR SPORTS PSYCHOLOGISTS

1. The sports world is fickle; yesterday's hero becomes instantly forgotten after a few bad games, with the exception of the team stars and the high-ticket players.
2. Most players go into training camp knowing they must fight for their jobs. The effect this has on a player's state of mind and career is evident.
3. For these players, training camp causes anxiety and fear.
4. The thought that one's career is always on the bubble, and the player is

always holding on by a thread, produces many wakeful hours in players trying to establish themselves.

5. The stress that surrounds each exhibition game is caused by the fear of making the crucial mistake that causes your team to lose, thus placing you in the coaches' doghouse.

6. Assistant coaches deal with the uncertainty of their survival when their unit becomes the weakest link in the chain.

7. Head coaches become the victim of second guessers and media attacks. The quip "Don't buy green bananas" is one that is constantly on the minds of many team members.

8. Being aware of the pecking order is also an unspoken truth. Most organizations follow a pecking order. The sports world isn't any different. It has one important criterion: years of experience. The pecking order was most evident in the treatment of rookies. *Rookies have their place, and don't forget it.* One unwritten rule for rookies is to curb their mouths. On some teams it seems there are members of the team who are on trial. The answer the trial hopes to expose is whether the younger person is worthy of being a stalwart alumnus.

9. Players, at least initially, look up to the men playing beside them who are more experienced. I listened in awe as rookie Dolphins would recite with excitement accounts of what linebacker Nick Buoniconti had relayed to them.

10. Each team has its own set of rituals and traditions. The older the team, the stronger and more revered are the trips down memory lane.

Some players became icons, while some others were instantly forgotten. Years later, during my first consultancy with the New York Giants, I was astonished about the adulation some former Giants players—Andy Robustelli (defensive end), Frank Gifford (running back), and Emlen Tunnell (safety)—received. Most other players have their moment in the sun and then receive as much attention as last week's headlines.

I heard the same thing from the young Miami Dolphins players like Mike Kolen or cornerback Curtis Johnson, who spoke of the prowess of their teammates—it was a revelation to me. Each player knew the strengths and weaknesses of the other players. After a while, they could predict which players would be called upon for special situations. I would hear player after player take great pride in recalling previous performances about their teammates; Shula had begun to bring his team together.

The team chemistry was evident and building. One of the most important acquisitions was offensive guard Larry Little from the San Diego Chargers. The move was a compliment to Little, since it underscored his talent. It was also a pivotal move for Shula, who saw unlimited potential in Little. One of the first moves by Shula was to get Little game-ready. He had lost the prescribed amount of weight and was able to establish himself as one of the game's premier run blockers. His efforts earned him a call from the NFL Pro Football Hall of Fame in 1993. Shula's hand was being played out. The first season ended with a 10-4 record. A loss to the Oakland Raiders in the conference finals slammed the door shut on a Super Bowl experience.

The second season continued the winning tradition. This time the team made it to the Super Bowl. Unfortunately, it ended in a convincing defeat to the Dallas Cowboys in their first championship game. Being so close and having it slip away was a bitter pill for Shula to take. He constantly reminded the players that he did not want to go through the pain of losing the big game again.

As a head coach, Shula had come up empty on both his attempts at winning the Lombardi Trophy. He was a man on a mission. He hoped the same fire burned in the belly of each of his players. The players and coaches responded well. Another winning season ended in a playoff experience. The team continued unbeaten throughout the entire playoff run. Despite the score of the Super Bowl, the Dolphins beat the Washington Redskins convincingly. In three short years, the Miami franchise, under Shula, was among the top teams in the league. The team's dominance continued for another year, resulting in a second Super Bowl victory. Shula's Super Record was now 2-2. He would make one more Super Bowl. The outcome was less than desired, leaving Shula with a 2-3 record. When the curtain fell on Shula's career he was, and remains, the winningest coach in pro football. Shula's years in Miami were exceptional, making him an icon of the southeast football teams.

I was fortunate to be close enough to the team during the early Shula years to have learned many lessons:

1. The most important lesson I learned during those years was how hard it is to survive a season, much less be successful by winning the championship game.
2. Another lesson was one that all fans should learn: Sunday's Spectacle is so finely orchestrated that no stone is left unturned. What is televised to millions of people doesn't just happen. It results from hard work, adhering to a plan, and a smile from the football gods.

My love affair with the Dolphins ended when the Shula era was over. Before the split was complete with the Fins, my son, Raymond, and I wrote a book on the Dolphins, *But We Were 17 and 0*, and interviewed many of the players from the undefeated team. As we interviewed the players, we were taken by the repetition of one comment many of the team members made. It was like an apology for going undefeated but, in fact, it was not. It was merely an assessment of the team. Players talked about the talent on the team. They realized, position by position, that the team, at least on paper, did not compare well to other teams. The final conclusion was "But we were 17 and 0." That is how we decided on the title of the book. In the book, we tried to trace the paths players on the championship teams took. The responses were interesting:

- One of the most impressive stories was that of Foley and his wife, Connie. About midway through Tim's playing career, they entered the Amway world. Tim solicited new clients while Connie filled orders from the garage of their Miami Lakes home. From these humble beginnings, they were able to ascend to the pinnacle of the Amway Pyramid. Many of the other stories were equally impressive.
- Buoniconti turned the law degree he received, while he was still playing, into a successful venture in the business world.
- Little returned to his love of people to go back into education.
- Defensive back Dick Anderson opened a distributorship, which provided him with a more-than-comfortable living.
- Many others were in real estate, some in banking.

My interest in the Dolphins faded because of several circumstances. First and foremost, I thought of the Dolphins as "Shula's Team":

- The succession of coaches, front office, and general managers was impressive—Jimmy Johnson (head coach and GM, 1996-99), Bill Parcells (executive VP), and Dave Wannstedt (head coach, 2000-04)—but the team did not experience any trips to the podium.
- The second circumstance was the success of my efforts in securing consultancies. Since I now had my own teams, I no longer had the luxuries of being a fan. The success of my teams had far greater meaning than rooting interest. After all the years of planning, dreaming, hoping, and praying, I was finally where I had hoped to be.

There was much more stress than I had anticipated. I took the performance of my athletes seriously; winning and losing had taken on a new meaning. Repeated failure on the part of my client could lead to a consultancy not being renewed. I was beginning to understand the attitude of most coaches that, when a game was over, you went on to the upcoming one. "One game at a time" was the credo. The focus of the Dolphins coaching staff and the intensity of that focus was essential to their success. Shula ruled the roost during the early part of the 1970s. But observing people going through an experience was nothing like living through it. Fortunately, the knowledge I gleaned from the Dolphins players and coaches was the foundation of my practice.

CHAPTER 5

NEW YORK GIANTS (NFL)

DOC FRANK'S LESSON
4 PRINCIPLES OF VERBAL, NONVERBAL, AND WRITTEN COMMUNICATIONS

In order to improve communication skills and to approach total psycholinguistic harmony, four principles should be employed:

1. Integrate the verbal with the nonverbal.
2. Gauge the level and attitude of your audience.
3. Promise only what you can deliver.
4. Beware what you communicate.

PRINCIPLE ONE: INTEGRATE THE VERBAL WITH THE NONVERBAL

Above all, mean what you say. The goal here is to produce total psycholinguistic harmony.

Great communicators, such as Don Shula, Phil Jackson, Gregg Popovich, and Claude Julien can attribute their success not only to their knowledge of their respective games but also to their communication skills.

The use of regional idioms may impede communication. The rigid purist decoder may find it difficult to understand the underlying message. In addition to regional idioms, there are varieties of jargon, such as golf talk, tennis talk, football talk, hockey talk, real estate talk, legal talk, medical talk, scat talk, and reverential talk, to name but a few. A hidden purpose behind all of these "talks" might be to produce a subculture limited to those who know the jargon. In a particular sense this may make communication difficult if not impossible.

Excellent communicators know their audiences and deliver their messages appropriately. They know how to mix the rational and the emotional with the sentimental and the spiritual. Their talk is neither trite nor pedantic. It needn't try to impress; its very nature is impressive.

As Alan Greenspan said, "I know you think you understand what you thought I said but I'm not sure you realize that what you heard is not what I meant." There is so much mystery surrounding communication that, to understand all components contained in it, one must analyze all of its elements. Cultural differences may interfere with communication. Gender differences may also impede understanding. The insightful work in this area of author and linguistics professor Deborah Tannen should be consulted to help avoid these pitfalls.

Excellent communicators are gifted in the use of language and the means by which language is expressed. Their verbalizations are precise and terse. When the communicator and listener are on the same page, namely when the encoding and decoding mesh, communication is perfect. But this situation does not always occur. In fact, perfect or even near perfect communication is rare.

Those of us who have worked in the sports environment are all too familiar with players repeating the same mistakes over and over again and coaches vehemently claiming it shouldn't happen because the player has been told what he needs to do to improve his performance.

Consider the parent who shouts at their child, "I have told you not to do that a hundred times." Hopefully, the parent won't try for the 101st time, because the method is not working. The desired change in the child's behavior isn't taking place. Sometimes the communicator just doesn't get it.

Simply telling a person what to do does not ensure that communication has taken place. Sometimes the effect that is being demonstrated does not match the verbal production. At best, this produces problems in the listener. This, in turn, impedes learning. So say what you mean.

The same can be said of Don Shula's coaching and communication skills. His genius rested in the fact that he never asked players to do more than they were capable of doing. He evaluated players' skills, knew the limit of their skills, and developed a role for each player according to his ability. His communication was built on his knowledge.

Another interesting aspect of communication is its composition. Speaking persons use verbal communication. We say words, form phrases, and put them into sentences. This is one type of communication. Concurrently, we use nonverbal communication (body language). This generally is the effect that accompanies the words. Sometimes the two don't mesh. For example, one may nod in agreement with a point a speaker made, but one may also nod as if to say, "Here we go again; I've heard it all before." When the verbal and the nonverbal disagree, the listener must decide which message is correct. Ideally, when the verbal and nonverbal agree, a psycholinguistic integration occurs, resulting in accurate communication.

The question is "Do the words I am about to employ best communicate what I want to say?" This must be followed by asking whether the effect of being employed is compatible with the verbal message you are attempting to send. This is the problem of the King in *Hamlet* when he utters, "My thoughts fly up, my words remain below. Words without thought never to heaven go." Once compatibility has been dealt with, an important second step is communicating to the level of the audience.

PRINCIPLE TWO: GAUGE THE LEVEL AND ATTITUDE OF YOUR AUDIENCE

A pedantic vocabulary used on a less verbal audience is an act of vanity on the part of the would-be communicator. Trying to impress through your ability with words does not achieve the goal of communication. Some may think you are brilliant because they have not understood a word you have said. Most will simply turn you off or at least lower the volume so as not to be distracted by your pedantry.

The second aspect of being appropriate is to judge the pulse of your audience. Are they in a jocular mood? Do they intend to get a serious message? Do they want to be informed or entertained, or both?

Team members listening to their coaches want information. They want this information to be delivered in such a way that they can leave a meeting knowing full well that the coaches understand the problem and have developed a plan to deal with it so that success is probable. If you want to join the winner's circle, take the time to know your audience, your team, your family, your employees, and especially the vernacular. Then you will be on your way to victory. Remember, communication is not about the speaker. It is about delivering the message.

PRINCIPLE THREE: PROMISE ONLY WHAT YOU CAN DELIVER

Communication properly used can be informational and can also enable individuals to develop insight into their own needs and behavior.

One of the most important principles in the field of educational psychology is the principle of individual differences. An awareness of this on the part of the speaker may contain the key to that speaker's success. Each listener is unique. How they determine meaning may be the difference between success and failure.

When dealing with team members, a coach might do well to adequately assess the possibility of success and communicate clearly what has to be done to achieve the goal at hand. A weaker team may require errorless performance for an entire game to defeat a stronger team. This is worthwhile information to communicate. It enables the listener to appraise the task realistically and not think that victory is something that is going to be handed to them.

PRINCIPLE FOUR: COMMUNICATION IS CONSTANT — BEWARE WHAT YOU COMMUNICATE

Communication doesn't take place only between coaches and players. It also can be seen in the interaction with one's peers. Workers communicate with each other. Teammates communicate with each other. Coaches communicate with each other. Patients communicate with other patients. In general, the same principles apply to poor communication.

However, there may be greater latitude between peers. The commonness of their experiences, the similarity in background, and identical problems growing up may all call for a more relaxed effect. The intimacy and the time span of a relationship may also be an important factor. Sometimes poor communication, whether between coach and player, husband and wife, or parent and child, may cause a breech in relationships. This means that, though some restraints may be relaxed, caution is still a prudent road to take.

Our nonverbal behavior may serve as a model for other people. Some people may follow the lead of those who espouse adherence to a cause but whose lives contradict their stated beliefs. But more astute persons evaluate the nonverbal behavior of those spouting words and make their judgements accordingly. They understand that, if a person's life is a shambles, what he espouses may not be a panacea for him. One is impressed, for example, by Mother Teresa, because of her dedication to the poor and the example of her actions. One finds a politician who verbalizes virtue and then compromises his moral behavior to be less of a role model.

We must remember that we are constantly communicating either on a conscious or unconscious level. An uncontrolled yawn may signal boredom to the person to whom you are speaking. Tapping your fingers may be a sign to get on with it.

Every Thursday when the game plan for the following Sunday's game was distributed, a tight end would look over the plan and count the number of times he was scripted to receive the ball. If he was not content with his role, he would either turn his back on the coach who was conducting the meeting or fling his copy of the game plan across the room. Words could not have described his feelings more eloquently.

Frequently, married couples complain they do not communicate in their homes. They really mean they do not talk, because silence is also a means of communication. They are communicating all right. They are just not talking.

Winners communicate by executing their assignments perfectly. They don't simply "talk" a good game, they play it. Their communication is total. What they want to communicate—namely that they are good players—is demonstrated beyond a doubt by their performance. The winners—the Gretzkys, the Jordans, the Jabbars, the Birds, the Everts, the Lopezes, the Johnsons, the Williams—needn't say a word.

The message of their greatness shines through their deeds. Communication has taken place at the highest level possible.

STEP 5
LISTEN MORE, TALK LESS

WALKING THE SIDELINES

The time after the third Super Bowl (Miami Dolphins versus Dallas Cowboys) was the beginning of my pro career in sports. Bill Arnsparger became the head coach of the New York Giants. After he settled into the job, Foley mentioned my name to him. I followed up with a phone call, and Arnsparger invited me to speak about the possibility of consulting with the Giants.

I clearly recall the day of our meeting. My thoughts were clear; my emotions were running wild. As I drove to the Giants offices in Pleasantville, New York, I was in a constant battle trying to calm my anxieties. I was convinced this was the chance of a lifetime. I didn't want to blow it. I decided I would try to be low key, but to not betray the fact that I was confident my program would work.

There is a fine line between being confident and being cocky. I had to toe that line. In Arnsparger's office, I was trying to disguise my emotions. Once I began my presentation, a calm came over me. I went through the program step by step. I started out by identifying the types of testing programs that were available—learning styles were a topic in educational psychology gaining some attention. I pointed out how some of that information could help coaches communicate their information more effectively. This caught Arnsparger's attention.

He interrupted me and asked me to explain this further. He also inquired about some books he could read on the subject. I hit a chord that resonated with him. He was really into the presentation.

When I described the benefits, which added to the effects of practice by visualizing, he showed an eagerness to try this out. The potential use of hypnosis seemed to fascinate him. By this time, we had talked for over an hour. He was late for his next appointment. He asked for a copy of my presentation, promised to read it, and told me he would call me in a few days. He was as good as his word; a few days later, he asked me if I would like to speak to his coaches about my proposal, and we arranged the date.

My journey to become a psychological consultant to a pro team was transitioning from a dream to a reality. The door was opened—a door that had previously been locked. Later in my career, as I looked back on that proposal, I was shocked to think about how incomplete it was when I compared it to a later proposal. Thank God it was adequate for the times.

In the Giants training camp that year, the journey took off. I was a consultant to a pro team. Imagine me, a Giants hater from my early youth, now expected to help that team win. Life surely plays its own brand of funny games. I was so awed by the honor that I completely forgot my antipathy toward the men in blue. The circumstances that led to this situation make for the well-known Horatio Alger "rags to riches" type of story.

My dream to become a psychologist for an NFL team, which began in the late 1950s, was realized for the first time in 1973. I used to pass the Giants' training facilities at Pace University in Pleasantville every day during my commute from Newtown, Connecticut, to Manhattan College in Riverdale, New York. When I did not have to be at work until later in the day, I stopped by to see Arnsparger and whichever coaches and players happened to be around.

One Monday morning, I stopped in and headed toward Arnsparger's office. He was pouring himself a cup of coffee, one of many he would consume that day. He invited me to join him in his office. He was preparing to view the tape of Sunday's game. Nothing could hide my "aw shucks, gee whiz" look. It was one of the few times in my life I was at a loss for words. I had no idea what he expected from me. He didn't explain; he was a man of few words. Silently, we sat in front of the large screen. As the tape rolled, he paused it many times to replay some downs while taking copious notes.

On occasion, he would make a brief comment, but it was never intended to start a conversation. It was as if I wasn't present in the room. This went on until he had viewed the offense, defense, and special teams several times. Then he said, "Let's see it one more time," using the phrase he made famous. He rewound the tape and took notes until the tape had played itself out, not just once but several more times. Finally, after rewinding the tape, he stood up and politely indicated that I was excused. As I was leaving, he thanked me for stopping by and said something to the effect that I should stop by again.

In the parking lot, I got into my car and sat stunned over what had just happened. What did it mean? I let out a hoot. Whatever it meant in the long run, I wasn't sure. My foot was in the door; a door that is usually shut to outsiders was now ajar. As I left, the one thing I knew for sure was, with Arnsparger, silence was golden. By saying nothing, I had successfully negotiated the first rung of the ladder that led to access to the NFL. I let out another hoot.

As the days passed, Arnsparger and I became more comfortable working with each other. We couldn't have been more different. The adjustment was uncomfortable at first, and he remained somewhat reserved for the rest of the relationship. Throughout my entire career, Arnsparger's intensity, focus, and ability to concentrate were the benchmark by which I would rate others and myself. Among his many football talents, he had several traits that stood out. His only response to a loss was, "We didn't play good enough."

THROUGHOUT MY ENTIRE CAREER, ARNSPARGER'S IN- TENSITY, FOCUS, AND ABILITY TO CONCENTRATE WERE THE BENCHMARKS BY WHICH I WOULD RATE OTHERS AND MYSELF.

One day, prior to a game against the Oakland Raiders, I asked him how he planned to stop the receivers we were to face. His answer was simply, "We don't have to beat them; they have to beat us. If we all do our jobs, we will win." The importance he placed on the team was impressive, though not unique. Shula and Coach Bill Belichick of the New England Patriots also echoed this thought. He frequently told his players, "Do your job." In the Patriots locker room, there is a reminder prominently displayed, "PLAYERS WIN GAMES. TEAMS WIN CHAMPIONSHIPS."

People who did not know Arnsparger found him distant, perhaps shy or aloof. Always football first, he was one of the most focused people I have ever known. Whether it was watching a game film or a movie, playing racquetball, or for that matter performing any task at hand, all his attention was goal-oriented. He abhorred distractions. I asked him one time after a Giants game at Shea Stadium, during the renovation of Yankee Stadium, if he wanted to watch the second game of a Sunday doubleheader in the club. He declined politely by saying, "That is not the way I like to watch a football game." The message was clear: if you watched a football game you did it exclusively by watching the game, not by becoming distracted with drinking or idle chatter.

My early recollections of him were that he was never completely relaxed, always serious.

One day, my impression of him changed after a Giants game at the Yale Bowl in New Haven, Connecticut (another temporary home for the Giants during the renovation of Yankee Stadium). Since we lived in Newtown, Connecticut, we invited him and his wife, Betty Jane, along with their two children, David and Mary Susan, to dinner. They accepted, and we arrived in Newtown about two hours after the game. As I mixed drinks in our kitchen, the children played outside. I explained the origin and the makings of a Kir cocktail (white wine plus crème de cassis, which became popular after World War II). As I went on and on, he sat on our kitchen floor with his back up against the refrigerator. He was the most relaxed I had ever seen him. He was laughing, making jokes, and permitting me to see a side of him I never knew existed.

From that point on, our relationship evolved. I was much more comfortable in his presence than I had ever been, and it seemed he felt the same way. The next time I was in his office, I didn't feel like an intruder taking his time from more important tasks. He continued to reveal that he was a caring man—warm and involved with the people he would permit into his inner circle. He reveled in the lives of his two children. The more I knew him, the more I appreciated his talents.

I began to think that, as profitable as his association with Shula was, it did not permit him to shine completely on his own. The Dolphin's experience certainly helped not only him but all who were even indirectly involved. Still, in my mind, he was entitled to much more recognition than he received.

One night, Betty Jane called me to announce Bill was receiving a Vince Lombardi Award. Betty Jane had given the organizers my name as a friend of Bill's. Apparently, they asked her to contact any of Bill's friends who might be interested in attending the event. Once off the phone, I called Foley and told him about the event. He was happy to have been invited. He took down the details and was added to the guest list.

The bus was a convenient way for the group to travel to the event, and it was a party both ways. The event was held on a Sunday night at a restaurant in New Jersey, which was opened exclusively for this occasion. As one would expect, the evening was top-shelf. A cocktail party preceded the dinner. I had withheld the information from Bill about Tim's coming to the event. Betty Jane also had not told Bill of my presence.

Later, Bill commented that he was not surprised at seeing me there, but was taken aback when Foley walked into the room. Foley brought greetings from Don Shula and the "No Name Defense" from Miami. During the evening, the MC strived to entertain the crowd with material that was bawdy. Arnsparger took offense at the comments. In his opening remarks, he mentioned to the MC that he hoped he would clean up his act in the future. He had his standards and was critical of those who would fall short of them.

After the event, Foley and I drove to Bill's home in Chappaqua, New York, where the three of us talked well into the night. Foley and I continued to Newtown, and he spent a few days with us. He visited my children's school and made a visit to Lincoln Hall, an institute for boys to which I was a consultant.

One night, I picked up Arnsparger from his home and drove with him to New York City to a basketball game at Madison Square Garden, a trip we had made several times before. This night was different. I started the conversation with him about how much I was enjoying my experience with the Giants and how I felt I would like to continue in that type of work. The conversation that followed was a revelation to me. He began talking about his days after college and being undecided about his future. He tried a few things, none of which grabbed him. Then he got his first coaching job. The light went on. He discovered this is the way he wanted to spend his life—working in sports, football to be precise. He knew the work would be difficult to get into and that there would be ups and downs. Still, he was willing to pay the price. As he looked back, he had few regrets, made many friends, and had many memories to look back on. I felt, for the first time, that he was comfortable with me and felt he could share private moments with me.

TED PLUMB, RECEIVER COACH, NEW YORK GIANTS

The year was 1973. The Miami Dolphins had just won the Super Bowl, completing an undefeated season by going 17 and 0. Arnsparger served under Don Shula as defensive coordinator, and in 1974 was hired by the New York Giants to become their 10th head coach. Among his many tasks as new head coach was assembling a coaching staff. His staff contained a newcomer to the NFL coaching ranks, Ted Plumb, the receiver coach. In those days, the coaching staff in the NFL was not composed of an army of coaches.

In 1973 the money from television and a brilliant marketing campaign on the part of the NFL had not yet begun cascading funds into the pockets of NFL owners. Assistant coaches were among the first to feel the pinch. This financial situation opened coaching opportunities to young coaches with no NFL experience who eagerly took jobs with relatively low financial compensation. These factors all combined to produce the birth of Ted Plumb as an NFL coach. His career was launched in New York as the receiver coach under head coach Bill Arnsparger, and took him to Atlanta, Chicago, Philadelphia, Phoenix, and St. Louis while earning him a Super Bowl ring in Chicago in 1985 and in St. Louis in 2000.

When first meeting Plumb, one is impressed by his openness, friendliness, and dedication to his profession. He was as cordial to me as anyone could be to an absolute stranger. He guided me through rough waters. Though he had less experience than I had at the time, his life had been in football. He knew how to tell where the bodies were buried and what pitfalls to avoid. When other coaches would shy away from revealing information to me, Ted was always there telling me what I needed to know and suggesting ways to use the information for the good of the team. I was sure I was going to be protected by Plumb, if ever the need arose, and I was right. No matter which job or city he was in, he always shared my name with the coaching staff. He was responsible for me working with the field goal kicker under Philadelphia Eagles Head Coach Buddy Ryan.

One of my responsibilities with the Giants was to compile a profile on the rookies. As I compiled my data, I concluded that one of the rookies was uneasy about camp and was likely to bolt. He did. Eventually, he returned to camp after numerous phone calls, and resumed his pursuit of a job on the team. Little did I know, until I was told by Plumb, that my prophesying was derided among the coaches, most vociferously by none other than Plumb himself. As he told me the story, we both laughed about it. It did nothing to put a monkey wrench into our relationship, which grew from a workplace liaison into a social one so close as to qualify as being referred to as "family" by his wife, Maryanna. His sons, Loyal and John, and his daughter, Molly, remained close friends with our family.

"Coach K is right. 'It is all about relationships.'"

Forty-four years later, our phone calls to each other shed light on great memories and joy. Duke University Basketball Coach Mike Krzyzewski "Coach K" is right: "It is all about relationships." From the meetings Arnsparger arranged for me with the assistant coaches, a friendship began to develop between Plumb and myself—one that never ended. He was aware of how green around the edges I was when it came to pro sports. He took it upon himself to fill me in about information I needed to have.

When others greeted my inquiries with silence, Plumb spoke up. An example of this was at breakfast in training camp one morning. I was going over the roster for the day, and a player's name whom I had spoken to Arnsparger about the previous day was missing. I asked why he was not on the daily roster. No one answered. After they left and Plumb appeared, I asked him the same question. He informed me that the player had become intoxicated the night before, was involved in a fracas, and was no longer a member of the team. He had been "shipped out to another team who owed us a favor." This incident demonstrated many things to me. Less than 24 hours earlier, the head coach had said to me, "If I had 10 other players like him, we would win the Super Bowl every year." The lesson here is that no matter how much talent you have, if you tarnish the image the team hopes to project, you are a goner, never to be remembered again.

My relationship with Plumb hit a bit of a snag after I tested the Giants draftees of the class of 1976. That group of young men represented one of the best crops of players ever taken by the Giants. Among the draftees were Troy Archer, Gordon Bell, Harry Carson, Dan Lloyd, Jerry Golsteyn, and Craig Brantley. Bell, Archer, Carson, and Lloyd soon became starters. Archer's career was cut short by a fatal car accident during training camp at the beginning of his fourth pro season. Lloyd's career was shortened by cancer, and Bell was traded after one season. Golsteyn suffered a serious knee injury and had a so-so career. Carson was the only one to reach the coveted NFL Hall of Fame.

After testing the rookies, I suggested that Jerry Golsteyn was uncomfortable and could possibly leave camp. He did just that. He went back home, causing Arnsparger to ask me to call him. When talking with Golsteyn, I assured him that I was not interested in trying to persuade him to return, rather I was there to help him make the best decision for him and his family. Golsteyn had already considered returning, and he did. My part in this irked Plumb. He thought I overstepped the limits of my involvement. All of this changed, however. Plumb was not only pleased by the outcome but impressed by the series of events. He became my strongest supporter.

The rookies in 1976 were impressive, and hopes for their contribution to the team ran high for a long time. Optimism was the order of the day. Several of them would become standouts in the NFL. My relationship with Arnsparger and his family had blossomed into a social one. We attended basketball games together for many years and continued after his departure from the Giants. The only taboo topic was speaking about the Giants.

During one of those games, Arnsparger was scouting a Manhattan basketball player for the position of defensive back or receiver for the Giants. After a brief courtship, the marriage between the New York Giants and George Bucci, the Manhattan player, never took place. Bucci remained a basketball player, had a championship career with the New York Nets, and was successful after playing basketball in Italy. He made the right career choice and profited from it.

Nothing is forever. After a bad start early into the season in 1976, Arnsparger was fired. His unemployment did not last long. He was to return to one of his greatest and dearest attachments, the Miami Dolphins. During his brief but unwelcomed hiatus, Arnsparger and I met on Fridays to play racquetball at the Danbury Racquet Club where I was a member. I was no challenge to him. Time after time he won with ease. Afterward we headed to a local watering hole and downed a few beers. Our conversations were mostly about family and football in general. The Giants never popped up in our talks.

Upon reflection about our experience at the courts, I realized that, in life, some people are athletes and some "play at athletics." I drew that conclusion from an evaluation I made about my play. There was no comparison for the talent of each of us. He was focused throughout each of our games. Both his experience and understanding of the game far exceeded mine. He planted himself in the middle of the court, barely moving from side to side, while I frantically raced from side to side, back and forth to return his shots. I was sure that if he had something better to do, he would not have agreed to meet me.

Without inquiring about my status with the Giants, I assumed that my days with them had ended. Because of my close association with Arnsparger, I feared that his successor, John McVay, may have been uncomfortable with me hanging around. Instead of asking about my status, I just disappeared from the scene, waiting for the phone to ring. And it did.

JOE GALAT, LINEBACKER COACH, NY GIANTS

The first call was from Andy Robustelli, the general manager, who inquired about my whereabouts and well-being; the second from none other than linebacker Harry Carson, inviting me to visit the Giants' training facility in Pleasantville. At noon time, Carson asked McVay if I could stay for lunch. Permission was granted. At that lunch table, McVay and I talked about my return. I assured him that even though I was a friend of the ex-coach, I would not be second-guessing McVay's moves. It was also in that dining room where I first met linebacker coach Joe Galat, with whom I would be working on my return to the Giants.

At that time, I had no clue as to how important Galat would become in my career. McVay asked us to explore the effects that psychological intervention could have on sports performance using the Giants' linebackers as subjects, if the players agreed.

They agreed. We were on our way. With the linebackers, Galat and I developed and analyzed tasks, as well as teaching techniques to communicate these tasks more effectively. All was going well until that day against the Philadelphia Eagles when my Giants career would end a second time.

This blow proved fatal. Quarterback Joe Pisarcik and fullback Larry Csonka mishandled the ball, which was immediately recovered by the Eagles' Herm Edwards, who raced into the end zone to defeat the Giants. The call, the handoff, and the subsequent fumble led to the immediate firing of offensive coordinator Bob Gibson and the end of his NFL career. At the end of the season, the remaining coaching staff followed through that same door.

HARRY CARSON, LINEBACKER, NY GIANTS

The star of the 1976 rookie class, Harry Carson became an icon among Giants players and was inducted into the Pro Football Hall of Fame. We met on the first day of training camp when everyone was assigned specific responsibilities. Mine was evaluating players. As soon as Carson spoke, I was impressed by the gentleness in his voice and the insights revealed in his conversation. Several days passed before I met with him again. By this time, all of us were settled into life at training camp.

Tedium was already beginning to set in. This was not the tedium one experiences while reading the daily posts in social media, but tedium nevertheless, which leads to spawning rumors. Most are unfounded, but they help people cope with camp. One rumor circulated about Carson receiving the number 53, which was supposedly requested by the head coach, Arnsparger. For those of you who may have forgotten Miami Dolphins' history, 53 was the number of a new defense created by Arnsperger during his days in Miami. The question around camp was whether Arnsparger had spotted something in Carson that set him on the path to stardom.

Of all the rookies I tested, Carson was the most curious about his test results. In our talk, he had mentioned some feelings of insecurity over whether he was going to make the squad. All reports I heard were that his camp was better than average and he showed promise. I reassured him as best I could and introduced the topic of his number 53. "I know all about its history," he said with a smile. He knew that linebacker Bob Matheson had worn 53 in Miami and was the player that the defense was built around. The rest is history.

Carson's start was a rough one, with five consecutive losing seasons. A disgruntled Carson weighed finding a way out. But he stayed. His leadership abilities came forth, and the Giants, under what some consider the greatest New York Giants captain ever, began to improve.

During his 13 seasons with the Mara Men (named for Wellington Mara, the Giants' owner), Carson was captain for 10 years, and with nose tackle Jim Burt, was credited by some to have invented the Gatorade Shower at the end of victorious games in 1985. The price Carson had to pay for such an illustrious career was disproportionately high. In 1990 he was diagnosed with post-concussion syndrome, which explained his frequent headaches and depression. All of this led Carson to state that if he had known the consequences of playing football he would never have played.

He authored two books, *Captain for Life* and *Point of Attack: The Defense Strikes Back* (with James E. Smith). Carson was honored with inductions into the Division II College Hall of Fame in 2000, the College Football Hall of Fame in 2002, and the Pro Football Hall of Fame in 2003, an event which my son, Raymond, and I attended as Carson's guests. The pride we both felt for him, and the gratitude for his years of friendship, made the occasion an event that will be forever remembered.

Knowing Carson is one of the perks that I was fortunate to receive during my career in sports. For this one, I am especially grateful and I often think of my relationship with him. From the first day I met him, I was impressed by him, his demeanor, and the articulate way he told me of his past. He seemed to be as comfortable with me as I was with him. I attribute the bond that tied us together as the respect we had for one another. Even after my time with the Giants ended, I closely followed his career. We spoke from time to time about the good old days and about our doings. Our most intense conversations were those that centered around our families.

ANDY ROBUSTELLI, GENERAL MANAGER, AND WELLINGTON MARA, OWNER, NEW YORK GIANTS

My part of the New York Giants experience would not be complete without the mention of two wonderful people: Giants owner Wellington Mara and general manager, Andy Robustelli. Wellington was the epitome, the benchmark, of what a sports owner should be. He was a kind man, football savvy, concerned about people, and approachable. His presence lit up the day. Robustelli was rigid, conservative, determined, task-oriented, and definite.

I met both Robustelli and Mara on two separate occasions in New York City. Robustelli was at the Toots Shores Restaurant in eastside Manhattan, then a popular watering hole for athletes and celebrities; Wellington was at a college basketball doubleheader at Madison Square Garden. But when I was introduced to them at the Giants training camp by Arnsparger, neither remembered having met me.

Robustelli embraced me even though he was extremely skeptical about my profession. He had been exposed to psychology in sports in Los Angeles. Robustelli's coach in LA would hang a picture of the next Sunday's opposing lineman in his stall with the player's characteristics, tendencies, strengths, and weaknesses. Robustelli felt this was an idea that helped him in his preparation for the next game. This brief exposure piqued his interest in psychology, though he was not an advocate yet. He asked me for books to read, and invited me into his office, his home, and his social life.

One of the books I gave him to read was *Altered States of Consciousness* by Charles T. Tart. It generated several afternoons of discussions, from which an interesting conversation ensued. Andy inquired about the possible causes for an experienced receiver dropping a catchable ball. First I offered the obvious answer: he took his eyes off the ball and didn't see it into his hands. Then I suggested that he was angry at the coach and unconsciously dropped the ball.

To this Andy replied, "Doc, if I live to be a million, I could never believe that."

This was Robustelli at his best—honest, direct, to-the-point, no-nonsense, black is black, and white is white. Those qualities, as well as his accomplishments on and off the football field, made his memory a fond one.

Wellington, on the other hand, always kept the few conversations I had with him on neutral topics. He was always congenial and welcoming, but you knew he was never going to consider you his buddy. The more you got into the Giants' family history, the more stories you heard about Wellington's generosity and caring. It was not uncommon to run into an ex-Giants coach who would tell you that, years after he left the Giants, he received a note from Wellington complimenting him on his accomplishment.

Former Giants players expressed their appreciation for the care and concern shown to them by the owner. Remember the Mara family (NY Giants), the Halas family (Chicago Bears), the Rooneys (Pittsburgh Steelers), and the Bidwills (Cardinals) were early owners in the NFL. Their collective leadership paved the way for future owners. Wellington built a great organization in New York. He is owed a round of applause for that.

JIM TRIMBLE, OFFENSIVE LINE ASSISTANT COACH AND SCOUT, NEW YORK GIANTS

Jim Trimble and I met late one afternoon during my first training camp with the Giants. I mention him because his willingness to spend time with me made me feel accepted. Remember, I was new to this. I didn't feel I had a right to be there. Trimble helped make that a little easier. He had 20 years of experience in the CFL where he led the Hamilton Tiger Cats to the Grey Cup. I knew next to nothing about the league. Little did I know that, in the future, the CFL would be the center of my professional life for almost 40 years.

While coaching in the NFL, Jim earned the honor of Coach of the Year. His creativity was responsible for the creation of the slingshot shape of the goal posts—an idea he created with a friend that was adopted by the CFL in 1966 and in the NFL in 1967. He also knew a lot about the league's history.

While he was a scout for the Giants, we talked a long time about his early experiences, one of which I found intriguing. Jim, in the late 1920s or early 1930s, had the opportunity to purchase the Detroit Lions franchise for $600—yes, $600. He solicited his friends. After many contacts they found they could not raise the money. He concluded the story by saying that, even if they had been able to raise the purchase price, they would not have had the money to run the team. The Detroit Lions today are valued at $1.7 billion, according to *Forbes* magazine. Trimble taught me many things about the sports world. We spent many hours together. His lessons were much appreciated. They helped me navigate rough waters in both the NFL and the CFL.

CHANGING OF THE GUARD

Arnsparger's departure and the circumstances surrounding his dismissal became rough waters to navigate. The day it occurred I was giving a lecture in Fall River, Massachusetts, to a group of educators. On the drive home I stopped for coffee and saw a picture of Arnsparger, his carry-on bag over his shoulder, exiting the Giants' complex. I suppose people who were more acquainted with these matters saw it coming. I chose to remain in denial of the possibility. There is always intrigue when a firing takes place. This was no different. I never knew the details, nor the reason for the hard feelings that ensued. The only thing that was apparent was that there was a split between the Arnsparger loyalists and the McVay followers. Beyond that, I was completely in the dark.

McVay was followed by head coach Ray Perkins, who after four years produced another unimpressive number of wins. Perkins left the Giants and was followed by Bill Parcells. My Giants career was almost resuscitated, or so I thought, when I got a call from Parcell's secretary inviting me to appear for an interview. After I hung up the phone, I was certain the call was a gag being played on me. It was not. Parcells, at the suggestion of three of his players—Harry Carson, George Martin, and Danny Lloyd—considered bringing me back. It was clear throughout the interview that I was underwhelming the coach. The interview went nowhere.

Recently I ran into Parcells, who spends his winters in a nearby town, in the waiting room of the acupuncturist's office where we both go for treatment. I mentioned that he had interviewed me. He asked in disbelief why he would ever interview me. Before I could answer, we were interrupted.

My Giants experience was eye-opening, informative, fun, full of some lasting friendships, and unforgettable. It caused me to take stock of the entire sports picture as I was beginning to know it. I didn't expect it to be so competitive on the coaching and management level. The politics stunned me. Talent was not the only thing that mattered. Being favored by someone on the coaching staff or in upper management was a bigger factor than I had thought. The men that I have mentioned—Arnsparger, Foley, Plumb, Robustelli, McVay, Trimble, and Carson—each were instrumental in helping me establish a career in the sports world, which would last for decades. It was one that would produce unbelievable memories and consultancies, which ended in championships and lifelong friends.

I left the Giants with the firing of John McVay. Along with an assortment of Giants shirts, I took with me many experiences and memories that shaped my career. I was surprised to learn how many people worked behind the scenes and how important they were. It is unfortunate that their efforts are not recognized more fully. We all owe them and the fans a debt of gratitude.

Some memories, in particular, made my time with the Giants special. These include the afternoons and evenings when quarterback Jerry Golsteyn and his wife, Nancy, visited our home in Newtown, Connecticut, and the hospitality they showed my son, Raymond, and me at their home in Florida where we spent time getting to know their son.

I frequently reflected on social occasions spent with the Arnspargers and the Robustellis. I was always in awe of the attention each of them attracted in restaurants, at sporting events, or on the street. Many disparate thoughts came to mind that caused me to focus on the players and on the influences people and places had on players' lives. Remember, my time with the Giants was my first real official involvement with a pro team.

Respect Your Position: To me, at that time, a locker room was just a room where players hung their street clothes and changed into their work clothes. I couldn't have been more off the mark.

Despite the fact that I had more personal contact with players than the average fan had, I still had lots to learn. To me, at that time, a locker room was just a room where players hung their street clothes and changed into their work clothes. I couldn't have been more off the mark. It was due to Ted Plumb that my lessons began. With the Giants, I didn't have unlimited access to the locker room. In fact, it was sacred space to the players. Even the coaches would enter only with cause. You, the reader, might think this is trivial information. Let me tell you, it is not.

After a while spent working in pro sports, many bits of information are revealed to you. My information about the locker room grew with each consultancy.

On some teams, the rules for admittance were stricter than in other rooms. As I became more experienced, I made certain that I cleared my status with players early. On teams where the coach announced that I was to have access to the locker room my job was made easier. On other teams, I would meet with the team captain and ask him to ask the players about my roaming the room. Most agreed that I was welcome, though this was not universal.

JUST AS IT IS A GRAVE ERROR FOR CONSULTANTS TO SEE THE PLAYERS AS TEAMMATES, THINKING THAT ALL PLAYERS ARE HAPPY TO HAVE YOU IN THE ROOM WHERE THEY EXPRESS CONFIDENTIAL INFORMATION WITH THEIR TEAMMATES CAN ALSO BE ERRONEOUS.

Just as it is a grave error for consultants to see the players as teammates, thinking that all players are happy to have you in the room where they express confidential information with their teammates can also be erroneous. Players expect to have space where they can discuss collective bargaining agreements with other players, last night's goings-on, or dissatisfaction with coaches—and they are right. Fans place all their attention on the players. I referred, earlier, to the role of many players in my development. This may appear as an exaggeration—believe me, it is not.

Fans sometimes overestimate their knowledge of a particular sport. A good play is one that benefits your team enough, though it has resulted from a mistake on the part of the opponent. I didn't know the responsibilities of each position in football. I am certain that most fans who are objective can recite the same litany. So when I say that my education in sports was aided by many players, I am serious.

Being educated in the mechanics of kicking a football by punter Dave Jennings was priceless. I felt a sense of privilege over the fact that he took time to instruct me. He patiently explained, and made certain that I understood, how important the drop of the ball was during a kick. To the reader, this may seem like an exaggeration. However, to one who was hungry to learn anything and everything I could about the mechanics and techniques of sports performance, it was an asset.

I had many conversations with Dave about football, each yielding some insight. In addition to football, we talked about other sports. Dave was an avid Celtics fan, and I followed the Knicks. No matter the issue, we each held steadfast to our teams. Dave became a "must see" on each of my visits to the Giants. He was a source of information that helped increase my knowledge and appreciation of the finer points of athletics. I felt satisfaction for the many accomplishments of Carson, who was one of my most enthusiastic followers from his first days with the New York Giants. His success and loyalty continued to bring a feeling of warmth.

To say that several people contributed to the success of my career would be an understatement. But the following people stand out as being pivotal to my success:

- Bill Arnsparger provided the road map I was to follow not only in navigating the rough waters of professional football, but other sports as well.
- Andy Robustelli was influential in my learning about the role of a general manager. I sat in his office when he was speaking to an agent on the phone.

He trusted me enough to permit me to hear his sensitive conversations. His availability and directness helped me feel comfortable and welcome.

- Dave Jennings, through his many conversations with me, laid the foundation for the intervention I would employ in working with kickers.
- Harry Carson was key to my working with other players who would otherwise ignore me. His approval gave me instant credibility.

After I left the Giants, Harry and I discussed issues surrounding other players and their welfare. His experience was invaluable to me as I tried to help players by introducing programs for their benefit after retirement. My plan was considered by the players' association, but never implemented. A similar plan was adopted many years later. The league was becoming more stable financially and owners felt they could implement such a program. If one is to break into pro sports, there is no better place to start a career than the NFL.

COMMENTARY FROM HARRY CARSON
MIDDLE LINEBACKER, NEW YORK GIANTS

I was drafted in 1976. Fresh out of South Carolina State University, I attended a rookie training camp. I was surrounded by people I didn't know, plus the coaches. Coach Marty Schottenheimer drafted me, and he referred me to Frank to talk with him. When we met, we just had a conversation—just talked. I realized he was just asking me general questions.

Later, I found out that Marty wanted me to change positions. "I want you to come back and learn a different position," he said. I was a little put off at first. He wanted to try me at middle linebacker.

I returned to South Carolina and realized that Frank was a psychologist (before that, I never had any interactions with a psychologist). I figured that Frank was an intermediary between the Giants and me to see if I could learn a new position. I started to understand. It wasn't just "Can you play the game physically?" but also, "Can you play the game mentally?"

The interactions with Doc always felt like small talk. He always picked my brain about certain things, and it was always a pleasant conversation. Marty could have drafted whoever they wanted in that round. They had back-to-back fourth-round picks. They first drafted Gordon Bell; with the 105th pick, they chose Harry Carson. Marty had to stand up in the draft meeting room to declare who he wanted to pick. When he drafted me, he could have drafted anyone. He chose me, and he chose me to play a position I had never played before. They knew I could stop the run. They didn't know if I could deal with the pressure of being a middle linebacker.

Marty was my teacher, and I learned from him. He shared with me the fact that there were some people who didn't know if I could make the adjustment from defensive line to linebacker. If I had gone to a different school, they wouldn't doubt it, but because I went to a small black college in South Carolina, there was doubt that I would be able to do the position.

During training camp, Frank spent most of the time in the upper level of the locker room with the staff and coaches. In retrospect, I got a sense that the small talk we engaged in was about me being on the couch, but I wasn't on the couch. He picked my brain about what I thought about certain things. During the season, I had made the shift to middle linebacker, and I was learning the position by watching other guys play the position. (It was a lot of pressure in the biggest television market.) To be able to call the signals and be able to read the pattern of the offense–that was a different story.

As time went on, it got better and better. In 1976 the Giants did not open their stadium until October. We practiced at Pace University in Pleasantville, New York. I lived in Ossining, and it wasn't far from Pleasantville. I would walk over to him and say, "Doc, I'm going crazy, I'm going crazy." I'd get a laugh out of him. And I said, "You've got to be crazy to play this game." I didn't fully know what his role was, but I knew it was about the mental part of the game and whether someone was smart enough to make the change to another position.

Marty said, "The position that you're playing is normally reserved for white guys." I appreciated him saying that. It was one of the things that was usually unspoken.

At the time, the QB role was reserved for white guys, as was the center and the middle linebacker, because those are the "thinking man's positions." People ask me what I'm most proud of, and I say, "to make that transition and play a position I had never played before." If I had not succeeded, it would have been on Marty's shoulders. I didn't have a lot of room to fail. I was able to make the transition. Everything Marty asked me to do, I was able to do; and he allowed me to play the game and help the team. Frank always said, "If you ever need me, let me know."

I needed him down the line.

Around 1980 or 1981 we were playing against the Philadelphia Eagles. It was a Monday night game. I was on the field playing, and for whatever reason, I wasn't tackling the way I should be tackling. I hit the guy with the ball but did not wrap up on him. There were a lot of missed tackles. We lost the game to Philadelphia. By this time I had become a good player, and had earned the National Football Conference Linebacker of the Year award. I was no longer impressionable and young. I played pro bowls. But I missed tackles, and I couldn't understand why. The game ended, and I went into the locker room. I was disgusted with myself. I played a lousy game in front of everyone to see on Monday Night Football. There was a guy walking around with everyone's check in white envelopes. I said, "I don't want it, and I don't deserve it."

And he said, "You have to do something with it. You can donate it."

I argued, saying, "I didn't deserve it or earn it."

When Ray Perkins was the head coach, I talked with him before we were on the bus. "I'm not doing the team any good," I said. "I'm going to retire."

He was shocked, and he said, "Don't do anything until you come into the office and see me."

I went home, and the next day, I went back to Giants Stadium. I had my daughter with me, who was two years old. He said, "Don't make any hasty decisions." The media had gotten hints of what I was thinking. There was a flock of media outside of Giants Stadium. There are photos of me holding my daughter and some of Perkins and me walking out. He said, "Work harder, and don't worry about it."

My next step was to talk to Frank. I told him that I was kind of desperate and didn't know what had happened with my ability to tackle. He put me through task analysis. I was going through the motions. I was doing on the field what we did in practice. With task analysis, you visualize each step:

1. *You see the ball carrier.*
2. *You get to the ball carrier.*
3. *You take it two steps further in your head.*
4. *You visualize yourself tackling the opponent.*

I went through this program. I watched the film. In my mind, I visualized hitting the guy and tackling him. So it would show in my game.

That is how Doc stepped me through the process to get back on the right track.

The reality is, there is a lot of room for mental coaching in football. A coach at the University of South Carolina said, "When you're in college, football is 20 percent mental and 80 percent physical, but in the NFL it's 20 percent physical and 80 percent mental." That was important for Frank Lodato to share that with me.

A lot of guys don't want to acknowledge that there is some deficit in how they play. I use task analysis in everything I do now. When I talk with younger players, I talk with them about task analysis, saying, "If you want to be the best of the best, you need to visualize and understand what the other team is doing and going to do. You need to be able to play the game in your mind."

Doctor Frank made me a better player. We had fun in the times we shared together. He was a very good friend.

CHAPTER 6

PHILADELPHIA EAGLES (NFL)

STEP 6
KNOW YOUR PLACE

In 1986 wide receivers coach Ted Plumb and defensive coordinator Buddy Ryan had hardly finished celebrating the Chicago Bears' dominant win in Super Bowl XX (46-10) when new opportunities in Philadelphia arose for both coaches. The Bears' win was made possible by Ryan's highly touted 46 defense that held the New England Patriots' offense to 10 points and set a record for sacks (7), fewest rushing yards allowed (7), and margin of victory (36). Then the door opened to greater things.

Ryan's tenacity and ingenuity had passed the test. He was now able to firmly assert himself in the company of highly regarded NFL coaches. Plumb and Ryan had a close working relationship during their days under the tutelage of head coach Mike Ditka of the Chicago Bears. Many stories were circulated about the conflict of egos between Ditka and Ryan. If they, in fact, existed (and I am relatively certain they did), it is a credit to these two men that they put their differences aside and triumphed in the Super Bowl.

As in every walk of life, egos also pop up in sports. Where and when it happens almost always ends in disaster. That was not the issue in Chicago during their winning season. That doesn't mean evidence of it did not show itself from time to time. Soon after the Bears' victory in the Louisiana Superdome in New Orleans, Ryan was offered the head coaching job with the Philadelphia Eagles.

One of his first moves was to name Plumb his offensive coordinator. Postseason wins for the Eagles in green and white had become hard to come by. The Eagles boasted the fact that they had Ron Jaworski, Reggie White, Keith Byars, John

Teltschik and Paul McFadden on their roster. There was enough talent to form the nucleus of a competitive team. However, Buddy Ryan, Ted Plumb, Wade Phillips, Jeff Fisher, and the rest of the Eagles coaching staff had a slippery slope to climb.

Once Plumb became ensconced in his new environment, and in consultation with the special teams coach, he contacted me to work with placekicker Paul McFadden. We met a number of times during training camp and throughout the regular season. McFadden was a bright, eager client, known for his barefoot kicking. His kicking improved due to his intense concentration and eagerness to excel. His post-playing career saw him rise to the position of director of development for Youngstown State University after a successful career in coaching there.

An interesting story about the kind of person McFadden is centered around one of our meetings. Paul arrived with an inflatable goalpost and Nerf football. He set it up on the floor and then invited me to kick the ball between the goal posts. He explained the reason for this action: "You told me you had never kicked a field goal in your life. Now you can tell your kickers you have."

I was constantly in awe of Buddy Ryan even though I had few one-on-one encounters with him. I vividly remember each one. Years later that memory would pop up when I reviewed the application of a young man with a new master's degree in sports psychology. He was seeking employment with the Calgary Stampeders and suggested in his proposal that his plan was different from other practitioners, as he met each day for a half hour with the head coach. I first laughed at the suggestion, and then I recalled the time I was also just as naïve.

One encounter with Ryan occurred in training camp at Westchester University in Pennsylvania. Morning drills were just about to begin. Ryan and I were exchanging stories with Lem Burnham, who had just been hired as the team psychologist. Later Ryan left, and the reporters, who thought we might have been people of clout, approached us. They knew Burnham as a former player; still they inquired about our roles with the team. Burnham, who had just finished his internship in psychology, described in great detail his role and credentials. When it came to my turn, I blurted out in my usual smartass way, "I write Buddy's ad libs."

Each of you readers may have at one time or another found yourself in this situation, where you would have done anything in the world to retract your statement. But as Shakespeare once wrote, "What's done cannot be undone." Were the words to appear in print? Would they be transmitted to Ryan another way? I had to wait until this saga played itself out. In my mind, I created scenario after scenario, all ending badly for me.

The coaching staff often gathered for drinks before dinner. On rare occasions, Ryan would attend. That night was one of those rare occasions. As I walked into the room Ryan was holding forth, the center of attention. He looked over at me and continued his story. So far, so good. Security wasn't called to usher me off campus, and no one seemed to be ready to call for my execution. I was beginning to relax. Wrong call. As he finished, he walked toward me, showing neither signs of camaraderie nor anger. As he approached me, he said tersely and rather firmly, "You smart ass. I write my own ad libs."

My insecurity over this incident would not leave me. I was certain that this stint with the Eagles would be short-lived. Again, I was wrong. The incident never came up again.

During training camp, I encountered resistance from one of the Eagles players, defensive tackle Jerome Brown. It seemed there was a floor where the black players met during their free time. Not knowing this area was off limits, I found my way up to it, looking for a player. As I entered the floor, I was met by Brown, who inquired about my reason for being there. Before I could answer, he made it clear to me that my presence there was not welcome. Segregation still existed to some extent.

I later had a similar experience in Canada where three black players with whom I interacted many times were sitting in a corner of the room together. Since there was an empty seat, I sat in it. One of the players said, "You can't sit there. This is the hood."

"If this is the hood," I replied, "I'm staying. I lived in the hood before you were born."

The "hood" is a term used to describe part of a neighborhood. Some consider the hood to be a reference to a ghetto. My hood was populated by Italian immigrants. Nevertheless, it was still the "hood." The players laughed and we interacted throughout the meeting. Granted, opportunities in the CFL were always more equal for players of color, but these three were Americans. Things have gotten better, but the NFL still has some work to do to increase equity, diversity, and inclusion.

On the flipside of the coin was Reggie White, who harbored hostility toward no one. Whatever aggression was in him was reserved for the playing field, where he could be as fierce as possible. To White, we are all God's children, and he treated us that way. Some people die too young in the eyes of those left behind. White was one of those people. Unlike those who struggle to find 15 minutes of fame or glory in a lifetime, White's was filled with both fame and glory. A standout player wherever he played—whether in Philadelphia or Green Bay—White touched the hearts of fans. He was the coaches' favorite on and off the field, and his talents soon made him an iconic figure in the NFL. Ryan once said, "What this man does to inspire his teammates is unbelievable. His was the booming voice in the defensive huddle, on the sidelines. His demands on his teammates were only exceeded by the expectations he had of his own performance."

I remember the first time I met White at the Eagles' Training Camp. His infectious smile, his genuine enthusiasm for life, his good humor, his kindness, his overall demeanor is forever implanted in my mind. He played with teammates who lived their lives diametrically opposed to his values. He respected them as teammates while praying for their well-being.

One day in training camp I was sitting alone in the lounge going through my items for the day. He came in looking for someone. He sat down at the table and began to ask me about my role. Before long we were talking about family, God, relationships, everything but football. I saw in him a passionate, committed man who wanted to do the right thing for himself and others.

This brief conversation gave me insights into a side of football players other than their sport. A new path had been forged for me. Players are more dimensional than fans know. Sports is what they do, not how they live their lives or who they are.

The loss of a great man and player in the NFL came with the untimely announcement of the death of the "Minister of Defense," Reggie White. He suffered a fatal cardiac arrhythmia. On that day, December 26, 2004, football lost one of its shining lights. Reggie was truly a man for the ages. His shoes may never be filled. As an ardent fan of Reggie's as a player, family man, gifted athlete, a fierce competitor, Super Bowl XXXI winner with the Green Bay Packers, and all-around good guy, I was happy to find out that he was to be inducted into the NFL Hall of Fame in the same class as Carson. I was privileged to be a guest at that induction.

My time with the Eagles was short, but my recollections were many and varied. I became a fan of Ryan, profanities, and all. Controversial and impulsive, he shot from the hip and always said what was on his mind, yet never in my experience had a hidden agenda. You might not like what he said, but you always knew what he meant. Qualities like this were refreshing to me. Too many of the people in the sports business do not reflect this candid approach to either their jobs or their lives.

WADE PHILLIPS, COACH

Another coach who was on his way to a prominent career in the NFL was Wade Philips, whose career through the NFL required its own atlas. One of the reasons I focused on Wade Phillips was to demonstrate the importance of being accepted when one is new to a different work environment. The sports world is a world unto itself—small and clannish, with its own culture, traditions, and rituals.

When I was about to enter the world of work, my oldest brother advised me, "As you begin to ascend the ladder to success in a field, be respectful of the people you meet on the way up. They are the same people you meet on the way down." This message always resonated within me. On first meeting Phillips, I was surprised at how comfortable he made me feel. After all, I was an outsider—one who had never played organized football on any level.

Let me be clear here, the reason I was so readily accepted was because I was a friend of Ted Plumb. His outgoing personality made him extremely popular with his coworkers, and his accomplishments made him someone to be respected. I was, in a sense, riding his coattails. The lesson this taught me and the influence that lesson had on my career was, in part, one of the reasons I was cautious about entering a new sports environment. This was difficult enough in itself without a guru, without someone tooting your horn. Thinking that you would make it on your own in sports was a pipe dream.

AS I BEGAN TO ASCEND THE LADDER TO SUCCESS IN A FIELD, MY OLDEST BROTHER SAID, "BE RESPECTFUL OF THE PEOPLE YOU MEET ON THE WAY UP. THESE ARE THE SAME PEOPLE YOU MEET ON THE WAY DOWN." THIS MESSAGE HAS ALWAYS RESONATED WITHIN ME.

Remember the sports world in many ways is elitist. If you don't earn your spurs after you have been given an opportunity, your career will soon become a memory. Sports careers are notable for their short lifespans. Not so with Wade, the son of the colorful head coach of the NFL's Houston Oilers, Bum Phillips. Wade Phillips retired after 42 years of coaching.

One of the interesting facts in Wade's career is that he was fired and then later rehired by the Denver Broncos. Usually you get one shot with a club, and then your resume goes into the dead file. It was a good move for the Broncos to sign Wade both times. In his first stint, the Denver team went to the Super Bowl Finals. In his second, the team won the Super Bowl. His career also included stops in Houston, New Orleans, Philadelphia, Atlanta, and Dallas. There are few, if any, defensive coordinators in the NFL today who gain more respect from their peers than Wade Phillips. Plumb once told me that Wade's manner helped cool conversations between coaches at meetings—conversations that were approaching the boiling point.

Always committed to improving, Wade took every opportunity to learn. During practice, the drill often involves handing the ball to a running back, as defensive players try to stop forward progress. This drill was refined by Wade to create a defensive strategy called, "pursuit."

Wade continued to bring the same enthusiasm, good spirit, and learning mindset to the Los Angeles Rams. With him on board, the Rams made it to the Super

Bowl, but unfortunately lost to New England. He was inducted into the Pro Football Hall of Fame in 2018.

COACH K, DUKE BLUE DEVILS

Coach Mike Krzyzewski ("Coach K") of the Duke Blue Devils is right. It is all **about relationships**. Let me develop this thought:

> *Sports, in my mind, is more than merely winning or losing. There is no denying how important that is to people whose livelihood depends on the number of Ws they accrue. I respect that idea, but to me there is another side to sports, which has to do with relationships. There are many people who, simply by being in your life, have a profound influence on you. I couldn't tell you the scores of most games I was involved in. But in many of those games, what I remember is the people on all levels who made the outcome possible. How they impacted my life, not only at that moment but for many years after the event, is unforgettable.*

I remember, for example, the last Grey Cup I was involved with. I remember how I felt the cold of that Canadian night—a cold I had not experienced during the game. But more importantly, I remember how the players, aware of my limited physical mobility, looked out for me. We were on the podium accepting the Grey Cup from the commissioner of the CFL. Two players signaled to other players to assist them as they carried me off the platform to the ground below. That memory remains as vivid as if it occurred yesterday.

I recall standing on the sidelines after the Boston Bruins had defeated the Vancouver Canucks in game seven of the Stanley Cup finals. After the players had their turn on the ice with the Cup, the team captain, Zdeno Chára, a player I had worked with closely, skated over to me and hugged me as we exchanged congratulations. Not all memories were the outcome of winning.

In another Grey Cup, one in which we were favorites to win, I recall walking into the dressing room where crying players, aware of the fact that they would never have that experience again, sought me out to console them. One rookie cried out to me, "How did this happen? Please explain it to me." The fact that I was turned to when someone was grieving made my presence special to me.

Another memory that goes into the "extra special file" was of Jason Claremont, a receiver for the BC Lions. He came toward me on the sidelines after he had scored a touchdown, excitedly telling me, "That was exactly the way I visualized it last night."

Those memories and many others like them show the importance of relationships and were, to me, more important than the outcome of the game.

From left to right: Tim Foley, Bill Arnsparger, and
Frank Lodato, 1974

Calgary Stampeders Training Camp, 1990

Turner Cup Championship
Back row: Peter Horachek, Jim Hughes, John Weisbrod,
and Frank Lodato, May 26, 2001

Orlando Solar Bears 2001 Championship Team

Harry Carson and Frank Lodato,
Pro Football Hall of Fame ceremony, 2006

Frank Lodato and Wally Buono

Frank Lodato, an 80-year-old sports psychologist, has flown north from Florida to help the Lions prepare for the Argos.

Winning mind games

PSYCHOLOGY | Frank Lodato has an impeccable read on the mental state of players

Vancouver Sun, 2006

Front row, left to right: Marco Sturm, Marc Savard
Back row, left to right: Patrice Bergeron,
Frank Lodato, Glen Murray, Zdeno Chára, 2007

Boston Bruins golf outing

Frank Lodato with the Stanley Cup, 2011   *Frank Lodato raising the Bruins Stanley Cup banner at the TD Garden Arena in Boston, October 6, 2011*

Frank Lodato and Claude Julien, 2012

Frank Lodato and René Paredes, 2014

From left to right: Kay Ackles, Janice Lodato, Ray Lodato, and Scott Ackles
BC Football Hall of Fame Special Award for Frank Lodato, 2022

Handwritten list of championships

Frank Lodato's championship rings

PART 3

CANADIAN FOOTBALL LEAGUE (CFL)

CHAPTER 7

MONTREAL CONCORDES (CFL)

DOC FRANK'S LESSON
5 PRINCIPLES TO KNOW ABOUT TRADITIONS
AND RITUALS

Traditions and rituals play an important part in people's lives. Traditions are often unspoken; rituals are the ways in which the tradition is observed. The way in which holidays, birthdays, and anniversaries are celebrated is significant to young and old.

Corporations, sports teams, and even small businesses are full of tradition. Some enterprises are almost rigidly set in their ways. Others are somewhat more flexible. Dress codes, pecking orders, acceptable language, opening times, closing times, and vacation schedules all attest to the esteemed place traditions occupy. The following principles relate to traditions and rituals:

1. Know which traditions exist and why.
2. Know the rituals that flow from these traditions.
3. Acquaint yourself with the names of persons associated with each tradition.
4. Distinguish between traditions that are untouchable and those that can be altered.
5. Keep your negative comments about traditions to yourself.

PRINCIPLE ONE: KNOW WHICH TRADITIONS EXIST AND WHY

There is probably no poorer way to enter into a corporate or team setting than by violating the existing traditions of that organization. Corporations and sports teams with a long history are replete with traditions. The corporation that has been run by a family for many years may be micromanaged by the present owner, who is a third-generation family member. The team owner who observes each practice and has not missed a regular or postseason game is a tradition. Fans, players, and the media all expect to see him or her.

Photos of generations of the family who founded the business or of players who were fan pleasers are commonplace on the walls of corporate headquarters or team locker rooms. Company outings, leave days for employee birthdays, and hazing activities all stand as monuments to tradition.

Sometimes there is a contradiction between what is espoused as tradition and what is actually practiced. This is highly recognizable in educational institutions. These institutions verbalize loyalty to traditions or missions. If one were to scrutinize these institutions, one would notice that adherence to traditions is merely a verbalization with no substance attached to it. The lofty statements about educational integrity and concern for student welfare may be the message that is sent. But the real message is survival and financial security. This may cause one to note a contradiction between what is sold as tradition and what is actually practiced. Tradition in these places pales to insignificance. Knowing that these traditions exist, and how and why they came into existence, is a good first step.

Not only is it good politics to know the history of the organization, but this knowledge can also prevent you from putting your proverbial foot in your mouth.

It's important that, once a tradition has been established, one knows its present status.

Search committees have become a popular device to fill vacancies. Many times the search committee members will choose the person they think will shake up the place. Next, the newly appointed hire tells an employee of many years that he will be moving to another floor. Then the new executive, just recently hired, becomes the enemy. He is interrupting what has become company history. Tradition has been changed. This in itself may be too threatening to be acceptable. When one gets to know tradition, one understands lines of communication, why an organization has been only moderately successful, or why an organization has experienced tremendous growth. Change is difficult for many people. Don't start by shaking the rafters.

PRINCIPLE TWO: KNOW THE RITUALS THAT FLOW FROM THESE TRADITIONS

A number of behaviors may seem odd to the outsider. These generally stem from some tradition that has been long revered. An office may always take vacations in July. In some industries this is logical, since machinery must be geared up for the upcoming year. In others, it makes no sense. A holiday may be given because it commemorates the birthday of the founder. There may be a picnic every year on a certain day for similar reasons. One may be expected to attend a function for which no absence is acceptable. Rituals become dear to people. When they are altered, much turmoil ensues. If you are in a new environment, it would be time well spent to learn the rituals that are observed.

Sports teams have many rituals. Rookie night is one of the most common. One night early on during training camp, rookie professionals are called upon to sing their school song. Their singing is usually accompanied by catcalls and various verbal forms of disapproval from the veteran players. This type of hazing is harmless and even fun.

PRINCIPLE THREE: ACQUAINT YOURSELF WITH THE NAMES OF PERSONS ASSOCIATED WITH THE TRADITIONS

Ex-players who have caught the eye of the media become icons in the history of sports teams. Andy Robustelli and Frank Gifford long stood high above the rest in New York Giants football traditions, as Bobby Orr and Bill Russell still do in Boston sports circles. Can a true Yankee fan not know the exploits of Babe Ruth or of the consecutive game streak of Lou Gehrig? Is there a 49ers fan who doesn't know the name Joe Montana?

This factor is true in almost all aspects of life. There is the one person who truly embodies the tradition of a particular institution. One way to succeed in a new environment is to become familiar with the names of people who have made the present possible. Winners take the time to learn from the past so as not to repeat errors in the present.

PRINCIPLE FOUR: DISTINGUISH BETWEEN THOSE TRADITIONS THAT ARE UNTOUCHABLE AND THOSE THAT CAN BE ALTERED

You may be called upon to sit on a planning committee. Being unaware of the sacred traditions of your organization may be fatal to your career. You may unknowingly step on the toes of those so wedded to the past that any change is considered heresy. You may chafe at the words, "But, we did it that way from the beginning."

This statement often indicates that this tradition is a sacred cow. To offer compelling arguments for change is a waste of time. The cliché of being between a rock and a hard place applies here. Don't try to convince scouts that the way they have been compiling a draft list for years can be altered. The tradition may be so deeply embedded that even such a menial thing as a meeting site cannot be altered. On the other hand, there are things that are done in many organizations in the name of tradition that are easily altered. In fact, a suggestion to change might be welcome. Tradition raises the comfort level of many rigid people.

While changing for the sake of change makes little sense, change that can improve a situation is always worth considering. Just make sure that what you are trying to change is not so deeply ingrained that it cannot be altered. A simple rule may help distinguish between what is changeable and what is not: If you hear a story about the fabulous exploits of the team founder, like he could leap tall buildings or swim against the tide for two days without taking a break, let it be. On the other hand, if there is a better time or date for the office picnic, this might be able to be changed. Listen, observe, and learn.

PRINCIPLE FIVE: KEEP YOUR NEGATIVE COMMENTS ABOUT TRADITIONS TO YOURSELF

Traditions and rituals are comfortable places. Whether the rituals take place in a family, a school, a team, a church, or a corporation, they are consciously and unconsciously observed. Their value is subjective, and that subjectivity is where the conflict generally arises. The man whose mother prepared a Sunday dinner banquet for all the family may find it difficult to adjust to a wife whose mother saw Sunday as her day off and expected all family members to fend for themselves. Neither might respect the other's rituals. Each might insist that his ritual should be followed.

Comments, particularly negative ones, could cause serious fractures in interpersonal relationships. Negative comments about traditions or rituals are best left unspoken. Know the traditions. Know their origins. Understand the depth of these traditions and the hold they have on the people you are with. Avoid criticizing them, and don't try to change the unchangeable. Some traditions are perpetuated simply because no one ever questions them. Others have a logic cast in marble.

STEP 7
ALL SPORTS AND TEAMS ARE NOT THE SAME

MONTREAL CONCORDES

During my first trip to Canada, I fell in love with its beauty, its culture, and most of all its people. I had visited Montreal on one of my vacation trips, but I did not get to know the city. I remember being fascinated by the inhabitants returning from the stores with their baguettes early in the morning. I was disappointed by my inability to handle the French language despite five years of courses spread out over my high school and college years. No matter how hard I tried, I wasn't understood. I continued trying, and I can only report slight progress.

There were many people I met in Montreal who were instrumental in my longevity in the Canadian Football League (CFL). In 1982 the Montreal Alouettes folded for the first time and were immediately replaced by the Montreal Concordes with Joe Galat as the head coach. I worked with Galat at the New York Giants. I was delighted to hear his voice on the other end of the phone line and further delighted by the content of his call.

"What do you know about the Canadian Football League?" he inquired.

"Not much, I've seen a game or two on television, and that is about it," I responded.

"How would you like to join me and my staff and learn about the league? There is no money. But I can pay your expenses when we are at home and for some games on the road," Joe offered.

Exactly what I was to do was unclear. I suggested that I put together a proposal. We talked about a week later. In my proposal, I stated that I was going to assist the coaching staff in building team chemistry, do concentration exercises with the players, teach the players about visualization, and support the coaches in making their presentations more effective. After Galat reviewed it, he called me with excitement. I couldn't wait for him to stop talking so that I could enthusiastically shout out a resounding "YES!"

The years that followed seemed, to outsiders, like a journey with no road map. Galat, who knew where he was going, appeared to be flying by the seat of his pants. This was a function of his personality. He gave the impression that he was always ad-libbing. He was not. He always tried to see the bigger picture. The hail-fellow-well-met persona that he exuded got him through. He was extremely popular with the press, always giving them a quotable one-liner. Considering his record, his press conferences were less confrontational than many.

He was generous enough to introduce me to the beat reporters, which was a shot in the arm to my career. I was soon becoming, if not a celebrity, an item of curiosity. I was interviewed by the reporters of the Montreal media and before home games by the visiting press corps. There may have been other psychologists who worked in the CFL, but they didn't have Galat blowing their horn. When I was in town, he introduced me to everyone he came across.

Joe Galat was head coach of the Canadian football team the Montreal Concordes, and previous linebacker coach of the New York Giants.

How do I thank a man who is responsible for introducing me to the Canadian Football League? Do I buy him a yacht, a Mercedes, a home on the Riviera? These suggestions sound great, but they are not within my grasp. The next best thing is to let people know how many football coaches and football administrators got their start in pro football under his tutelage. Many became outstanding coaches in the NFL, the CFL, or in colleges. My list of names will no doubt be incomplete. It will serve as an overview of coaches he impacted.

Dave Ritchie had a Hall of Fame (CFL) eligible career, serving as:

- Head coach of the Montreal Alouetttes
- Head coach of the British Columbia Lions, where he led his team to a Grey Cup Victory
- Defensive line and special teams coach of the Winnipeg Blue Bombers, who appeared in one Grey Cup under Ritchie

He was also awarded The CFL Coach of the Year in 2001. He completed his career with 108 wins, placing him seventh among all time winningest coaches in the CFL.

Wally Buono is a Hall of Famer and is known as the "Winningest Coach in CFL History." In 2018 Buono was honored with the Bob Ackles Award, as he was retiring from football with the most wins as a coach.

Chris Palmer had a memorable career in the NFL.

Tom Rossley was the head coach at Southern Methodist University. In addition, he held positions with Holy Cross, San Antonio Gunslingers (where I worked with him briefly), Atlanta Falcons, Chicago Bears, Kansas City Chiefs, Green Bay Packers, and finally with Texas A&M.

Eric Tillman earned Grey Cups as general manager with the BC Lions, the Toronto Argonauts, and the Saskatchewan Roughriders, and he was also the executive director of the Senior Bowl.

George Cortez had an outstanding career in the CFL, as well as stints in college football and the NFL. He saw his career take shape in Montreal.

Stan McGarvey won the NAIA Division II Coach of the Year Award while at William Jewell College. He honed his skills as a pro coach under Joe Galat.

Doug Sams broke into pro coaching while he worked on the Montreal Concordes' coaching staff.

Add to this incomplete list my name. Joe Galat opened for me an entirely new area of the sports world. Instantly, I became a fan of the game as it is played in Canada, a lover of Canada in general, and an admirer of Canadian football fans. Forty years later, my ardor has not dampened.

The last time I had contact with Galat was in Montreal. I was in town with the Boston Bruins, who were in the NHL playoffs with the Montreal Canadiens. He had become a successful businessman providing artificial turf to college and pro stadiums. He had lost none of his good humor. Life had treated him well, and he was basking in it. Joe, thanks for the opportunity and the memories.

SAM ETCHEVERRY, GM, MONTREAL CONCORDES

Sam Etcheverry was a very important person in the early days of my career in Canada. He had a following from his days as a player and was an influential person in the league. Remember, I was an unknown commodity. Psychologists in sports on any level were few and far between. Etcheverry was our general manager at the Montreal Concordes. He greeted me warmly and made this American feel comfortable while learning the Canadian scene.

Etcheverry was one of several people who helped me find my way through the mazes of the CFL. A football legend in Canadian football lore, he was known as the "Rifle." My initial impression of him was that he was goal-oriented and expected success. Over the time I knew him, I found my initial impressions to be correct. His frustrations grew with what was occurring on the field, as the losses began to become regular and expected. It must have taken a toll on him.

Etcheverry was born in Carlsbad, New Mexico, of Basque farmers from Spain. He excelled as a college football player at the University of Denver where he still lays claim to many of the offensive records. An inaugural candidate and subsequent inductee into the University of Denver Athletics Hall of Fame, he remains highly visible in the annals of Pioneer football. His passing records are mind boggling. He broke a record held by NFL Hall of Famer Sammy Baugh when he threw for 3,610 yards in a single season. He is remembered for his on-the-field feats throughout the CFL.

In his first year as head coach of the Montreal Alouettes he led the team to victory in the 58th Grey Cup. Montreal also remembers him as one who tried to bring the NFL to Montreal. Any idea of the NFL expanding to Canada was one that I strongly resisted. I feared for the death of the CFL should that occur. Sam shared with me many times that one of his greatest moments was when he was inducted into the CFL Hall of Fame. To him it was the culmination of a successful career.

DON SWEET, PLACEKICKER, MONTREAL CONCORDES

Little did I realize it at the time, but Don Sweet became a strong influence on my career in Canadian football. He spent hours teaching me kicking techniques. Gaining this knowledge cleared the path for me and helped me establish some credibility in working with kickers in the league for many years. Sweet, our outstanding place-kicker, taught me tons about the intricacies of kicking. Whether it was in education, on the field, or among friends, most of his life was spent helping people.

After retiring as a player, Sweet traveled throughout Canada, helping aspiring kickers achieve their goals. His calm, quiet, and consoling demeanor made him approachable and sought after. His career was a roller coaster, reaching the heights with the Montreal Alouettes and plummeting to the depths with the Montreal Concordes. With the Alouettes, he reached the coveted Grey Cup five times, winning once in 1974 and again 1977. His greatest performance was in the 1977 Grey Cup, often referred to as the "Ice Bowl." Cold weather didn't bother Sweet. In that game he scored 23 points with a record number of six field goals. The Most Valuable Canadian award found its way into his trophy case three times in 1974, 1977, and 1979. His mark on the Canadian Football League is indelible.

NICK ARAKGI, TIGHT END, MONTREAL CONCORDES

I often joked with tight end Nick Arakgi about his being the only person I ever knew personally who was born in Cairo, Egypt. Arakgi's talents exceeded the success that the Montreal Concordes had as a team. Had he been on a winning team, his achievements would have been far greater than recognized. Nonetheless, his on-the-field accomplishments are noteworthy. Playing in a Grey Cup game is the goal of all players in the CFL. Arakgi accomplished this early in his career with the Montreal Concordes. His awards include:

- CFL All-Star recognition in 1982, 1984, and 1985
- CFL's Most Outstanding Canadian in 1984

Years later, I saw Arakgi when he attended his son Jason's CFL games with the British Columbia Lions. Meeting Jason was a thrill for me. When his father and I were with the Montreal Concordes, there was a promotion of some sort. A button with a picture of Arakgi holding Jason on his shoulders was widely distributed in Montreal. The continuity between players and their children always fascinated me. It added to my sense of history with the CFL. Interestingly enough, I not only worked with Arakgi and his son, but with Arakgi's teammate, Willy Hampton, and his son. These two men gave me a stronger sense of belonging in the CFL. In some small way, I was becoming part of the continuing face of the CFL.

GLEN WEIR, DEFENSIVE LINEMAN, MONTREAL ALOUETTES / CONCORDES

Some people are significant in starting a career when entering a new domain. Others are significant because they help perpetuate one's place in a league. This was how Glen Weir also contributed to my career. He was a respected veteran—a team leader who smoothed the way and endorsed me to have access to the players. Teams are generally constructed so that there is a balance between veterans and younger players. The Concordes were such a team. Most of the older players had played in Montreal wearing an Alouettes uniform. Because I embraced and studied history, traditions, and rituals, I was one of the few "outsiders" who knew the Concordes were previously the Alouettes. Knowing this bit of information and being a recipient of it made me more acceptable to the players. After all, I was brought in by the head coaches.

To many players I was considered the coaches' "plant," and Weir quickly helped stifle that notion. He had a storied past in Montreal's history and in the CFL. His accomplishments during those years with the Alouettes and Concordes are numerous. Having been a teammate of Don Sweet's in the Grey Cup years of the Alouettes, he was quick to share stories about Sweet and his teammates. His stellar year was in 1975 when he was nominated for the Schenley Awards Outstanding Defensive Player. That year saw him chosen as an Eastern All Star and Canadian All Star. The years of hard work, blood, tears, and sweat led to Weir's being called to the Canadian Football League Hall of Fame in 2009. It is rumored that the song "My Cousin Has a Grey Cup Ring" was inspired by the fact that the songwriter was a distant cousin of Weir's. I ran into Weir at a Grey Cup about 10 years ago. He was still the life of the party and enjoying his post-football life.

OTHERS WHO MADE A DIFFERENCE

Chuck McMann's path and mine crossed several times over the years, leaving me with fond memories spent with McMann and his wonderful wife, Margaret. He was a serious but humorous person. He continued his coaching career in the CFL, and at McGill College where he was named Coach of the Year. During our years together, we held group sessions with his athletes to teach them stress-reduction activities and help them learn to use visualization to aid in performance enhancement. McMann had many talents; one of his projects was constructing a kayak in his basement. I never did hear how he got the vessel out of there. Our coaching staff was replete with talent.

Chris Palmer was a first-year coach who later became a successful NFL coach. When the Cleveland Browns were resurrected, Palmer became the head coach. Among others, he invited John Hufnagel to join his staff. Hufnagel was a true offensive genius despite the disparaging picture that was painted of him by Eli Manning. He still turned his entry into the NFL into a successful career, which included winning a Super Bowl ring with New England.

Wally Buono, our linebacker coach, fresh from a career with the Alouettes, became the all-time winningest coach in the CFL. I worked with Buono throughout his entire career as head coach and general manager. More about Wally Buono later.

Peter Dalla Riva was a tight end and wide receiver with the Montreal Alouettes. I was fortunate to get to know Dalla Riva, a Hall of Famer and outstanding player for the Montreal team. Born in Treviso, Italy, he arrived in Canada at the age of eight. He and his family settled comfortably into their lives in Hamilton, Canada, where Dalla Riva graduated to football from being a worker in the Hamilton Steel Mills. His career in the CFL resulted in three Grey Cup Rings and an election to the CFL Hall of Fame. Dalla Riva is one of the icons of Canadian football in the Montreal area. He spends much of his time promoting junior football in Canada as a way of paying back the opportunities presented to him.

In 2018 he was selected to the Gridiron Greats Hall of Fame, in recognition of 51 years of service to the Montreal Alouettes Football Club. When I was first told I was going to be nominated into the CFL Hall of Fame in 2014, I demurred. Then I thought of calling my old friend Dalla Riva to ask for his advice. We hadn't spoken for years, but the conversation flowed as if it was the continuation of one held the day before. He insisted that I permit the nomination to be made and expressed optimism for its passage. From that moment on, I wanted so badly to be admitted to the Hall. It was not to happen. Some love affairs are one-sided. It seems I loved the league more than the league loved me. Dalla Riva shared that he was surprised at the rejection. Despite the outcome, it was great to know Dalla Riva was supportive of my nomination. His generosity, positive attitude, and humility helped make him the outstanding citizen that he is.

KAY BROWN, OPERATIONS

Kay Brown, the business guru for the team, became my guiding light in learning to navigate the Canadian waters in areas outside of football. I knew little about the business operations of pro sports. Brown helped fill that void. She taught me about the important roles of competent people in the office staff. She was loyal, passionate about her work, and one of the team's greatest fans. Her job was complex, and she handled it with grace, charm, and competence. She was a close associate of mine and remains a good friend.

THE DIFFERENCES OF CANADIAN FOOTBALL

The game itself as played in Canada was, at first, difficult to follow. Everything happened at breakneck speed. The longer, wider field, three downs, and a slew of rules unique only to Canadian football were a challenge. Some of my American friends ridiculed the league. How could a small league with two teams named "Rough Riders" be taken seriously? They didn't know there were two different spellings of the word. "Rough Rider" and "Roughrider" each had different meanings. Working for the league in those days was treated as a part-time job. Salaries were low and were supplemented by players working as substitute or regular teachers, firemen, policemen, or whatever was available to them. Practice schedules were often adjusted to accommodate the players' work schedules.

Over the years, the league became more financially stable. The work conditions improved at first for the players, and then many years later, for the assistant coaches. In fact when the issue of my being paid a consultant fee came up, I refused payment, hoping that what was offered to me would be spread among the assistant coaches. I am not certain that is the way it played out, but I sure hope so. Our games were fun. In the beginning few ended in the win column. For me it was a great learning experience. I became acquainted with Canada and its people and quickly became hooked on the CFL games. I treasured each visit to home games and the opportunity to explore Montreal, its many neighborhood restaurants, its delights, and culture. I began to feel I was a welcome part of the Canadian Football scene. Decades later I remained a fan of the league, friendly with many coaches, in touch with former and current players, coaches, and members of the media, and happy over the opportunity to have had the experience. My gratitude to Joe Galat knows no bounds.

CHAPTER 8

CALGARY STAMPEDERS (CFL)

STEP 8
ALWAYS BE AVAILABLE

CALGARY STAMPEDERS

Calgary was one of the cities that intrigued me. I had heard about the Calgary Stampede and was convinced that the Canadian Rockies had to be high on my bucket list for travel. If you have never been to Calgary, add it to your wishlist. On my first trip there it was a growing city, which for some reason reminded me of Denver, Colorado. A "cow town" was my first reaction, which was expanded by the spectacular views of the snow-capped Rocky Mountains. Couple this with the fact that, within a few hours, you could travel to places like Banff, where caribou, at that time, walked the main streets. Then travel to Lake Louise, to see its (now) melting glaciers for a sight to behold. You'll see the reasons for my admiration of the city when you go. Downtown Calgary, with its shops of native crafts and the work of local talent, added to its charm.

My first visit to Calgary was in the early 1990s, when I was asked by management of the National Hockey League's Los Angeles Kings to interview a prospect they were considering for the upcoming draft. I spent most of my time there becoming familiar with Calgary.

Later, when I returned for the CFL Stampeders, the city had sprawled by incorporating some of the neighboring communities. It seemed to me it had tripled in size. Another factor that cannot be overlooked was the warmth exhibited by the people who resided there. Their pride in the Stampeders and its proximity to winter sports were talked about openly and appreciatively. Families looked forward to each season, which brought new activities, including crops to be canned and enjoyed throughout the long winter months.

In addition to that, the Calgary Stampeders had the best logo in the Canadian Football League, running a few laps ahead of the second-best logo, that of the Hamilton Tiger Cats. What made these two logos special for me was their simplicity and imagination. They stood out from other logos in the CFL, which were too often only the capital letter of the host city. I had secretly wished one day to be decked out in Stampeders apparel. The odds against that ever happening were running pretty high against me. Then one day it happened. But, as with all roads that were difficult to navigate, this one was winding, and my presence on it came only by chance, in a most unlikely manner.

The year was 1990 and I was still under contract to the Los Angeles Kings. The NHL draft was successfully completed in Vancouver, British Columbia. One of the highlights of the draft was that the Kings gained the rights to defenseman Darryl Sydor. Sydor had a long and star-filled career as a player and coach in the NHL. Bob Owen, a chief scout of the LA Kings, and John Lindegren, who was a Swedish-based scout, formulated the plans for a roadtrip through a series of late-night phone calls. Lindegren, who was always eager to explore more of Canada, asked if it could be arranged for him to visit Owen's home in Calgary. Since Lindegren and I had become close friends, Owen decided to include me.

The three of us rode in Bob's car. Despite numerous offers from both John and me to share driving time, Bob drove all the way—all 600+ miles. Did he think it was easier for him to drive than to give us directions, or did he simply not trust us with his car? These are questions I cannot answer.

To anyone who has not made this trip, it's difficult to explain the wonders, if not impossible. The scenic beauty is breathtaking, and the history of western Canada that one learns along the way, priceless. One stop on the trip was in Kamloops, a city I would visit many times later, as the British Columbia Lions Football Team held their training camp there. On the golf course, our threesome coincidentally ran into Darryl Sydor, whom we had just drafted for the LA Kings (NHL). His home was in Kamloops. We stayed overnight in Kamloops, and the next day found us in Calgary, at the home of Bob Owen.

After a day of many laughs and unending conversations, John Lindegren expressed interest in watching practice at the Stampeders Training Camp (CFL), which was at McMahon Field at the University of Calgary. Wally Buono had recently become the head coach of the Calgary Stampeders. For me, this was more than just OK, since I had already made plans to visit the camp. I called Wally a second time to tell him of our plans. He welcomed the suggestion and gave us his schedule for the day.

At the Stampeders' training camp we were greeted royally by Montreal Machine General Manager Gordon Cahill, with whom we had worked with in Montreal, and by the new head coach, Wally Buono. After the practice, we met in Wally's office. The two scouts excused themselves, and Wally and I had the opportunity to renew a relationship we both thought had run its course. During that conversation, the matter of me becoming associated with the Stampeders came up. No commitments were made. I left feeling that the opportunity to become associated with a CFL team was a real possibility. That training camp was the first in a string of training camps that went on for more than 20 years. My relationship with Wally was rekindled. The consultancy became a reality, and we developed a plan that included me in his team. That season I met the Stampeders as they came east to play in Toronto, Hamilton, and Ottawa. This was the beginning of a working relationship between Buono and me that lasted over 30 years.

WALLY BUONO, HEAD COACH, CALGARY STAMPEDERS

In 1983, after a six-hour drive from Newtown, Connecticut, I arrived at the Montreal Concordes' training facility just as a preseason practice was ending. I was, at the time, the consultant psychologist to the Montreal Concordes. Unshaven, attired in blue jeans and a plaid flannel shirt (I was comfortable and this had become my usual attire), I had driven by car through the Adirondack Mountains.

It was the beginning of a new season, which meant new coaches, new players, and new aspirations. I walked into the coaches' dressing room to the sound of a new loud voice that dominated the conversation. It was the voice of our new linebacker coach who had retired recently from the Montreal Alouettes, Wally Buono. A two-time Grey Cup Champion, as well as a former linebacker and punter, Buono was neither shy about nor reluctant to offer opinions on many matters.

As I was introduced to each of the new coaches, I noticed skepticism on the part of some and had the feeling that I was underwhelming others. My feelings were quickly confirmed as I was introduced to Buono, who greeted me with the words, "You don't look particularly professional to me." What a way to start a new season. My immediate reaction was that a know-it-all Italian was going to have to cope with another know-it-all Italian. The prospect was not appealing. I decided I would walk cautiously around the new coach.

As the camp progressed, Buono was the first to offer assessments of the previous session. At first I dismissed his comments. As the days passed, though, I began to listen more closely and came to realize that this man was making valuable contributions to the team. He was worth being taken seriously. While the messages were great, the manner in which they were delivered was grating.

It was not too long before I realized that this man had many inherent leadership qualities. His assets could easily have been overlooked because of the way they were presented. We survived one another for an entire season—really just tolerated each other. Neither of us disliked the other, but we weren't bosom buddies. I attributed it to the fact that we were both Italian-know-it-alls whose respective egos were beginning to blossom. But who knows the real reason?

After that, the franchise began to fall apart. Soon after it folded, Buono and the rest of the employees were out of work. During my final years with the Concordes, my role became miniscule and my trips to Montreal infrequent. I lost track of Buono and many others. It all changed in Mobile, Alabama, in 1986. I attended the Senior Bowl in Mobile as a guest of then-executive director Eric Tillman.

One day in practice I ran into Wally who, like many other attendees, was looking for work. We talked briefly and went our separate ways. The next day at breakfast I encountered him again. This time he had a request. It so happened that Wally's roommate snored rather loudly and interrupted Wally's sleep. He asked me if I had an extra bed in my room and wondered if he could move in with me. I agreed, not certain as to how this would work out.

That night after dinner, I returned to my room to find Wally stretched out on the bed, reading his Bible. We talked for hours in deep, meaningful conversations about God, being Italian, family, and yes, even football—anything that came into our minds. We talked late into the night. My opinion of this man changed completely after our talk. The next morning, he was reading his Bible again and discussed a passage with me. I left him to go to breakfast and was eager to speak with him again that night.

Each day during that week was the same. Long, deep, heartfelt conversations. Each morning, we discussed the Bible reading he had just read. I had just developed a new friend. Oddly enough, it was a revelation to me. Here I had discovered a man of deep faith and moral conviction. His devotion to family was commendable. There were even traces of humility, which had been well hidden before. I began to feel a closeness to him and sensed that he was developing an appreciation of me. He was not, at first, a real advocate of a psychologist working in sports. That I could handle. He was in the majority of sports people in that regard. After our conversations, he became interested in my role, which he had originally not seen a need for nor understood.

At the end of the week, we parted ways, certain that we would continue our relationship by phone. We did just that. Every few weeks we called each other and continued to solve the problems of the world.

In 1990 Buono was hired by CFL legend Norman Kwong as the head coach of the Calgary Stampeders. He called and asked me if I was interested in working with him. No details, no nothing. I agreed, but did not expect anything to come of that conversation until we met at the Stampeders training camp. Over the years our relationship developed into a strong friendship that served both of us well. We shared many laughs, faced many crises, solved a multitude of problems, created an even greater number of them, learned about each other's families, shared cooking recipes, won a good number of football games, took part in nine Grey Cups (won five), and generally enthusiastically participated in creating a strong emotional bond between us.

Each year in Calgary the respect we had for each other grew. We experienced a Grey Cup together and lost. But eight more appearances followed, five of which were successful. I learned many things about this man over almost 40 years of association with him. He is not the hard-nosed, insensitive person some think him to be. Instead, he is a caring, warm, and loyal person who cares for his players and enjoys their success. I admire him mostly for his faith, his emphasis on the importance of family life, and for his many kindnesses to me. He was there for me through the ups and downs of my career. His frequent phone calls and his concerns made him a very special person in my life. Thank you, Wally. It was one helluva ride. Too bad it had to end. Enjoy many plates of al dente pasta, glasses of fine wine, and countless hugs from your family.

ERIC TILLMAN, GM, BC LIONS, TORONTO ARGONAUTS

Eric Tillman, with whom I had worked with in Montreal, became the executive director of the Senior Bowl, which some said was experiencing many problems and was in danger of folding. During Tillman's tenure he successfully turned this event, which was flirting with failure, into a huge success. Soon after his appointment he invited me to Senior Bowl week. Eager for every and any new experience, I accepted the invitation. The Senior Bowl was an excellent place to study human nature, and a great place to see GMs and coaches let their hair down. I don't know how many of these weeks I attended.

The Senior Bowl was kind of like a coaches' convention. The demands on the attendees were minimal. It provided coaches the opportunity to catch up with their friends, exchange war stories, hear the latest gossip, and if they so chose, create some of their own. It also provided those men whose contracts had been terminated an opportunity to seek employment. Those seeking to improve their status also hopefully attended. Too bad most of the unemployed men who attended the Senior Bowl left Mobile, Alabama, still unemployed, carrying the added anxiety of how they would support their families.

To a lesser degree, those seeking advancement experienced the same thing. I had three experiences with this situation. One indirectly affected me, the other two directly. These events are not in chronological order.

EXCEPTIONS TO EVERY RULE:

In 1994 Jeff Fisher was named interim head coach of the now defunct Houston Oilers (NFL). Ted Plumb had a long history with Fisher, dating back to their glory days with the Chicago Bears and later with the Philadelphia Eagles. Fisher worked under Buddy Ryan with Plumb and me in Philly, where Plumb hoped to be named offensive coordinator. As was his way, Plumb had hoped to bring me with him. But the best laid plans of mice and men were again thwarted.

After their meeting, the first day we were in Mobile, Fisher stopped returning Plumb's phone calls, and Plumb began to suspect that the scenario he had created as offensive coordinator with me on the team would never be acted out. When phone calls are overlooked in sports there is usually only one reason for it—the person who received the call is not interested in the caller.

I learned that there are exceptions to the rule. One, Peter Chiarelli, with whom I worked in Boston, was notorious for disregarding messages requesting he return a call. So much so that his colleagues would simply shake their heads when the matter came up, commenting, "That's Peter." Luckily, Chiarelli's many positive qualities overrode the call-back phobia.

In Fisher's defense, he had to pick the person he thought was best for the job. He owed that to himself, the owners, and the fans. Emotions should have no role in these decisions. At the time, I thought that he had made a mistake. As it turned out, I think Plumb and I were right.

The second incident occurred between Allan Webb and me when we worked together at the New York Giants. There was a highly touted running back, newly drafted Gordie Bell, who exhibited some concentration difficulties. Together, we developed a program for Webb to meet with Bell during lunch every day to review the morning practice. The experiment worked. Webb did a great job teaching a willing and eager subject.

When Webb was with the San Francisco 49ers, he had a running back with similar problems. He asked me if I would be interested in working with this person in the same manner as New York. Of course I agreed. There was one glitch: the deal had to be approved by John McVay. At the hotel, we found that John had checked out and was returning home. I never heard anything further from the organization and never knew where the plan died. The lesson I learned from that was simple: the sports business is fickle. Yesterday's flavor of the day is instantly and unceremoniously replaced with neither apologies nor explanations to anyone.

My 13 years in Calgary proved that one of the values in sports is the relationships that are engendered. I could fill the pages of an old Manhattan telephone directory with the number of people I met who moved in and out of the CFL. During my time there, many new relationships were formed, and some from Montreal were reignited. The CFL is a small world. Players, coaches, and people in all walks of life who work in the league are recycled. Many ended up in organizations they passionately despised. New loyalties were de rigueur. To name and to recognize each of these men and women would be impossible. Some memories have been dimmed by the passing of time, which in no way diminishes their value.

Get ready for a ride down memory lane! How many of these folks do you remember or have you heard about?

EZZRETT "SUGARFOOT" ANDERSON, DEFENSIVE BACK, CALGARY STAMPEDERS

Ezzrett "Sugarfoot" Anderson was a legend in the lore of the Calgary Stampeders. You may ask why he was significant to me. If you looked for any tangible gain from knowing him, there was none. But his knowledge of the league, his willingness to share it with me, a stranger, and the patience he demonstrated in our discussions makes his memory precious to me.

Remember: By this time I had many years of experience in sports. I was, if not always respected, always tolerated. Still, deep down in my soul, I did not feel I belonged. I had no history of achievement in any sport. I never played competitive sports on any organized level. I couldn't skate, kick a field goal, take a block, or be tackled. So when someone with a history of success in sports like Anderson spent time with me and included me in their inner circle, I naturally reveled in their acceptance.

Sugarfoot's playing accomplishments were underscored by his inclusion in the Calgary Ring of Honor. He was one of the most approachable men I have ever met. After five minutes in his company, you felt as if you had known this man your entire life. His many careers were private to him. Few knew he was an actor and an all-star football player. He was kind, lovable, and a joy to be around. His death at age 97 on March 8, 2017, represented the end of an era. Few lives will ever be as memorable as the life of this man. He was of utmost importance to me, for he was a walking encyclopedia.

NORMIE KWONG, PRESIDENT, CALGARY STAMPEDERS

Calgary football was full of legends. Was there ever a more accomplished man in so many fields than Normie Kwong? Try to name one. Upon first meeting him, you would never assume that this quiet, humble man was renowned in a variety of fields. I was privileged to have met him early on in my years with the Calgary Football Club. He was magnanimous, gracious, witty, loyal, honest, driven to perfection, affectionate, and successful. Whatever the field—football, industry, or politics—Kwong plunged wholeheartedly into it, although he never neglected the roles he loved best—those of husband to his wonderful wife, Marie, and father to their children.

At the start of training camp, Wally Buono informed our assistant general manager and director of player personnel, Roy Shivers, and me that Normie wanted to take us to lunch at a time convenient to us. It surprised us that the president of the Calgary Stampeders found the time to entertain us. We agreed upon a date, and Roy and I headed over to the restaurant. As it turned out, the place was upscale, full of businessmen and women dressed to kill. We, on the other hand, had come directly from morning practice, and were disheveled and in our sweats. Ordinarily, we would have been denied entry into the place, but we were with Normie Kwong, and the door was wide open to us.

On many other occasions, Normie took several of us to dinner in Chinatown, where he explained, in detail, the origin of many dishes. He took pride in introducing us to menu offerings we would have never tried. Since this "man for all seasons" was private, it took a while to become familiar with his many and varied deeds and honors. He stood five feet seven inches tall, not what one would expect of an all-star running back who, over a 12-year stint in the CFL, amassed a total of 9,022 yards rushing and scored 72 rushing touchdowns. In addition to the rushing stats, he scored four receiving touchdowns and accumulated 903 yards as a receiver.

As the first player of Chinese heritage to play in the CFL, he made such an indelible mark on the league. His list of football honors pales to insignificance when compared to his non-football accomplishments. Three times (1951, 1955, and 1956) he won the coveted Eddie James Memorial Trophy. In 1955 and 1956 he was also named the Schenley Most Outstanding Canadian. Both Walls of Fame in Calgary and Edmonton carry his name.

Outside of football, he was partially responsible for bringing the Calgary Flames

(NHL) to their new home in the Saddle Dome. The Flames became the Stanley Cup Champions, earning him a Stanley Cup ring to go along with his Grey Cup rings. He shares, with Wayne Gretsky, the honor of having his name inscribed on both the Stanley Cup and the Grey Cup. I share with them both the distinction of having both Grey Cup and Stanley Cup wins. Mine are with the BC Lions and the Boston Bruins. Gretzky's are with the Edmonton Oilers and the Toronto Argonauts. Normie's are with the Calgary Stampeders and the Calgary Flames.

Politics fascinated Normie. He was appointed lieutenant governor of Alberta by Queen Elizabeth II. She later honored him with the insignia of a Knight of Justice in the Most Venerable Order of the Hospital of St. John in Jerusalem. To his amazing list of accomplishments, he also swore in one of the prime ministers. Meeting this man and getting to know him was one of the many highlights of my time spent in Canada.

JOHN HUFNAGEL, OFFENSIVE COORDINATOR, CALGARY STAMPEDERS

John Hufnagel's reputation as an offensive guru was beginning to grow. Together with the defensive genius of head coach Wally Buono, he put together many double-digit winning seasons and two successful trips to the Grey Cup. The respect between the two men continued to grow. After many years in the Arena League and after earning a Super Bowl ring in the NFL with the New England Patriots, Hufnagel returned to the CFL. Buono was heard to say, "The CFL just became a better place because John Hufnagel returned to it."

Considering the coaches I've had the pleasure of working with, it might appear to be an exaggeration to say that John Hufnagel is one of the most creative offensive minds in pro football. Believe me, it is not. I have stood next to him on the sidelines in Calgary, and have gone shoulder to shoulder with him in the cramped boxes of the Arena Football League. I saw the determined, optimistic look on his face as he orchestrated the rhythm of a football game. I felt the intensity and confidence he instilled in his players. I always concluded that, if something was left in Hufnagel's hands, it had a pretty good chance of success.

Of course he didn't win every game, but he was competitive for 60 minutes every time he walked onto a football field. He suffered losses badly. He bled a little after each defeat, then put it to rest, and went on to the next challenge. Hufnagel is restless by nature and bears fools not at all. Small talk is never on his agenda, even during his relaxing moments. Fishing and golf are the only fun activities he willingly engages in. Picture a man in motion, and you get John Hufnagel.

He and I became close friends over the years. This relationship was fostered by Wally, who encouraged Hufnagel to speak with me when he was considering a career change. He was offered a job in New Jersey with an Arena League Team, the Red Dogs. Wally hoped that when I talked with Hufnagel, it would help him to make a decision about leaving the CFL. Wally had strong feelings for Hufnagel. Privately he may have hoped that Hufnagel would stay with him. Still, he wanted Hufnagel to look at any opportunity to improve his career.

One day on the road, Hufnagel and I talked at great length and explored options, one of which was for him to accept a job with another CFL team where there might have been an opportunity to advance in the distant future. I suggested to him that any lateral move was unacceptable. John was interested in my observation. After giving my suggestion some thought, he decided to take the lateral move off the table and focus on one job, which was clearly a step up.

A few days later, after he returned to Calgary, he called and told me he had accepted the New Jersey Red Dogs position. Officially he was general manager and head coach. In reality, he was also travel coordinator, babysitter, chief scout, surrogate parent, counselor, or whatever else came his way. Our experience in New Jersey permitted us to form a strong bond—both professionally and personally. It was, for me, one of the experiences I felt most involved in and one that was the most fun.

Each morning of our first season, Hufnagel called to give me an update on the day's activities. When possible, I made the drive from Newtown, Connecticut, to New Jersey and spent the day at practice meeting with players and with Hufnagel. He had a quarterback who played in the CFL, Ricky Foggy, who was considered by many observers a streak player. Once he got hot, beware. Foggy did more than live up to his reputation. The first season we ended up in the playoffs, but the rings from that season bore neither our logo nor our names.

After several years, Hufnagel left to join Chris Palmer, with whom I had worked in Montreal. Chris only knew of Hufnagel by reputation. Chris was named head coach of the newly resurrected Cleveland Browns. That move started a series of jobs in the NFL for both men. One of the highlights in Hufnagel's career was with the New England Patriots, which ended in a Super Bowl victory and a gigantic Super Bowl ring. His relationship with Tom Brady and the memories of that association, coupled with the appreciation Brady expressed to Hufnagel, remains precious to him.

His exit from the NFL was less than he had planned, but sports politics demands the opportunity to raise its ugly head. This one bit hard. Hufgnagel returned to the CFL, where he served as GM and head coach for many years. During his first year in Calgary, his team won the coveted Grey Cup. My wife and I were invited to Montreal for Grey Cup week. After British Columbia was defeated by Calgary, with Buono's approval, I was free to pursue opportunities with other CFL teams.

Hufnagel invited me to join him in Montreal to address his team and work with the players. With the players, I covered a recap of my program, including relaxation, focus, concentration, and visualization. I also strongly emphasized to the players that this was, for some of them, a once-in-a-lifetime opportunity, one which eluded most players throughout an entire career. I told them how I felt about being in the Grey Cup and losing.

After I completed my talk, several players asked me if I would be available on the morning of the Grey Cup. I agreed, and invited anyone who was interested in coming to the session. Later John told me he was amazed at the number of players who attended. Watching the game from the sidelines helped me feel that I contributed in some small way to the win. At times on the sidelines, I have felt like an intruder despite the many expressions of gratitude I received from the players.

There is a story worth telling, since it helps capture the tenor of the man. One day apropos of nothing, Hufnagel asked me, "Throughout your career, which athlete do you think you have helped the most?" In all honesty, I could not come up with an answer. (Many years later I still could not find the words necessary to give the question an answer.) After a pause Hufnagel said, "What about Tony Stewart? You made him a football player." At first I drew a blank. Then I recalled Stewart from New Jersey, who also played for us in Calgary. Stewart was a talented running back who had trouble holding on to the ball. Each substantial run ended with a fumble. Through a series of concentration and visualization sessions, his performance improved considerably. Hufnagel concluded that I helped Stewart become successful.

Hufnagel repeated this theme when he wrote a letter in support of my nomination to the CFL Hall of Fame. He added Tony Stewart to his initial list, along with the names of Allen Pitts and René Paredes. For both of these players the same protocol was followed. This is another of the endearing qualities of John Hufnagel: his appreciation and loyalty are gratefully received. John and I continued to remain in contact and see each other whenever possible. He continued to send players to me until I retired. His friendship and respect are treasured. Our relationship enriched my career, and I'll always be grateful.

Relationships with quarterbacks of note were also part of this journey: **Danny Barrett, Doug Flutie, Jeff Garcia, Dave Dickenson,** and **Henry Burris** were at one time or another Calgary Stampeders. With the exception of Barrett, all four of the others had stints in the NFL. One learns from each experience. Fans marvel at the precision with which a quarterback under pressure can complete a pass. Even now I am amazed at the skill these men and their receivers have. Having the techniques explained to me by some of the best in the business was essential to my effectiveness in assisting players at enhancing their performance.

Linebackers Otis Floyd and **Matt Finlay** were two players I had many conversations with throughout the season. When Floyd was trying to make the team as a rookie, he was in close competition with another linebacker. The competition perplexed the coaches, who felt that, talent-wise, the players were of equal ability. Buono asked that I interview both players. My choice was Floyd. The decision turned out to be the right one. Buono once described Otis as the best team leader he ever knew. Finlay and I spoke often.

In 1995 the Calgary Stampeders played the Baltimore Stallions in the CFL Grey Cup in Saskatchewan and Matt Finlay made a prediction about the outcome of the game. As we were approaching the fourth quarter, we were behind by one point. We were getting so beaten up by the Baltimore Stallions team, which was stacked almost exclusively by American players and were a force to be reckoned with. Finlay's prediction became reality and Baltimore ended up winning the game (37-20), the only American-based team to have won a Grey Cup. I often wondered if, after Buono's experiences in BC with Travis Lulay, Rolly Lumbala, Geroy Simon, and Jason Clermont as leaders, Finlay might be asked to share the distinction as a leader in Calgary.

Alondra Johnson was spectacular in the Grey Cup win against Winnipeg. His early game heroics helped swing the momentum into the favor of the Stamps. I hope that their interactions with me added to their success.

My work with them ran the gamut from A to Z. For some, the issues centered around athletic performance, for which I integrated techniques on how to relax and visualize, and evaluated the value of the technique for each of the 11 individuals. For others, we addressed interpersonal problems with parents, siblings, girlfriends, and coaches. Since one technique does not fit all, individual protocols were established for each player.

ALLEN PITTS, RECEIVER, CALGARY STAMPEDERS

Allen Pitts, a talented and sometimes troubled receiver, led the receiving corps of Vince Danielsen, Travis Moore, and Dave Sapunjis. The demons on the field, for Pitts, were in the form of linebackers and defensive backs who tried to contain him.

Off the field, the demons were present, but rarely identified. To those who worked with him, Pitts was, at best, a complicated man. As a competitor he had no peers. As a leader he was forceful and direct, somewhat quiet and taciturn, perhaps, and some would say withdrawn. He appeared to many as a man who carried tons of baggage with him, someone seeming to withdraw from his past. This man was generous to a fault, humble about his accomplishments, and appeared shy to the point of being aloof. In spite of this assessment, he on rare occasions could also be a prankster.

Our sessions led him to rely on me in his moments of need. Unfortunately some of these moments were during the off season, thousands of miles away from support. He was cooperative, respectful, eager to learn, and constantly seeking ways to improve. He was grateful for the time I spent with him and always greeted me with enthusiasm and warmth.

As I watched him play, I felt that he was always on the brink of breaking another record. His head coach in Calgary, Wally Buono, said of him, "With Allen, whether you liked him or didn't like him, as a contributor to the Calgary Stampeders, I haven't seen anyone greater." Buono has spent his adult life among the greatest in the CFL. His words for Pitts are the highest compliment I ever heard him utter.

Dave Dickenson, now head coach of the Stampeders and the man who threw the ball to Pitts, felt that Pitts was able to use the motion of the CFL game better than any other receiver. Pitts held the record for most 100-yard games in a season (11) and most 100-yard games overall (64).

Roy Shivers, who is a brilliant judge of potential football talent, discovered Pitts at a tryout camp in California. Pitts paid his own expenses to attend, and this native of Tucson spent 11 seasons in the CFL, was inducted into the Canadian Football Hall of Fame in 2006, and was honored by having his jersey retired on the Stampeders Wall of Fame. He is the owner of two Grey Cup rings, one in 1992 and another in 1998. All told, he played in five Grey Cups and was nominated for the CFL's Most Outstanding Player Award. This was no mean feat, considering he was up against the likes of Doug Flutie, to whom he lost in 1991, Jeff Garcia, and Dave Dickenson. He may have been the quiet man in the locker room and generally off the field, but his on-the-field performance spoke of his greatness loud and clear.

Praise from one's teammates ranks high in the estimation of most athletes. No one who played with Allen Pitts had anything but praise for his performance. His behavior was sometimes labeled "goofy" by his head coach, but superstars function on a long leash, and goofiness is often overlooked as the player keeps putting up the big numbers. Despite some opinions, Pitts always brought it. He, like all of us, was defeated by Father Time.

In 2000 he retired, leaving behind him a legacy of records still waiting to be broken and respect from those who played and worked with him. Images of this tall, slender man with sure hands, gifted with speed and stamina, streaking up and down the football field, remain in the minds of all who were fortunate enough to have seen him play. As Dave Dickenson stated, "Unequivocally he was *the best*."

DR. TOM SAUNDERS

Not all the Calgary memories were involved with football. Spring had come early to Halifax, Nova Scotia, during the year I met Tom Saunders. The Annual Meeting of the American Society of Clinical Hypnosis had once again chosen a pleasant venue for its gathering. I was fortunate to have the paper I submitted accepted. After I presented my paper, a slightly built, soft-spoken man with a fringe-type beard approached the podium. After waiting to talk to me, he introduced himself and offered congratulations. He thanked me, excused himself, and went on to the next session.

It often happens at these functions that you meet someone, exchange ideas, and never see that person again. This turned out to be slightly different. That afternoon in the hotel pool, I met this man again. This time, we talked for longer. He was a physician from Calgary, Canada, and an avid golfer who had written a book on applying psychology to performance. Before we parted ways, he offered to send me a copy of his book when he returned to Alberta.

Weeks later, the book came in the mail. I acknowledged receipt of the book and complimented him on his many insights. This seemed to give momentum to our relationship. It was not until many years later that I encountered him again. I arrived at the University of Calgary for the start of the Calgary Stampeders' training camp. A beat reporter, Mike Petri, interviewed me and wrote an article about me for the next edition of the paper.

Two days later, as I entered the Stampeders' office, I was told there was a phone message for me from Dr. Saunders. It wasn't too many hours later that he appeared at training camp. Immediately I recognized him, and we had a long conversation. I invited him to join us for lunch. This time, the relationship was not to be touch and go, but one that lasted until his death. Dr. Tom Saunders, with his lust for life, his optimism, and his untiring energy, was magnetic, and his life was full of adventures:

- He flew reconnaissance missions over the North Sea in World War II.
- He helped develop the Ambulatory Care Center at Foothills Hospital.

- He was a catalyst in founding the faculty of medicine at the University of Calgary.
- He was the Calgary director of the postgraduate training program for rural Napali physicians when he and his wife lived in Kathmandu for eight months.
- He simply enjoyed his granddaughter's company to and from her voice lessons and her singing in between trips.

Whether Dr. Saunders engaged with military or medical personnel, was traveling or with family, his focus was always on the task at hand. He was not wishy-washy. He held strong beliefs, which he never tried to force on anyone else. Over the years, he became one of the first people I called when I arrived in Calgary. Golf, dinners, and trips to the track and casino became routine. One year he was in the process of updating his book, *Golf: Lower your Score with Mental Training,* and he asked me to write the foreword. This opportunity exposed me to a new group of athletes. Needless to say, after his diligent approach to the task, the book was well received, and led some people to refer to him as "Doctor Golf."

Our relationship grew; I became acquainted with his wife and some of his children. I ran into him on Sundays at Mass. Impromptu meetings all over Calgary were common, as were dinners or lunches at La Brezza, a restaurant run by our friend, Marco Abdi. The fluent Italian that flowed from Marco's tongue made us feel as if we were in Tuscany. Abdi was born in Somalia and learned Italian as a child in his homeland. Somalia was an Italian colony for many years. Italian language and customs lasted long after the nation's emancipation. Marco's good humor and enthusiasm added much charm to the great food he presented. He hosted many of the players and coaches.

"This is Tom Saunders," the voice on the line offered. "I am in Florida playing in a golf tournament. I would like to see you and spend some time with you." I picked him up that day, and we drove to my home in Florida. We spent an interesting week together, discussing religion, sports, and any other topic that was hot at the moment. A few months later, he called and told me he had been diagnosed with cancer. I offered my condolences, which he immediately refused, saying instead, "No, I have had a good life and have no regrets." He battled the disease as best he could. Eventually, the disease and Father Time, who is undefeated in his encounters, claimed one more victim. The world was left a better place because Tom Saunders was in it. Rest in peace, Dear Friend.

ROY SHIVERS, GM, CALGARY STAMPEDERS

There were many other people whose roles in my career were notable. No two people in the world could be more different or more diverse than Roy Shivers and myself. Roy and I were roommates for many years in Calgary. To say he was different would be an understatement. The word "unique" in its highest sense would be closer to the truth.

Shivers, the first black general manager in pro football (Saskatchewan, 1999-2006) was not an ardent proponent of a psychologist interfering in football matters. Since we enjoyed each other's company and respected each other's frankness no matter the topic, he cut me some slack. His ability to spot young talent was an asset to the teams he served. His behavior was unpredictable; mine was more planned. He showed up where you would least expect him, had opinions on everything, and was not shy in expressing them. Though we were both proponents of social justice, we had different ideas as to how this could be achieved.

Our friendship grew over the years in Calgary and then BC. During his tenure in Saskatchewan, he sought permission from Wally Buono for me to assist his players. Shivers sent me the names of players who needed words of encouragement and a shot in the arm to boost their confidence. My one requirement was that the players initiated our contact, as this enabled me to test their commitment. Our times together were filled with amusement and pleasure.

TOM HIGGINS, GM, CALGARY STAMPEDERS

Tom Higgins was head coach in Montreal and an executive in the CFL offices in Toronto, and he led the Calgary defense for several seasons. Higgins, a soft-spoken man off the field, was creative in his teaching approach and highly regarded. The many hours I observed of his teaching were priceless in my development. As a coach, Higgins employed many of the techniques championed by psychologists. He was an expert at applying the principles to coaching. He was conversant with ideas about relaxation and employed those techniques prior to his game plan sessions with the players. Higgins taught me ways to tweak some of my own thoughts, and how to make my offerings more applicable to defensive players.

While Higgins worked in the league offices, he asked me to submit a testing program for the screening of on-field football officials. My program included clinical interviews with the candidates, personality testing, aptitude testing, and performance tests through the use of tapes and video. Before it could begin, Higgins left the league offices for another position. It was an important part of my career, and the second time I was asked by the CFL Office to supply a proposal. Neither time the proposal was accepted. It is a compliment to be asked, and a disappointment to receive no reply.

OTHERS WHO PLAYED A ROLE IN MY CAREER

As fate would have it, the ill fortunes of one man sometimes become the bonanza of another. **Jim Daley**, an excellent coach for the Stampeders and even finer person and friend, undertook the tutelage of an aspiring young coach, Mike Benevides. When Daley suffered a health issue, Benevides stepped in apprehensively and adequately covered Daley's role. Upon Jim's return, he found that all was in order and Benevides had attracted the eye of general manager and head coach Wally Buono. Benevides then climbed the ladder of success one rung at a time. He became the head coach of the BC Lions after Buono's first retirement. He served as the defensive coordinator of the Edmonton Eskimos, as a football analyst for The Sports Network (TSN), and then was employed by the Ottawa Redblacks of the CFL.

Trainer **Pat Clayton** was, for years, a faithful and diligent employee of the "Red and White" Calgary Stampeders. He and his coworker, **George Hopkins**, were exemplary in their attention to and execution of the details of their jobs. They both played an essential role in the success of that franchise. There was a standing joke between Clayton and myself. Each time we met, he greeted me with, "I don't have your per diem." The memory brings a chuckle. The comment resulted from the fact that one of Clayton's duties was to distribute the per diem allowance to the members of the traveling team. In addition to that, Pat was a gold mine to me. His talent for spotting and assessing problem behaviors in players helped me with intervening in areas that affected the welfare of the men who played the game.

Ron Rooke, the team publicist during my tenure, spent endless hours bringing the franchise name to the public. Player interviews and coaches' appearances ran like clockwork through his office. He arranged many interviews for me on Radio, TV, and print media. His recommendations to the media went a long way to open the door for me to appear on TV sports shows and morning drive-time shows, all of which helped spread my name.

Stan Schwartz came on board as an executive. His leadership was recognized when he was elected to the coveted CFL Hall of Fame. No honor was more deserved. Schwartz was a pleasant man to be around and generous to me. During one Gray Cup final, I had two of my friends accompany me to Montreal. Thanks to Schwartz, they were able to enjoy the winning experience at the game, and later in the locker room. This was typical of Schwartz, always willing to help while expecting nothing in return.

During my tenure in Calgary an assistant coach was brought on to lead the offensive line, **Dan Dorazio.** In no time he established himself as an outstanding coach who, luckily for us all, followed us to BC. Dorazio, an intense, knowledgeable man, was extremely helpful to me. He shared his wisdom gained from many years of experience on many levels of football. His knowledge of football was encyclopedic; his passion for it and his impact on the players was an ongoing tribute to the man.

Angus Reed immortalized him in a book titled *Thank You Coach*. Reed, too, was an important link to me as a conduit to the players. His wit, charm, talent, and innate goodness was evident to me from the moment I met him during training camp in Chilliwack, Canada.

No list of associates in Calgary would be complete without the mention of the straw that stirred the drink, **Jane Mawby.** John Hufnagel's tribute to her after her passing says it all: "This is a great loss for both the team and me personally. She was a beloved member of the Stampeders family and a welcome female presence in a male-dominated world. Her gentle manner and warm sense of humor made her a favorite of anyone fortunate enough to work with her. Though she worked quietly behind the scenes and was not familiar to fans, Jane nevertheless made vital contributions to the team's success. She will be greatly missed." AMEN!

One last memory, and with apologies to those who were omitted, includes:

Rod and **Liz Hennessey.** I knew Liz through her brother, Jim, who was an NHL player. Her husband, Rod, was one of the leading horsemen in harness racing.

Many nights in Canada were spent with placekicker **Mark McLoughlin** and punter **Tony Martino**, with the help of Liz, trying to beat the odds at Stampede Park. Though the escapades were loads of fun, they never ended in significant financial gain. These outings took place about two times a year at training camp. The nights generally ended at the casinos, which were adjacent to the track. I mention them for the simple reason that social contacts, when you are away from home, help round out the working day. They add to one's enjoyment and effectiveness.

As you may have gathered, my experience in Calgary was outstanding and successful on so many levels:

- Three Grey Cup Championship rings
- Many friends inside and 16 outside of football
- Numerous memories of trips around the Calgary area
- The thought, upon leaving Calgary, that I was able to make a difference

Each time someone asked me about memorable Grey Cup moments, the first memories that came to mind occurred with the Calgary Stampeders. Buono always preached that the outcome of each game hinges upon three or four pivotal plays. Of the eight Grey Cups in which Wally and I appeared, the one that stood out most vividly in my mind was the Grey Cup: Calgary against Winnipeg in 2001 in Montreal before a sellout crowd. Winnipeg had just completed an outstanding season. The Blue Bombers, led by head coach Dave Ritchie, and on the field the brilliant quarterbacking of Khari Jones, were more than formidable opponents. Five plays were most memorable:

1. A sack by linebacker Alonzo Johnson on Khari Jones early on in the game for a significant loss of yards
2. A blocked punt by Aldi Henry
3. An important first-down run in the waning minutes of the fourth quarter by Kelvin Anderson
4. A play that George Cortez told me later on was suggested by backup quarterback Mike McCoy
5. The play of all the Stamps players, which sealed the win for Calgary

The second memory that comes quickly to my mind was also with Calgary. This was my first Grey Cup. Calgary versus the Toronto team, owned at that time by Bruce McNall, John Candy, and Wayne Gretzky. As I sat in the press box, I could not get used to the rarified air that accompanies each Grey Cup. I couldn't believe I had finally arrived and was a part of a Grey Cup contender. Regardless of the fact that another of my consultancies was the Los Angeles Kings, also owned by Bruce McNall, there was no question as to where my football loyalties lay. Optimism ran high, inspired by the Calgary Special Teams Unit that had an outstanding regular season, and that one of Toronto's strengths was in the return game fueled by the exceptional speed of Notre Dame Heisman winner Raghib "Rocket" Ismail.

But in sports the only stat that really matters is the current one. Past performance means nothing if you don't execute today. That optimism waned quickly after QB Danny Barrett was picked off on his first pass, which was returned for a touchdown. But a football game has many downs and many plays that can quickly affect the outcome of the game. Our special teams were doing a good job in keeping the Rocket from exploding. But explode he did. The sound resonated all over Canada after an 87-yard kickoff return orchestrated by the Rocket and the Toronto's Special Teams Unit. Calgary's special teams, which were dominant all season, had been victimized.

Toronto went on to win the Grey Cup. My disappointment over the loss caused me to ignore the opportunity to congratulate the Toronto ownership, all of which I had interacted with many times before. My lack of sportsmanship at that moment was one of the low points of my career. We, the Calgary Stampeders, had been defeated. No disappointment should be used as an excuse for bush-league behavior. My move was small and petty. I regret it.

Other Grey Cups, particularly the five where three were in Calgary and two were in BC, held a special moment shared with players and coaches.

COMMENTARY FROM RENÉ PAREDES
CALGARY STAMPEDERS

Dr. Frank started helping me in 2011, and to this day I'm blessed I called him. I only met him in person once and on phone calls for four to five years. He helped me so much with the mental part of the game. My favorite memory with him was our weekly conversations before each game, talking about football, the mental part of the game, and our families.

I know we both looked forward to our call each week. He always ended by saying he was close to his phone on game day if I needed anything. I will never forget his genuine care. He didn't have to take those calls, but he just loved helping me, and I'm sure helping others was something he loved.

CHAPTER 9

BRITISH COLUMBIA LIONS (CFL)

DOC FRANK'S LESSON
4 PRINCIPLES TO REMAIN FOCUSED AND REACH YOUR GOALS

One must do a task analysis in order to improve a skill. This consists of going through the desired activity step by step so that the necessary form is followed. Anyone who has gone through this knows how cumbersome this can become. Perhaps this can be best understood if we use the example of one attempting to teach a physical skill to one who has never attempted the activity before. What is the primary step? What is step two, and so on? This is where the discipline comes into play. It takes concentration and perseverance to follow a task analysis effectively.

There are four principles that must be followed if one is to accomplish anything in life:

1. Know your goals.
2. A goal must have meaning for you.
3. A goal must be a realistic challenge.
4. A goal, once achieved, must give satisfaction.

PRINCIPLE ONE: KNOW YOUR GOALS

Setting goals and focusing on them are the secrets to success. Know your goals and then set out ways to achieve them. The end must always be in sight. The road to it must be clear and uncluttered. In order to do this, you must remain focused. The first requisite in becoming focused is to know where you are going and where you want to be. Joe DiMaggio, Karrie Webb, Michael Jordan, Oscar Robertson, and Cal Ripken all shared God-given athletic ability. They also shared the capability of focusing on the task at hand. They knew where they were going. In my own experience, some of the most gifted at focusing were Bill Arnsparger, Wally Buono, Robbie Ftorek, Claude Julien, and John Hufnagel.

Bill Arnsparger, as the defensive coordinator of the unbeaten Miami Dolphins, was gifted in his ability to detect the most minute details present in every offense he faced. There was little doubt in the minds of Dolphins fans that Arnsparger would make necessary adjustments to continue the Dolphins' undefeated run. Arnsparger, like the other great ones, never sought excuses. He sought only the reasons for any momentary lack of success. In many ways Arnsparger, like Buono and Ftorek, made the game as simple as possible, while providing the necessary motivation to guarantee victory.

One night in Glens Falls, the Albany River Rats were losing to the Adirondack Red Wings after the second period. Ftorek's only words to his Albany team were: "We're the better team. Go out and show it." The victors shared a bus ride back to Albany.

Ftorek, Buono, Julien, Hufnagel, and Arnsparger share the particular gift of getting the attention of their players and then of convincing them that victory is within their grasp. Their method works like this: "This is the plan. Now go out and do it." Without a doubt they all believe that if you do it the way it has been planned, losing is impossible.

None of the men I've mentioned, those with whom I've interacted or have interacted, ever did any relaxation exercises, visualizations, or other focusing techniques. Nevertheless, something in their makeup made them capable of shutting out all distractions, concentrating on the task at hand, and staying with it until it was successfully completed. Each clearly set out realistic goals, found the ways to achieve them, and, more often than not, saw their goals attained. They were single-mindedly focused on the goals they had set. In each of them was a particular rigidity enabling them to stay focused. Each person had internalized his goals, and thus could pursue them without veering from his course.

It is possible to generalize from this experience that the first requisite in being able to focus is to know where you are going and where you want to be. The end must always be in sight. The road to it must be clear and uncluttered. In order to do this, you must remain focused. In other words, know your goals and then search for ways to achieve them.

PRINCIPLE TWO: A GOAL MUST HAVE MEANING FOR YOU

Ask the next hundred people you meet where they see themselves five years from now, and many will have difficulty giving you a cogent answer. They live their lives day to day, and, at the end of 5, 10, or 20 years, all they have achieved is to have gotten older. In a nutshell, they have no short- or long-range plans for their lives. They are not active participants, but passive observers of the changing scene. Their life happens, changes, and ends without their full participation in it. They are unable to focus because they have nothing to focus on—no goals, no plans, no thought-out direction.

Perhaps setting goals is more difficult than it appears. Goal setting requires a knowledge of oneself. This self-knowledge must be pure—free of rationalization and denial. This may be the rub. Too many people live their lives in partial or complete denial of the realities at hand. In a way, they become enablers in their own failures, which is perhaps the result of their consciously or unconsciously overlooking the severity of their situation.

For example, some women in abusive situations refuse to admit or recognize the gravity of their abusive situation. The wives of many athletes find themselves in this category. The O. J. Simpson scenario occurs more often than we may be willing to admit, the only difference being that most abuse does not end in murder. I was told of a conversation between the girlfriend of one athlete and the wife of another. The younger woman, the girlfriend, was physically abused by her live-in mate. The older woman, the wife, counseled the girlfriend to be patient, explaining that athletes have to let out their aggressions, sometimes at home. Fortunately, the young woman did not heed the advice.

Anyone employing rationalizations as did that wife would be incapable of adequate goal setting, either for themselves or others. Goals must flow from a knowledge of honest self-discovery. This self-knowledge is important in the development of goals, because a goal superimposed on someone unwilling or unable to accept its value is meaningless. A goal must either be a means to a meaningful end or an end in itself.

PRINCIPLE THREE: A GOAL MUST BE A REALISTIC CHALLENGE TO AN INDIVIDUAL

If you do not know what is important for yourself in life, if you are unaware of what gives meaning to your life, realistic and meaningful goal setting is impossible. A question I almost always pose to athletes is "Why do you play?" This is far more difficult to answer than it first appears. Many skirt the issue. Those who have self-knowledge come up with far more profound reasons than "because I love the game."

A wonderful example of the application of this was former Los Angeles Kings Forward Scott Bjugstad. Scotty kept a diary of his daily activities as they related to his hockey career and his life. It was a most honest assessment of his goals, his aspirations, and the limits to which he was willing to go to become and remain a success. Most of his athletic goals were achieved simply because he knew himself and set achievable goals for himself. Professional hockey lost a great person when he was forced to retire after a series of concussions late in his career.

What, then, makes a goal realistic?

- An end or goal is realistic when it is achievable by a particular individual who adopts it as a goal.
- A realistic goal must be achievable by the individual, while at the same time it must cause the individual to make some effort to reach it.
- The goal should not be impossible to accomplish, nor should it be accomplished with little or no effort.
- The goal must be a challenge for the individual.

Goals must be challenging. Observe children shooting at the basket during school recess. If they can easily make the basket from a particular spot on the court, they almost instinctively move further away. The easily achieved basket is no longer a challenge. While there is little satisfaction from scoring from the easier point, the one basket from farther out is an achievement.

PRINCIPLE FOUR: A GOAL ONCE ACHIEVED MUST GIVE SATISFACTION

Finally, a goal—one that enables a person to focus and ultimately achieve—must give satisfaction once attained. One reason that athletes retire, in addition to age and physical condition, is that there is nothing left for them to prove. In other words, all their athletic goals have been achieved. For some minor league players, goals are reframed so that the new goal becomes to play as many games as possible on the next highest level of play. Once this goal is achieved, it may give closure to some players. For example, older players who recognize that the players on that next level are faster, stronger, bigger, and generally more talented may decide to move on to the next step. Those who felt that they competed adequately on the next level may revise their goal to seek more opportunities on the next level. Expansion teams have made the achievement of that goal possible, even if just for a short period of time.

To restate the principles involved in goal setting and its consequent effect on focusing, we must begin with self-knowledge. This knowledge of self permits one to understand his or her needs and to know beyond reasonable doubt what they require for success and contentment. Focusing requires goals that are clearly understood by the individual, that have meaning to that individual, that are challenging to that individual, and that, once achieved, give satisfaction to that individual. It is impossible for a person to be focused if there are no established long- and short-range goals for his or her life. Career goals are extremely common, while goals of a broader nature may be less clear. Focusing, like everything else in life, must have a purpose. This purpose comes from the goals one sets for oneself. Keep your eye on the goal, learn how to get there, and who knows? The success that has always eluded you might be just around the corner.

STEP 9
KEEP THE MAIN THING THE MAIN THING

Changes in ownership of a football team can be either insightful and forward look-ing or static and retrogressive. Where there is trust with new ownership, everyone could continue without skipping a beat. That was not the case in Calgary. What was a harmonious and pleasant environment turned toxic. The turmoil led to the departure of Wally Buono and most of his staff to greener pastures in Vancouver.

Moving into a new environment was not easy. It was tough on families, coach-es, and just about everyone who would now have to relocate and rebuild. There are always pluses and minuses. But with a new leader in town, change was inevitable. The first few weeks required hours of probing, listening, and setting the direction for the coming season. The new GM had to be prudent to not throw out things that could lead to his success. On the other hand, he had to be courageous enough to make changes, many of which would not sit well with the employees from the previous regime.

Then rebuilding would take place, position by position, unit by unit. The cul-ture would soon change. Coaching staff had to be evaluated. Some capable coaches would be retained, while others, for whatever reason, would not be rehired. Head coaches like to surround themselves with people they admire, respect, and above all, get along with. Coaching staff spend countless hours together over the course of a season; harmony is essential.

In Calgary, we left behind a team that boasted three Grey Cups. We certainly were in "The Company of Champions." Each of us wondered if the football gods would also shine on BC. Several opportunities began to emerge with the lines. Head coach Wally Buono was already an established and revered name in the CFL. His coaching staff was mainly intact. Since all offensive plays begin with the offensive line, emphasis was placed on their development.

In BC, the offensive line featured Cory Mantyka, a respected veteran; the re-liable Kelly Bates; Angus Reid, a fixture at center; and Marc Pilon, a big, steady lineman. With Coach Dan Dorazio orchestrating each move, success was expect-ed. There was no limit as to what these men could achieve. Dorazio, one of the most respected coaches in the league, had proven to all that he was "the real deal." The "Men Who Caught the Ball Players" would have to be graded and office staff would be reshuffled.

Concerning the players, not all was gloom and doom. There were many simi-larities between the caliber of player Buono left behind in Calgary and what he in-herited in BC. His receivers in Calgary included Allen Pitts, a future Hall of Famer.

Travis Moore was a reliable "go-to man," as was Vince Danielsen. Dave Sapunjis was not to be overlooked. Examining his new roster, Wally saw a glimmer of hope. Geroy Simon and Jason Clermont, both potential Hall of Famers, led the receiving core of Ryan Thelwell and Bret Anderson. They were fortunate enough to have the talented and cerebral Dave Dickenson throw the ball their way. Dickenson was on the path that led him to the Canadian Football Hall of Fame (CFHOF).

The quarterback position was set. The backup was Casey Printers, who raised the hopes of Lions' fans. With the QB position settled, restructuring of the offensive line became the priority. The QB is of no value if he is lying on his back on the ground due to a porous line. Remember the action of the offensive line begins each play.

GEROY SIMON, RECEIVER, BC LIONS

The BC Lions receivers coach, Jacques Chapdelaine, invited all of his charges to meet with me. Many of us had worked together in Calgary with Wally Buono, who left Calgary for Vancouver in 2003. One of the men was Geroy Simon. I am not certain that the players I encountered for the first time were eager for the meeting, but they were cooperative and receptive. This was as talented a group of football players as one could hope to work with. Along with Simon, there was Jason Clermont, a Hall of Fame nominee, the multitalented Bret Andersen, the fleet-of-foot, sure-handed Ryan Thelwell, the ever-dependable Paris Jackson, Frank Cutolo, and Chris Brazzell. The meeting, from my point of view, was successful.

Simon, Clermont, Thelwell, Jackson, and Andersen all continued whenever I was with the team. Simon was well on his way to stardom before I met him. It seemed every catch he made and every yard he gained either brought him closer to a record or increased his lead over the leading contender. Simon had taken to striking a Superman pose after each touchdown. To the BC fans, he was the real Superman and Clark Kent was reduced to: *Clark who?*

Simon spent a season with the NFL Pittsburgh Steelers and the Winnipeg Blue Bombers, and came to the Lions in 2001 as a budding superstar who lived up to expectations. With the Blue Bombers, his stats were noteworthy. He caught 51 passes for 725 yards and seven touchdowns. Under the tutelage of Chapdelaine, and with his own determination to improve, these stats became CFL records.

In BC, Simon was an important contributor to two Grey Cup victories. After he was traded by the Lions to the Roughriders, he added another Grey Cup ring. Upon his retirement he became a CFL Hall of Famer and a member of the BC Lions "Ring of Honour." His contributions to the league were impressive. He ended his career with a total of 237 regular season games and 22 playoff games. His regular season receptions (1,029) stood as a record until they were topped by Nik Lewis. His regular season yardage gained (16,3520) still stands. Add to this the total number of touchdowns recorded (103) in a regular season and (7) in playoffs, and you have a first ballot Hall of Famer.

Simon's post-playing career was as director of scouting for the BC Lions. Canada Post used his image on a commemorative stamp of the 100th Grey Cup. Simon remained a treasured friend. The loss of his wife was a difficult blow to deal with and, in true form, he stepped up to his responsibilities in solo parenting his children. With his cape flowing in the air, his journey through the CFL was a "super" accomplishment.

JASON CLERMONT, SLOTBACK, BC LIONS

Simon was complemented by Jason Clermont, a big slotback who was capable of powering for extra yards after every catch, while stacking enough accomplishments of his own to earn him a nomination to the CFL Hall Of Fame. One of the many things I liked about Clermont was his directness. During our talks, he became a believer in what I was selling in terms of performance. He and Simon were two of my best clients. In one game, Clermont scored a crucial touchdown. As he reached the sideline, he came toward me and said, "That was just the way I visualized it last night." He gave me more credit for his success than I really earned. When he retired from football, he worked with young people in sports. He informed me that he solicited the services of a sports psychologist to help the kids. Popularizing psychology and its role in sports was one of my career goals. Thanks, Jason, for being one of those people who helped me achieve it.

> **AFTER HE RETIRED, JASON CLERMONT INFORMED ME THAT HE SOLICITED THE SERVICES OF A SPORTS PSYCHOLOGIST TO HELP THE KIDS. POPULARIZING PSYCHOLOGY AND ITS ROLE IN SPORTS WAS ONE OF MY CAREER GOALS. THANKS, JASON, FOR BEING ONE OF THOSE PEOPLE WHO HELPED ME ACHIEVE IT.**

BRET ANDERSON, PLACEKICKER, SLOTBACK, BC LIONS

The nifty Ryan Thelwell was also sure-handed and graced with better-than-average foot speed, making him an additional threat. Rounding out this corps was Bret

Anderson, who was considered by many of his teammates to be the most gifted athlete on the team. Receiver coach Jacques Chapdelaine was so confident of this man's ability that he never hesitated to use him at several positions through the course of a game. Anderson was a slotback, receiver, punter, place kicker, and a backup quarterback. His versatility started in his youth when he was a star basketball player who also excelled in football.

In his senior year in high school he received many offers from both Canadian and US colleges in both basketball and football. He opted to stay closer to home. At Simon Fraser University he played both football and basketball. His versatility made him an indispensable part of a team. His approach to life and sports made him a leader in the locker room. He was part of the 88th and 94th Grey Cup teams. After he retired from football, he joined the fire department in Port Coquitlam, British Columbia.

OFFENSIVE BACKFIELD

There would be two major carryovers from the team Buono inherited in BC, and both were huge assets. Kelvin Anderson, who was elected to the CFHOF, and Lyle Green. Both men were important cogs in the BC Lions offensive for many years.

THE DEFENSIVE LINE

On the defensive line, things were looking up for Buono. His coaching staff included Steve Buratto as offensive coordinator who, as head coach in BC, was already the holder of a Grey Cup. Defensive coordinator Paul Arslanian and the ever-popular Richard Harris were both holdovers. Mike Benevides also joined Buono, Dan Dorazio, Chuck McMann, and Jacques Chapdelaine in the move to the Canadian West Coast.

THE DEFENSIVE BACKFIELD

The men on the defensive backfield who were carried over into the new regime had either established their place in the annals of the CFL or were in the process of becoming fixtures. Carl Kidd and Brent Johnson, who were elected to the CFHOF, and Javier Glatt, a linebacker, became better-than-average special teams' players. Add to this linebacker Kelly Lochbaum, and the Lions were in good shape.

Regarding defensive back Mark Washington: What more could a coach want in an excellent player and on-the-field leader? Mark was reliable, competent, and competitive. His was a voice to be listened to and was, for many years, as a Lion.

It was now time to get serious. Expectations for this team under Buono were exceptionally high. But, as in all changes, success was not a given. Personnel changes were made after the first year. Talented coaches found the new environment difficult to navigate, causing some to leave while others were simply not invited back. This had nothing to do with expertise or coaching ability. It simply was a fact of life. Real progress could not be achieved until everyone on every level was at ease and on the same page.

BOB ACKLES, PRESIDENT, BC LIONS

Fortunately for Buono, he answered to one of the most insightful, knowledgeable, pleasant, straight-shooting men in the business, Bob Ackles, who started his football career as a water boy. His talents carried him to many NFL locations, among them Miami, Houston, and Dallas. His book, *The Water Boy,* should be on the bookshelf of every football fan. It chronicles the life of Ackles from the beginning of his journey as a BC Lions water boy to his rise as president of the club.

The relationship between Wally and Bob lasted until Ackles' untimely death brought it to an end. Ackles would be difficult, if not impossible, to replace. He was truly a unique person—honest, knowledgeable, humorous, intelligent, football-wise, and gracious. His death was felt throughout the NFL and the CFL.

Fate once again shone on Buono. His next appointee was Dennis Skulsky, who had many of Ackles' traits and several good ones of his own. Wally and Dennis enjoyed a great working relationship. The genuine concern and kindness shown to all of us was gratefully received. Thank you, Dennis.

As for me, my time in BC was becoming more inclusive. After all the years of our relationship, Wally and I hit it off better than ever. He was even becoming a believer in psychology. He and I put together a leadership group of BC Lions players. The qualities of the players were so high that the group functioned flawlessly. During training camp that first year, I interviewed the players. Our coaches made the task easier for me as they expressed confidence in me and communicated it to the players. Geroy Simon and Jason Clermont told me they had looked forward to meeting me. The reception I received from most of the other players motivated me. I brought all of the tools of my trade to the camp.

There is always optimism at the start of training camp. This camp was no different. But reality was not to be denied; we were not ready to go for the Grey Cup ring. We were not as deep as we would become in some positions. This would be remedied over the next two seasons.

In subsequent years, Lions players were added and made their mark.

One of the players that led to the success of the Lions was **Aaron Hunt**, who was a valuable addition to the defensive line. Aaron was everyone's favorite. His overall good humor and his captivating laugh raised the spirit of the room. He left the Lions after five seasons as the bearer of a Grey Cup ring, a three-time Western Division All Star, and during the 2008 season, Player of the Month in October. After he retired he returned to Texas.

How do you describe **Travis Lulay**? As a leader of the BC Lions he stood out on and off the field and was everyone's favorite. His teammates admired his uncanny skills, his competitiveness, and his leadership. He led BC to a Grey Cup victory in 2011 and was named the Most Valuable Player in that game. He was also named the CFL's Most Outstanding Player that same year. As a person, he was bright, articulate, and interesting to converse with. His dedication and devotion to his wife and their three daughters was exemplary. The latter part of his career brought with it serious injuries, and helped him make his decision to retire. While contemplating his retirement, we talked many times about life after football and career opportunities. He worked in management for the BC Lions where he continued to root for his buddy, Lions quarterback Mike Reilly. Football was fortunate to have had such a talented representative in this man. Don't be surprised to find him in a leadership role again. This time in a business suit.

Rolly Lumbala is proof that stats don't tell the complete story of a person's career. The stats are not recorded for the number of blocks Lumbala threw at opposing defensive players, which enabled running backs to become prominent members of a team, nor the times those blocks prevented injury to QBs. Leadership participation doesn't appear on the data list. The number of fires he helped put out before they raged and became a smear on the image of a team are not counted. As for me, I knew the man well and was always an admirer of his. If I would have built a team, Rolly Lumbala would rank in the top of the list of players I considered to be one of my building blocks.

Jason Arakgi was one of Rolly Lumbala's buddies. They both played on special teams with a determination and intensity that gained the attention of opposing players. Jason is the son of Nick Arakgi, a player with whom I had worked in Montreal during my first year in the CFL. He holds the record for the most tackles by a special teams player (185), a record set against the Calgary Stampeders on August 19, 2016. The next year Jason announced his retirement from the CFL.

Solomon "Solly" Elimimian was an outstanding linebacker who spent nine seasons with the BC Lions. During that time, he was named the CFL's Outstanding rookie in 2010. In 2014 he was named the CFL's Most Outstanding Player. It was the first time this award went to a player who was exclusively a defensive player. After a disappointing release from the BC Lions, Solly signed with the Roughriders.

Angus Reid, a jolly, optimistic, determined, gregarious retired CFL player, is now enjoying his life as a sought-after speaker and successful author. He brings the same enthusiasm he did during his playing days. He played every CFL game from 2002-08. He holds a ring from the 94th and 99th Grey Cups. Never one to miss the opportunity to contribute to his team's success, Angus is quick to acknowledge the role that Dan Dorazio had in his success.

I teased **Marco Iannuzzi** that he was "Harvard's gift to the CFL." His determination, ambition, and unbounded energy made him an important cog in the wheel to success. Outspoken about many causes, he may at times have rubbed some people the wrong way. You may question his causes, but never his sincerity. His untiring commitment to numerous charities earned him the Sovereign Medal for Volunteers to go with his Grey Cup ring. His active participation in social media attests to his diverse interests. He is as active in his retirement from football as he was in it. I hope his optimism for a better world succeeds.

Buck Pierce, a quarterback, impressed everyone with his demeanor, talent, attitude, and desire to win. He carved out an enviable career in the CFL.

Mike Reilly was a backup to Travis Lulay. He became an outstanding player in the CFL, notching a Grey Cup with the Edmonton Eskimos, while becoming the Grey Cup MVP.

During training camp, at practice, and on the sidelines during games, I spent considerable time with defensive secondary **Korey Banks**, who held the interceptions record, as well as **Ryan Phillips, Dante Marsh,** and **Mark Washington**.

No recollection of people significant to the BC Lions would be complete without mention of the man who made it all happen, team owner **David Braley**. He is a patriotic Canadian, oft-time savior of the CFL, successful businessman, senator, concerned family man, and the guiding light behind the BC Lions. Braley not only helped keep his ship afloat, but led the CFL to its successful present. Canadian football owes David Braley a resounding THANK YOU.

It was during the year 2009 that I missed my first training camp during Wally Buono's tenure in BC. My wife, Patricia, had a serious accident, followed three weeks later by another one. There was no way I could go to camp. In addition to her disability, old age was beginning to take over some of my movements. Travel was becoming cumbersome. If you were to look it up on a map, you would see that Florida, my new home, was about as far from Vancouver as any two places on a map of North America. Add the trip to Kamloops, and you begin to see the problem.

Things were also changing with the Lions. Wally decided that he had had enough of walking the sidelines and spending countless hours watching and re-watching game tapes. He stepped down as head coach to devote his time to the position of general manager for the BC Lions.

Mike Benevides, his loyal sidekick, was handed the reins, and his first year as head coach was spectacular. Subsequent years were good by anyone's standards, but not as dramatic. The sports world can, at times, be brutal—neither good for your physical nor your mental health. So it was to Mike Benevides, who found himself unemployed.

Coaches know from the day they are hired that they are, regardless of previous performances, hired to be fired. If you have any doubt about this, simply google the names Don Shula, Tom Landry, or Yogi Berra. In sports, you can fire a legend. It is ingrained in sports lore.

Benevides was later employed by the Edmonton Eskimos as assistant head coach and defensive coordinator, and then by The Sports Network (TSN) as a football analyst. Later, he held the position of defensive coordinator of the Ottawa Redblacks. Buono's next choice lasted an even shorter time.

On paper, hiring an experienced, highly successful US college coach with ties to the CFL appeared to make sense. Reality once again raised its ugly head and proved otherwise. BC was again in need of a coach. The rapid pace of coaching changes caused instability in an otherwise stable organization. Once again, David Braley showed his leadership ability. He asked, perhaps pleaded with, Buono to return for two years as head coach. Reluctant at first, Buono warmed to the offer and immediately plunged himself into the task at hand. His loyal followers— Bill Reichelt, Ken "Kato" Kasuya, Dan Dorazio, Mark Washington, and Jamie Carmell—quickly circled the wagons and went to work. The first year back ended in a winning season, an appearance in the playoffs, a loss, and a quick exit.

The one big plus for the BC Lions was the talent level of the team. The receiving corps, **Manny Arceneaux, Nick Moore, Marco Iannuzzi, Bryan Burnham and Shaq Johnson,** ranked close to the top in the league. The two guys throwing the ball were well above average, **Travis Lulay** and **Jonathon Jennings.** Their ability to read defenses and make quick decisions once the ball was snapped by center **Cody Husband** meant sleepless nights for the defenses attempting to stop them. The ever-reliable **Rolly Lumbala** was ready to do whatever was expected of him. **Chris Rainey**, who complemented running back **Jeremiah Johnson,** was also a threat when receiving kicks. Both Rainey and Johnson were capable and sure-handed receivers. **Solomon Elimimian** was the leader on the defensive side of the ball. **Ronnie Yell, Loucheiz Purifoy, T. J. Lee,** and all the defensive linemen made this unit an issue to be confronted. Linemen, both offensive and defensive, are generally underrated. Most of the offensive and defensive success can be traced to the work of these men. So, to all the linemen, take a deep bow and be assured of continued appreciation for all of your efforts. Success is impossible without your contribution.

One man whose contributions were rewarded by being elected into the CFL Hall of Fame in 2018 is **Brent Johnson**. Little did this native of Kingston, Ontario, know when he was a Buckeye at Ohio State University that his future would unfold in such a way as to amass a Hall of Fame career in the CFL. For Johnson, the journey was a litany of triumphs. At Columbus, he was on the winning teams at both the Rose Bowl and Sugar Bowl.

His experience with the Jacksonville Jaguars was less than he expected, so much so that he was unable to make the team, despite being named a Big Ten player in college. The days of playing home games before 100,000 people in Columbus were over. There was one option still open to him—the Canadian Football League. At best, the enthusiasm he was able to muster was tepid. In his mind, he thought of giving the CFL one year, and then he would get on with his life.

The BC Lions, when he joined them, were not playing outstanding football. The team appeared to be in disarray. With Bob Ackles, who had returned from his two tours of duty with Jimmie Johnson in Dallas and Miami, and the hiring of Wally Buono as GM and head coach, all of what had transpired was about to change. New life was pumped into the organization. The team was once again competitive.

For Johnson, the desire to be a part of a winning organization relit the fire. He wanted to stay in BC and be a part of what he expected to be a winning team. Always desirous of being the best, the pace of his progress in Vancouver caused him concerns. He seriously contemplated leaving football. After a serious conversation with Buono, and being promoted to a starter, he was determined to try harder, to learn more, and to become the mainstay of a dominant defense. All these things paid off. His career lasted for 11 seasons, punctuated by his election to the Hall of Fame.

The defensive backfield (D-backs) also came into prominence. The D-backs were fun to be around. They were lively, talkative, and good naturedly drove each other. During training camp and practice I wandered over to the spot they convened in just to listen to their chatter. **Dante Marsh** and **Korey Banks** presented me with game footballs, each painted with an inscription and each representing an interception. These two footballs occupy a prominent place in my memorabilia room.

Barron Miles was, in many ways, the leader of the group. The D-backs constantly jawed and pushed each other to succeed. They were aware of the number of interceptions each had, and Barron Miles had enough to get him into the CFHOF.

Ryan Phillips rounded out this group. Was Ryan Phillips the player who was the missing piece in the jigsaw puzzle?

Korey Banks (DB) was named a divisional all-star in 2006 for the second time. (The first all-star selection was in Ottawa, where he had intercepted opposing quarterbacks seven times during that season, second only to his teammate, **Barron Miles** [S], who led the team and the league with a total of 10 interceptions, 2 of which were returned for touchdowns. **Dante Marsh** [CB] recorded 52 defensive tackles and four interceptions, one of which he returned for a major touchdown.)

Their leader was the personable **Mark Washington**, newly retired with a long list of stats for himself as their coach. Many moments on the sidelines with these men made practice less of a chore for me. They constantly jawed at one another, good naturedly belittling the contributions each made in the previous game. Banks needed no invitation to start the frivolity, which encouraged Miles, Marsh, and Phillips to enter the fray. Sometimes they called me over to mediate a dispute; I don't ever recall being able to give my opinion once called. I enjoyed the banter and the camaraderie. They seemed comfortable to have me in their group.

Each man made enormous contributions to the success of the BC Lions. They complimented one another and respected each other as teammates and friends.

Korey Banks finished his career with the Winnipeg Blue Bombers in 2014. In addition to the Blue Bombers, he spent time with the Washington Redskins, the Miami Dolphins, the Edmonton Eskimos, and the Ottawa Renegades. His career stats are impressive, his irrepressible personality even more so. Korey Banks was named a CFL All-Star four times, a CFL East All-Star once, and a CFL West All-Star a total of seven times.

Dante Marsh was pensive and, in comparison to his unit mates, quiet until he was riled up. A fierce competitor, with amazing football smarts, he amassed stats that gave him membership into an elite group of players. His 10-year tenure included two Grey Cups, four times being elected to the CFLPA All-Star Team, a CFL All-Star in 2008, and a CFL West All-Star four times.

Blocking kicks is an art. To be the all-time leader in blocked kicks is a gargantuan task; to do it 13 times is a record that someday will be broken, but not easily. The holder of that record is:

Barron Miles. In many ways, this man was the leader of the defensive backfield of the BC Lions. Miles was and is a pensive man, quiet in his demeanor, and definite when he had to be. Leadership came easily to him. After returning from a stint with the Frankfurt Galaxy in Germany, he spent six years in Montreal and four more in Vancouver. He earned several distinguished awards:

- Named six times as a CFL All-Star
- Named four times as a CFL East All-Star
- Named five times as a CFL West All-Star
- Awarded the 1998 Frank M. Gibson Trophy
- Received the 2002 James P. McCaffrey Trophy
- Received the 2004 Tom Pate Memorial Award

Add **Ryan Phillips** to this outstanding group of defensive players and you can see how they became such a dominant force in the CFL. Phillips' contributions to the league were outstanding, as were those of his three amigos. After 11 seasons with the BC Lions, Ryan ended his career with the Montreal franchise, having:

- Been named a Grey Cup Champion twice in Vancouver
- Been named a CFL All-Star four times
- Been named a CFL West All-Star five times and the holder of five BC records
- Achieved most interception yards (816) in a career
- Achieved most interception return yards in a season (299)
- Achieved most defensive touchdowns in a career (6)
- Achieved most interceptions and returned touchdowns in a career (5)

The football sage who first commented on the fact that "a good defense helps win games" had these four men in mind.

Barron Miles was defensive coach in Edmonton, and **Dante Marsh** is coaching college football in Oakland. Phillips, after spending time with the BC Lions scouting staff, joined the coaching staff as an assistant coach. Teams on any level of football would do well to add Banks and Marsh to their staff. Each would bring spirit, experience, and insight. To all four of these men, I say a heartfelt thank you. Each in your own way made our games exciting. It was fun and a privilege to know each of you.

As I was writing this, I realized that many of my memories of these two teams (the Calgary Stampeders and the BC Lions) became merged into one. I had fewer opportunities to make new friends in Vancouver. I met the team on each of their eastern swings. My trips to BC were less frequent than my trips to Calgary. In BC, the motel I stayed in was not close to the homes of coaches or players. So on nights when I was not the guest of the Buono family, I spent my nights reading or watching television. My rapidly advancing age also required more sleep in the recuperation project. Some nights I spent time on the phone with team chaplain **Dave Klassen** and we tried to right the wrongs of the world. Looking at today's world, you have indisputable evidence of our collective failure.

It looked like the final season of the union that Buono and I had together was upon us. For Wally's sake, I hoped it would end with a Grey Cup win in Ottawa come November. It didn't. It also turned out not to be our last season together. My retirement was postponed. In a formal way, my association with the CFL had come to an end. I was still working with individual players across the league.

Passion for the league ran through my bloodstream. I was undecided about my loyalties to particular teams. Many men with whom I worked were scattered around the league. I knew few of the players who remained with the Lions. **Mike Reilly,** the QB, was my closest association.

The offensive coordinator, **Jarious Jackson**, and offensive line coach **Kelly Bates** remained. So if I chose the Lions, it would be for that reason. But my good friend, John Hufnagel, was a prominent figure in the league, plus my star pupil, René Parades, with whom I had worked throughout his entire career, were both Stampeders. The ever-effervescent Mark Washington had become the defensive coordinator in Hamilton. It became hard to express my loyalty to any team. It seemed my loyalty was to individuals.

In addition to these men were **Craig Dickenson**, the head coach in Saskatchewan, assisted by Travis Moore. Dickenson's linebacker was the all-star Solomon Eliminian, and his receiver was Manny Arcineau. They all had to be considered.

Khari Jones, my buddy from BC, now led the Alouettes.

Don Dorazio and **Jacques Chapdelaine** put together an offense in Toronto.

Barron Miles was the defensive backs coach in Edmonton.

The Winnipeg team could not be overlooked; two of our standout players in BC were **Andrew Harris** and **Adam Bighill.** It's easier to root for individuals than it is to root for rivals.

The final chapter was even more disappointing. A slow start, numerous games where we shot ourselves in the foot, two decisive losses at the end of the season, and one humiliating loss forced down the final curtain. It was time to head off into the sunset. For Wally Buono, it was a time for deserved send-offs and honors.

For both of us, it was a sad ending to one helluva ride.

My quandary soon ended in terms of team loyalty. In conversations with Khari Jones of the Alouettes, it was decided that I would work with some of the Montreal players.

COMMENTARY FROM TY LONG
BC LIONS

I met Frank in 2017 during my first year with the BC Lions. I started with and stayed in the CFL for two years, and then three years in the NFL. The head coach, Wally Buono, saw potential in me, and knew Frank would take my game to the next level. When I talked to Frank, I told him, "If I'm not perfect, my career will be over; Wally will cut me." Frank helped piece me and my head together for the game and had me think the right way. He was the common denominator through every season in both franchises. Frank taught me visualization. I already knew some, and we met in the middle because I hadn't learned yet. He knew I was a very task-oriented person in the first place. I didn't struggle. He taught me not to get in my own way. He told me, in times of adversity or struggle, "Don't get in your way and let it happen." He was a good person, and I enjoyed my time with him. We were playing the Chiefs on Monday Night Football. I saved all his emails. I reread his emails, and I could hear him saying everything to me like he was standing in front of me. I'm thankful I had an opportunity to build the relationship we had and to be a small part of his career.

COMMENTARY FROM TRAVIS LULAY
BC LIONS

I met Dr. Frank my first year in the CFL in 2009. I don't recall if I met him at training camp right away or later on in Vancouver, but I could tell right away that he was someone I wanted to connect further with. I played quarterback for the BC Lions of the Canadian Football League, and my first impression was that I could tell Frank had a number of years of experience and that he was someone that was only there to genuinely help pass on knowledge.

The biggest thing Frank did was provide me with a little bit of perspective that improved my confidence. He reiterated to me how much the coaches believed in my ability based on his inside conversations with them, and it was the first time I felt "wanted" in pro football after several years of working hard, getting released, working out for new teams, entering new locker rooms, etc. He said something to the effect of "You wouldn't be here talking to me if they didn't believe in you and want to see you succeed."

The first time I met with Frank, we did a visualization technique designed to relax the mind from other busy thoughts and then focus on the feelings of success. As a quarterback, I focused on seeing the defensive coverage clearly, delivering an accurate throw, and watching my receiver make the play on the ball. The first part of the exercise was designed to calm the brain and become very relaxed, followed by a detailed visualization of the football environment. "Think of the color of the grass, the feel of the football in your hands, the roar of the crowd as the pass is complete. Look into your teammates' eyes in the huddle," etc. This was followed by the thought, "What's the toughest thing they could do? What's the most challenging defensive look you'll get? Picture a blitzing linebacker," etc. This was followed by "See the offensive line pick up that blitz; see yourself step into the throw and deliver an accurate pass to your receiver; see him catch the ball and score," etc.

These were techniques I used throughout my career as pregame jitters set in. I was able to visualize myself confidently making the plays. It was a very helpful exercise, and I regularly used it throughout the remainder of my career.

*I was curious about how psychologists could contribute to us but hadn't spent much time looking into the mental aspect of sport. I became more interested in the topic and bought a few books, some probably at Frank's suggestion. One of those books (*Mind Gym, *by Gary Mack) became a must-have for me, and I read a chapter before every game to boost confidence and decrease any pregame jitters.*

Frank and I stayed in touch via email until he passed away. But I use a line I got from Frank on a regular basis, in both my personal life and whenever I talked to young athletes: "Always keep the main thing the main thing." Such simple wisdom to remind yourself that if it's a peripheral or cursory thing, it's not as important as the primary reason for doing whatever it is you're doing. In sport, don't worry about your uniform, the fans in the stands, the opponent's record, etc. The goal is to Win the Game. If the task helps you win, it's worthwhile.

PART 4

NATIONAL HOCKEY LEAGUE (NHL)

CHAPTER 10

LOS ANGELES KINGS (NHL)

STEP 10
THE SPORTS WORLD IS A SMALL WORLD

I can't, for the life of me, recall what brought me to New Haven on that particular day in 1983. We had moved to Brookfield, Connecticut, from Florida in 1970. After three and a half years, we bought a house in Newtown, Connecticut, and lived there for the next 30 years. At that time, we had neither business nor social ties in New Haven.

Was I in the market for a car? The Budget sales lot was across the street from the New Haven Coliseum. We had bought a used car from them years before and were satisfied with our purchase and their service. Or was it the hand of God opening another opportunity? Whatever it was, it turned out to be one of the most important days of my budding career. As I started my drive home, I passed the offices of the New Haven Nighthawks. The nightly news featured the exploits of the hockey team, praising its ownership, management, players, and loyal fans. Contacting the organization was high on my list, but not easily accomplishable. I was teaching full time and doing educational consulting in New York City. My round-trip commute was three hours . . . on good days. Time in Newtown was scarce.

Today was a rare opportunity. My courage in approaching the team was all that was lacking. Instead of heading home, I circled the block and parked my car outside of the office. As I left my car, I took a deep breath, asked God for guidance, and went inside. Once inside, I was greeted cordially. I explained the purpose of my visit and was introduced to head coach Nick Beverley, who invited me into his office. At first, I was so in awe of this man that I was at a loss for words.

My only experience in hockey dated back to the 1930s when my sister, Jo, took me to games at the old Madison Square Garden. Our seats were generally in the last row of the bleachers. It took almost two full periods to get over the fear of being up so high. Most of the games we saw were between the New York Rangers and the New York Americans, a team that had preceded the Rangers but lasted only a few years.

Beverley proved to be intelligent, perceptive, innovative, and curious. It turns out he changed the course of my career in sports forever. He made me feel completely at ease. At first sight, I was impressed by this man. We talked about my involvement with the Giants, the program I hoped to initiate, and the fact that I was not seeking remuneration but merely experience. Nick then introduced me to Nighthawks Team President Roy Mlakar, who was also gracious and welcoming. Somehow, I felt that he was more interested in my affiliation with the Giants than with my psychological expertise. This proved to be untrue. Roy became, as did Nick, a valued friend. After a brief conversation, Nick assured me that I would hear from him shortly.

By the time I left the office, I had the names of players who were potential subjects.

I was hopeful that when his call came, it would be positive. I was certain that, regardless of the outcome, there would be a call. Two days later the call came, telling me that all parties agreed and I could begin whenever I wanted. In addition, there was an invite to the next home game. I was on my way. I was in a new world—hockey—and happy to be there.

When I arrived at the New Haven Coliseum for the game on Friday night, I was greeted royally, introduced to everyone whose path I crossed, and given a slip of paper with the numbers of three players on it. These were my first clients in hockey—center Bill O'Dwyer, left wing Phil Sykes, and right wing Dean Jenkins. I was asked to observe these players and to discuss my observations with Beverley. I was, for a moment, anxious about my assignment. Would my notes reveal my ignorance? Would they be a good starting point for evaluations of players? I tried to get my wits together.

A few days after the game, I met with each player individually. I introduced myself, discussed my credentials, and told them of my experience. Then we discussed my goals for each of them, and how our purpose was performance enhancement and not a clinical assessment of their personalities. The techniques I would use were discussed in detail, as well as a little bit about the success rate from people who had tried the program. I emphasized the fact that my role was like that of a teacher's. If they improved, it was due to two things:

1. The techniques work.
2. The subject has bought into the program.

To get their commitment:

1. I explored with them which elements of our talks would be confidential.
2. I then asked them to reveal the goals they had for their careers.
3. I explained the importance of relaxation, repetition, and visualization.
4. I asked each of them to commit to the program and to keep a daily log.
5. I insisted they take what we were doing seriously.
6. I committed to meeting with them after each game I attended.

After exchanging phone numbers, we scheduled our next meeting and went our separate ways. I remember focusing first on Bill O'Dwyer, who consistently reminded me that he was my first client in hockey. Fortunately, he and the other players bought into my program. According to Beverley, their play improved, and their mental errors were less frequent. As is always the case, when one player on a team buys in, others follow. In a few weeks, after several presentations to the team, I felt I was contributing and becoming relevant.

After one of the games in which O'Dwyer was named first star of the game, he was interviewed by members of the local media, and he revealed publicly, for the first time, my role with the team. This led to my being interviewed from time to time by both the local media and the media that traveled with visiting teams. This consultancy far exceeded my fantasies. As I look back on it, I realize that it was successful because of the players' enthusiasm and cooperation. It would never have happened without the courage of Nick Beverley and Roy Mlakar taking a risk on someone who literally came in off the street.

As was the custom of both Nick and Roy, they introduced me to tons of people. Their approval of me was like being given a key to an exclusive club. I was accepted merely from their say so. Every time there was a visitor in the lounge of the Coliseum in New Haven, my credentials and I were elaborately presented. After a few weeks, meeting luminaries in the hockey world was a normal occurrence. For starters, I met Rogie Vachon, Roger Neilson, Wren Blair, all in management with the LA Kings. My two daughters both became hockey fans and accompanied me to home games and an occasional away game. The Nighthawks became our favorite team, one from which we learned lots about the game of hockey and of the people who made their living in the sport.

Working side by side with Nick was one of the best learning experiences a neophyte could have. I literally knew nothing about the game. One year I tried playing the game on roller skates with a lot of other guys who also had no ability in skating, puck handling, or shooting. The experiment was short-lived. We all went back to baseball. My education at the hands of "Professor Beverley" started with a blank slate. Patiently, he explained to me what positional play was and why it was important. He taught me how to observe subtle aspects of the game that I never even knew existed. I thought every shot off the net was a failure, never realizing that players sometimes shot off the boards with the hope that a fleet-footed team-mate might be in position to tuck the puck into the net. I learned about the art of the penalty kill, the tic-tac-toe of the power play. I was slowly becoming a more astute follower of the game. Still, I missed important moves. Beverley patiently corrected me.

Many times, Beverly invited me to away games. It was through him that I learned of the perils and pleasures of bus trips in the minor leagues. Some were adventuresome, but drivers speeding on black ice was never fun. The bus trip from New Haven to the Canadian Maritimes took days. If you were in the AHL, bus trips were part of the deal. Being on the road helped me bond with the players and coaches. For the first two years, it was a welcome novelty. After that, less so. Different arenas presented different challenges and different breeds of fans. The one staple was the 50/50 raffle, a tradition that lives on.

My first hockey playoff experience came with Beverley at the helm. We were defeated in the second round. It was here that I learned playoff hockey was played at a faster pace, at a more intense level. Before each round, the optimism ran high for management, coaches, players, and fans. Winning a championship is an experience that eludes even some of the greatest players; it is a moment unto itself. It never gets old. Though we won our section one year, it would be many years before I would have that experience of a league-wide championship in any sport. Once I had it, I quickly became addicted to it. The bond it creates is never forgotten; outstanding plays are brought up each time those involved in a championship meet. It is great to be a fan of a championship team. It is a million times greater to be closely associated with the team and involved in the process.

NICK BEVERLEY, ASSISTANT COACH, LA KINGS, HEAD COACH, NEW HAVEN NIGHTHAWKS

Let me tell you more about Nick Beverley. If you were to walk by him, you would immediately conclude that this attaché-carrying, erect standing man was a college professor. Begin a conversation with him, and you would be certain of it. In spite of his being scholarly, insightful, intelligent, and inquisitive by nature, a college professor he is not. His numerous talents go beyond being intellectual. His father told me one night, when it came time for the younger Beverley to choose a path that would eventually earn him a college degree or a career in hockey, he opted for the latter. In 1963 he began his career as a defense man for the Oshawa Generals, and in 1980 ended it as a player with the Colorado Rockies. In between those years, he played for the Oklahoma City Blazers, the Boston Bruins, the Hershey Bears, the Boston Braves, the Pittsburgh Penguins, the New York Rangers, the Minnesota North Stars, the Los Angeles Kings, the Colorado Rockies, and the Fort Worth Texans.

Beverley's coaching career began in 1980 with the Houston Apollos of the Central Hockey League. Then he moved on to the Los Angeles Kings as an assistant coach, and then to the New Haven Nighthawks as head coach for three seasons. He replaced Pat Burns as interim head coach of the Toronto Maple Leafs in 1996, then took a position as chief professional scout for the Nashville Predators, who have also knocked on the elusive door leading to the Stanley Cup only to find it was slammed shut against them. As they used to say in Brooklyn, "Wait till next year."

Over the years, the friendship and respect between Nick and myself intensified. But, as with all human experiences, working conditions would change. In 1986 the New York Rangers became co-affiliates with the Los Angeles Kings in New Haven. Some of our players were now Ranger property. Roy Mlakar, the team president, who always tried to look out for his associates, decided that my services should be rewarded financially. Each team would make an equal payment to me. As far as I was concerned, the way I operated didn't change. My contacts and sphere of influence grew by leaps and bounds.

ROBBIE FTOREK, HEAD COACH, LA KINGS

Beverley was replaced as head coach by Robbie Ftorek. A new era had begun for me. I had no idea what to expect. Robbie was a player in New Haven before he became the coach. This is my recollection of my first meeting with Robbie: As I walked into the team locker room during training camp, one voice dominated. Looking over, I saw this small man (by comparison to the other players) holding forth—Robbie Ftorek. I was struck by his passionate defense of whatever the position was he held at the time. He was a brash, aggressive player who was born to lead. I was not certain of my feelings toward him. At that time, they were probably more negative than positive. I introduced myself to him, and if I recall his reaction properly, I would say he was underwhelmed. We talked from time to time throughout the season. Ftorek's season as a player was split between New York and New Haven, reducing the contact we had with one another. We both survived the season.

The rest of the story ends well. During his time in New Haven we worked well together. Why I was uncertain about my future, I wasn't sure. Maybe I thought that the bubble was about to burst, ending the dream. Well, it didn't pan out that way. On the contrary, the relationship grew into a great professional one and an even greater friendship. By January, rumors were beginning to float around the team that Ftorek would replace Beverley at the end of the season. I was not too thrilled by that prospect. By this time, Beverley and I had established a good working relationship. I did not want to see that end. In addition to that, the relationship I had with Ftorek was somewhat enigmatic to me. As a player, he often discussed team matters with me. His manner was direct, and I appreciated that. You always knew where you stood with him on the issue at hand.

Otherwise, Ftorek played it close to the vest. I wasn't sure that, if he were to become the head coach, he would be content with having a psychologist on board, particularly one he had inherited and not chosen. My presence did not seem to bother him as a player. What his thoughts would be when and if he became the coach were a mystery. I was fearful that my New Haven days were coming to an end. My position was secure in the eyes of the LA Kings, but what it was in New Haven remained a question mark. Ftorek was a different kind of cat—opinionated, never making excuses, with a hockey savvy that knew no bounds. But being insecure, I never knew where I stood with him. Were my days numbered? Was my hockey life abruptly coming to an end? Who knew?

After Robbie became head coach and we had been working together awhile, he included me in everything, even seeking my counsel in some areas and always encouraging players to visit with me. As Beverley was the person who taught the course for my hockey certificate, Ftorek became supervisor of my hockey internship. He requested my presence in his office between periods. He would challenge me with the words: "What did you see?" At first, I was timid in my replies, fearing I would embarrass myself with my non-insightful comments. He persisted. "I need all the eyes I can get," he explained.

As my comfort level grew, I was encouraged by his support of some of my observations. I became more vocal; still, I was unsure. I learned that you served at the behest of the head coach. If the man in charge was forced to keep you, your life could be a living hell. A hell that I experienced many times in hockey. A hell I didn't want to inhabit.

On December 9, 1987, all of my insecurities, fears, and second-guesses of my right to be there were removed. I received a phone call from Roy Mlakar, which went something like this: "Couch," he said (he referred to me as "1-800 Couch"), "Robbie has just been named head coach of the LA Kings. He is coaching his first game tonight in New Jersey and he wants you there. We are leaving at 4:00 p.m. See you in New Haven." Talk about an offer you can't refuse. I left Newtown with plenty of time. The high I was experiencing was indescribable. Words could not adequately communicate my feelings. The excitement of seeing Ftorek at the helm was dampened by a 2-1 loss to the Devils. A massive door had been opened for Ftorek; it also ensured my continuing in the NHL.

Hockey is a small world. In many ways, it is a closed environment; good to the people who have paid their dues, hostile to those who give the impression that they invented the sport. Humility is the virtue of the day for people new to hockey. During Robbie's time with the LA Kings, he had the good fortune of coaching none other than Wayne Gretzky. The cast of supporting stars was equally impressive: Luc Robitaille, Tony Granato, Tomas Sandstrom, Dave Taylor, Jon Tonelli, Steve Kasper, Larry Robinson—the list goes on and on.

As the years passed, Robbie mellowed. He was still the demanding perfectionist, the tireless competitor, the loyal friend, the prankster, the wise guy. The ups and downs of his career, the illogical timing of some of his firings, and the price one pays when optimism turns to despair weighed heavily upon him. But through subsequent jobs he was still his fiery self, a person who hated to lose but accepted the reality of it. Success came to him in Albany, New York, as head coach of the River Rats and later in New Jersey.

Our relationship was further solidified through the LA, Albany, and New Jersey journey, and it resumed in 2016 with the Norfolk Admirals of the East Coast Hockey League (ECHL). He continued to send me players to work with until he was dismissed. Larry Robinson was one of those players. He had signed on with the Kings and was finishing out his career. "Big Bird," as he was called, had a wingspan as wide as a Boeing 737. Robinson, an NHL Hall of Famer, was an encyclopedia of hockey. Each time you left him you knew you had learned something. His signing helped the Kings in their development of young defensemen. It seems each time the Kings played in Montreal, Larry was receiving some honor. He had established himself as an icon in the hearts of Montreal Canadiens fans. Many of us—players and support staff—attended each affair in his honor. His appreciation was shown by his attention to the details of where we sat and how we were treated.

The success that Beverley and Mlakar experienced in New Haven paid off. Their reward saw them both in Los Angeles—Nick as general manager, Roy as president of the LA Kings. They were reunited with Ftorek, who had preceded them to LA. The Kings organization, during the ownership of Bruce McNall, was to become one of the premier organizations in the NHL. I remember the day it all happened. The Kings would rise from being just another NHL team to a media favorite.

In August 1988 I was driving on Route 84 from Newtown, Connecticut, to Springfield, Massachusetts, to meet Paul Fenton, a player on the LA Kings. We were meeting to play a round of golf. I was listening to a sports radio show when an announcement almost caused me to lose control of my car. Wayne Gretsky had been traded by the Edmonton Oilers to the LA Kings. I remember being in shock over the news flash. I couldn't wait to get to the golf course to discuss the matter with Fenton. Like so many other sports fans, I was blindsided. I had no idea the deal was being brewed. I knew nothing about the other Edmonton players in the trade.

When I arrived at the Springfield Country Club, I was treated like royalty by the parking lot attendant and other staff members. I concluded that these workers were the most polite people in the business. It was a short while later that I learned the reason behind all of this. It seemed that Fenton had exaggerated my importance and had given me more credit for the success of his hockey career than I had deserved. The adulation lasted the entire day, despite the fact that my golf game, which was always bad, reached a new low that day. I was invited by the resident golf pro to speak to his members at a later date. I was also introduced to an aspiring woman golfer with whom I would later work, Michelle Dobek.

Paul was as eager as I was to discuss the Gretsky announcement. His concern was that he would lose status with the Kings organization because of Gretsky's presence. We both agreed this would impact hockey in California and throughout the league. Impact, it did. The flamboyant new owner put LA firmly on the NHL map. The star-studded LA scene would add another star who embraced and was embraced by the folks who dominated the environment. McNall's generosity became the talk of the league. Money flowed freely in the hope of putting together a winning team. The team vastly improved and reached the NHL Finals, only to lose in game six to the Montreal Canadiens. Some placed the blame on coaching; others preferred different reasons. Nevertheless, the Kings lost.

Bruce McNall, the flamboyant and ofttimes controversial owner of the LA Kings, produced many memories worth sharing. It was not uncommon for Bruce to come into the Kings' locker room before games. Bruce had an unspoken philosophy that money was the only motivator that you could depend on. He put this in practice by offering the Kings team a sum of money if they won that evening. The money was to be spent in celebration of the win. The practice ended abruptly, I think at the request of the league.

Stories abounded about the generosity displayed toward the players. One story I recall, the truth of which I cannot swear to and which was repeated many times, was this one: McNall often accompanied the team to away games. Since he and Gretsky had become business partners as well as friends, they spent time together. The story, as it was reported to me, was that one day they happened upon a team-mate who was trying on an expensive leather coat for around $5,000. Comments were made that the coat and the player went well together. The player commented that the price was too steep and that he would not purchase it. The story continues that Gretsky took McNall aside and said the player had been playing well. He asked McNall if he would consider buying it for him. McNall agreed and the player left the store with the coat. The only reason I tell this story is to point out McNall's generosity and Gretsky's loyalty to a teammate. It is compatible with other such tales.

I recall one night when we were playing the Washington Capitals the next day, and we were in Annapolis for a team dinner. For some unknown reason, I ended up sitting next to Bruce. The waiter approached him and asked for his preference from the bar. He immediately responded, "Bring 12 bottles of your best red and white wines." The coach, who was sitting on the other side of him, suggested that it was too much and the players would not consume that much. The order was reduced to six bottles of each. The dinner progressed, and all the guests appeared content (as people are at a command performance). But, as is always the case with high-profile people, restlessness was beginning to set in. McNall called for the check. After a perfunctory perusal of it, he reached into his pants pocket, pulled out a roll of bills, threw them on the table, and instructed the waiter to take what was needed to pay the tab. The waiter returned, saying he was sorry, but that was not enough. Bruce reached into his other pocket, took out another wad of bills and said, "Here." I was in total disbelief. Many times in my life, before credit cards, I was anxious about not having sufficient funds. The memory remains today as vivid as if it had just occurred.

But nothing is forever in the sports world. Dark clouds were beginning to form over the Kings franchise. McNall's legal troubles began to mount. The Kings were in disarray. One after another of us went by the wayside. The final curtain came down on our version of Camelot. The glamor of celebrities in the locker room, training camp, or impromptu visits by McNall with the celebrity of the week was coming to an end. Regretfully, an experience that started out in New Haven on such a high note, and reached many high points in Phoenix and Los Angeles, ended on a low note. Beverley and Mlakar had seen the signs of the impending debacle.

After they had been fired, I called the new Kings' management to inquire about my status. I was totally at sea. I introduced myself to the new GM of the Kings and told him of my contract, which left me one year and included a substantial raise. I was startled by his response. It was evident that he had no clue as to what I was contracted to do, nor of the legal rights my contract granted me. He said he would replace me with himself and that the contracts were only valid between players and the organization. First and foremost, he had no credentials that would enable him to function as a psychologist. Second, my contract was ironclad. He told me my contract did not bind the Kings to me. Ungraciously, I told him I was giving him his first lesson in how he should do his job, and that I expected to be paid. Two weeks later, the financial officer of the Kings called me. Starting in October, I would be paid the sum stipulated in my contract. End of story.

McNall had built an empire, which included at one time or another, producing movies, ownership in the Canadian Football League of the Toronto Argonauts, a stable of horses, and at its base, involvement in the rare coin business. It was soon to be discovered that the empire was a house of cards erected on sand. An article that appeared in *Vanity Fair* seems to have been the final piece of the jigsaw puzzle that enabled the FBI to close in on McNall's operation. In no time, the once proud empire began to crumble, and soon it came crashing to the ground. Coconspirators turned on Bruce and began to testify against him. He eventually pleaded to several charges and was sent to prison. The once proud LA Kings were in disarray, which plagued the franchise for many years. The hockey version of Camelot sang its last song.

Though we were paid by the same financial offices of the Kings, Gretzky, the legend, and I had almost nothing in common. Our longest conversations centered around the CFL. He was friendly, respectful, and occupied by many things. Watching him play the game was an extra perk of working with the Kings.

I knew many of the Kings players when they were ascending the ladder to the NHL in New Haven or in our second affiliate, the Phoenix Roadrunners, a minor league team in the International Hockey League (IHL). Glenn Healy, Steve Duchesne, Bob Kudelski, Todd Elik, Petr Prajsler, Ken Baumgartner, Ron Scott, Scott Bjugstad, Robb Stauber, Gord Walker, and Hubie McDonough were all, at one time or another, fellow travelers of mine.

I first met **Glenn Healy** when he was assigned by the Los Angeles Kings to the New Haven Nighthawks. Immediately upon meeting him, you knew he was headed for big things. Articulate and pensive, this graduate of Western Michigan University possessed all of the qualities that would ultimately spell success. He excelled as a goalie, lasted 15 years in the NHL, won the Stanley Cup with the New

York Rangers, and was the poster boy for three video games, each time pictured in a different team jersey.

I recall one of the very first conversations I had with Glenn. He expressed reluctance to become involved because he was fearful that by exposing his short-comings to me, his career would be in jeopardy if he were to be traded. After many conversations he agreed to give it a try. This led to a strong relationship—so strong that the Kings sent me to visit him in Toronto where he lived during the off sea-son, since they had high hopes for him in their organization. During his career, he played for the New York Islanders, Toronto Maple Leafs, the New York Rangers, and the Los Angeles Kings. After his playing days, he was a talented hockey analyst for both The Sports Network (TSN) and the Canadian Broadcasting Corporation (CBC). He has also held jobs with the National Hockey League Players Association (NHLPA) and a role as the director/president of the NHL Alumni Association.

Healy joined his Kings teammates, **Ken Baumgartner** and **Hubie McDonough,** after a trade to the New York Islanders. Baumgartner was a rugged left winger—quiet and gentle off the ice, a menace to opposing players on it. As reli-able as he was as a player, he was even more valuable as an enforcer. He was quick to defend his star players, who were less inclined toward fisticuffs. A winner of the Memorial Cup, his playing career lasted from 1987 to 2000. Always an excellent planner, he had degrees from Hofstra and Harvard universities, which prepared him for life after hockey.

One of my most vivid memories of Ken dates back to when he was a rookie in New Haven. As was my custom, I took the rookies to New York City. Many of them came from small towns in Canada. New York City was an eye opener for them. Kenny was from Flin Flon, Manitoba, Canada, a mining town with a population of about 5,000 people. He was flabbergasted at first seeing Manhattan. We visited the top of the Empire State Building, which was enshrouded with fog on that particular day. Fog or no fog, Kenny took picture after picture. I never knew what became of them, but this helped create a bond between this young winger and myself. My wife and I attended his wedding in Connecticut. Years later, when I was consulting with the Bruins, I met Ken in the press box at TD Garden in Boston. I was happy to learn that life after hockey was rewarding to him.

Another ex-King who became a NY Islander was **Hubie McDonough**. Small in stature, fleet of foot, this fierce competitor soon became a fan favorite. Our paths first crossed in New Haven, then in LA, and finally in Orlando. He played in 195 games. He later became the director of hockey operations in Orlando, followed by Manchester. It is hard to separate the NHL experience from the experiences afforded to me in New Haven and Phoenix. We might have been one of the only franchises to have an affiliate in both the AHL and the IHL. Most teams had only one minor league affiliate either in the IHL or the AHL. A few teams shared an affiliate in either league. As for me, I thought it was great. Though there were many changes in New Haven, the experience there was always top-notch, even after Beverley, Mlakar, and Ftorek had marched on.

Their successors filled the bill adequately.

Pat Hickey was an innovative GM.

Coach **Rick Dudley**, who was assisted by **John Tortorella**, was easy to work with, and each included me in team matters.

Marcel Comeau, one of the nicest men in hockey, was saddled by a mediocre team. His sense of humor helped him through. I would say to him, "Years from now, we will be laughing about this." Each time I met him, he greeted me with the statement, "We're still not laughing!" Comeau lives in Washington State. Our encounters were few and far between. It is one of the associations I truly missed.

Things in Phoenix were also rewarding to me. I was asked by Kings' management to offer my services to all three teams. **Ralph Backstrom**, my first coach there, was a gem. A knowledgeable man in many matters in addition to hockey, he was pleasant to be around. He was able to identify artists from the Big Band era after hearing one note. I had thought that I was pretty good at that; he made me look like an amateur. If I had any beef with him, it would be the pineapples on his pizza after games. It offended my Italian culinary tastes. The owner, Lyle Abraham, went the extra mile to make my trips to the Southwest successful.

TIM BOTHWELL, COACH, NEW HAVEN NIGHTHAWKS

My second coach with the Roadrunners was coach **Tim Bothwell,** with whom I had a history in New Haven. Barbara, his companion, shares his adventurous spirit and a passion for fitness. Theirs is a relationship that has not only survived the passage of time, but also the losing seasons, firings, hirings, and disappointments. In 1989 in New Haven, Tim was nearing the end of his playing days. He had a full career, which saw him with stints with the New York Rangers, the St. Louis Blues, and the Hartford Whalers. Many players in this situation sign on with an AHL team. It affords them time to plan their futures and develop a plan that permits them to enter into the next phase of their lives. Tim was not quite there yet. He needed one more year to decide whether or not to hang on for another year or retire. Father Time would decide whether that playing career was over and, from what I know, Father Time remains undefeated.

Bothwell was always in top-notch condition, and the fire in his belly was still burning. Would the legs and the rest of the body, and the passage of time, force a decision? In New Haven, there were several vocal fans who gathered in Section 14. Each year, the name of their target would change. Their victim was always a veteran defenseman. During the players' introductions for a particular defenseman, Section 14 would chant in unison, "Bothwell sucks." Anytime during the game when Bothwell's name came up, the chant would be repeated. When Tim and I were together, I always asked him why the fans in Section 14 in New Haven did not like his socks. To this, a scoffing Bothwell would smile and shrug it off.

Hockey was only one of the dimensions that constitute Tim Bothwell. Several others help us to understand this man. There are some people you meet in life where you instinctively become aware of their loyalty and talents. So it is with Tim. I often think to myself, if you want to get a job done and done right, involve Tim Bothwell. If you need a job that involves painful attention to detail, call on Tim Bothwell. If you need a task to be completed after many frustrations, your man is Tim Bothwell. Whether it is developing a winning game plan for his hockey team or dicing plum tomatoes and garlic for bruschetta, if Bothwell is on the case it will be done flawlessly.

Our professional paths crossed many times after New Haven. Tim was head coach of the University of Calgary's Men's Hockey team. I was working for the Calgary Stampeders. Our living quarters were on the campus. Each day I passed his office, and if we had time we had coffee together.

Being in Calgary also allowed me to get to know **Barbara Chambers**. Barbara and Tim have been a couple for an eternity. On first meeting her, she appears shy. But once she is comfortable in your presence she is an engaging conversationalist, humorous, bright, optimistic, sensitive, and loyal. In Calgary, we cooked lasagna, made bruschetta, used her unequaled recipe for tiramisu, and enjoyed many home-cooked meals together. Chambers has a Ph.D. in psychology, and we often engaged in detailed dialogues about mental health issues. Her experiences span many areas; one of the most unusual was that of a prison guard. Together, they formed a wonderful couple and were precious friends. I thank them for many memories.

It was during my time in Calgary that I met **Dr. Dave Paskevich**, an outstanding colleague in the field of enhancing sports performance. He worked with Canadian athletes during the Olympic games in:

- Salt Lake City (2002)
- Torino (2006)
- Beijing (2008)
- Vancouver (2010)

- Sochi (2014)
- Pyeongchang (2018)

Dave is also the performance coach for the Canadian Freestyle Ski Team, which won 7 Olympic medals and 42 World Championship Medals, and appeared on more than 300 World Cup podiums. Dave is truly among the top practitioners in the world.

While the experience with the coaches in the affiliated teams was a great working experience, the coaches in the NHL were different. Was it the pressure? The prestige? The egos? It was hard to tell. Many of the Kings coaches after Ftorek played it close to the vest, seeming to be cautious so as not to be surprised by betrayals. And there were betrayals: from staff, management, and players. This was not unique to the Kings. There were players on other teams responsible for the firing of coaches.

One striking example in LA was under the tutelage of **Barry Melrose**. He had little respect for some members of the support staff whom he inherited, and that was his right. One day in LA, he invited me and the coaches into his office to view a video. It turned out the practitioner was demonstrating a technique I had been using for years; one I had, in fact, taught in many cities to many psychologists. When I informed him of the matter, he tried to put me on the spot. "Why didn't you tell me?" he asked.

"Why didn't you ask?" was my only response.

The matter never came up again. Howie Bolger, who was a respected practitioner, resigned abruptly.

I was not included in playoff activities. My role had diminished so much that I spent most of my time in the minor leagues. Years later I ran into Melrose during game seven of the 2011 NHL finals in Vancouver. I introduced myself to him. He apologized for not remembering me. In my book, he became just one other person I underwhelmed. To his credit, after the Bruins defeated the Canucks, he saw me and came up to me, offered his hand, and said, "Congratulations, Doc." All's well that ends well, so they say.

JOHN LINDEGREN, SCOUT, LA KINGS

No report of the experience I had with the Kings would be complete without mention of two of the scouts in the organization. Picture a large man with a round face, a bald head, an impish smile, a love of life—someone generous and polished, with a laugh that was infectious—that's **John Lindegren**. He was one of the European scouts for the LA Kings. He functioned mainly in Sweden, lived in Stockholm, and was a clocksmith there. His shop contained the finest timepieces available.

I had met him briefly on several occasions. Once was during the journey from Vancouver to Calgary mentioned earlier. What a gift it was to be able to call him "friend." John and I shared many interests. He enjoyed playing golf as I did, appreciated fine dining, imbibed selectively, reveled in even the corniest of jokes, loved the adventure that traveling brought, and liked to second-guess our hockey coaches.

He sometimes was a guest at our Newtown home, where he met the other members of our family. He invited my wife and I to visit him in Stockholm. One September we accepted the offer. Fortunately, after a rainy summer in Stockholm, the weather had turned beautiful and stayed that way throughout our entire trip. Lindegren, always the gracious host and gentleman, introduced us to life in Sweden, which most tourists do not experience. Local restaurants, hidden historic monuments, and traces of Swedish lore were all revealed to us. A particularly important side trip for us was a Sunday visit to his lake house. One day on our own, we took the train to Uppsala, where we visited the university and ended the day with a fine dinner before we returned to Stockholm. John and I spent many hours on the phone after our visit.

By 1992 we were all gone from the LA Kings organization. I latched on to the New Jersey Devils while he went with Bob Owen to the newly created expansion team, the Atlanta Thrashers. Soon after, his health nosedived. Each phone call found him sounding weaker and in greater pain. Then the phone calls stopped. His friends all assumed he died. Unfortunately, his death was not confirmed until Nick Beverley came across another Swedish scout who was aware of John's demise. The time spent with him, the quality of his friendship, the memory of his laugh and good nature was another of the happy memories that my time spent among champions afforded me. May he rest in peace.

VÁCLAV NEDOMANSKY, SCOUT, LA KINGS

At this point, I would like to explain my inclusion of the following player and scout. After all my years, and after numerous contacts with the greats in sports, I have always felt humbled by being in their presence. Not only can I call this man, Václav Nedomanský, a friend, but he also recommended me to several coaches looking for psychologists. Though I worked closely with these men and women, I have always felt like an outsider. Being accepted by people of this stature helped me feel like I belonged. Call it hero worship. Call it name dropping. Call it whatever you want. Just know that I feel privileged to know this man and to call him "friend."

While not a household name in the United States, this man was and is revered for his hockey prowess. He is to Czech Hockey what Gordie Howe and Wayne Gretsky are to the United States and Canada. His extensive list of achievements are testaments to the adulation paid to him in his homeland. In what was once Czechoslovakia, **Václav Nedomanský** ("Nedo"), played for 12 seasons for Slovan Bratislava of the Czechoslovak Extraliga. He was also a member of the Czech National Team, where he contributed to the winning of a Silver Medal in the 1968 Grenoble games and a bronze medal in the 1972 Olympic games in Sapporo.

His pro hockey career began in 1974 in the World Hockey Association (WHA) with the Toronto Toros. Then came a stint with the Birmingham Bulls, also of the WHA. His entry into the NHL was with the Detroit Red Wings, and it lasted from 1977-78 until the 1981-82 season. He spent the final season with both the St. Louis Blues and the New York Rangers.

In Nedo's life, hockey was only one of the fascinating parts. He was the first player from the Iron Curtain to defect to the United States. In his day, he was considered one of the best players in the NHL. His harrowing escape with cliffhanging tales are all being compiled by his son, Vashi, into a full-length documentary titled *Big Ned*. He was inducted to the NHL Hall of Fame in November 2019. His nomination was, for many years, supported by David Conte and Nick Beverley. His induction was long overdue. But politics always rears its ugly head, causing the feats that have been achieved to be overlooked. Because of his defection, the Czech government temporarily stripped him of his citizenship, which has since been restored. No worries for Nedo; he enjoys being both a Canadian and American citizen.

This man, at 75 years of age, appears fit enough to play at least a few shifts among other seniors. He was also a scout for the Nashville Predators and the Las Vegas Knights in the NHL. His black hair is streaked with gray, his infectious smile and gentle manner are immediately captivating. He speaks softly, with remnants of his mother tongue still in his speech. Serious by nature, but with a great sense of humor, this man is a connoisseur of fine wines and even finer dining, and is a delight to spend time with. On many of my excursions with the LA Kings, I met "Ned," as he is known to his friends, for dinner and interesting conversations. Unfortunately, our paths crossed less and less. We had to be satisfied with long telephone conversations.

BRYAN LEFLEY, COACH, LILLEHAMMER OLYMPICS

While I was still active, Nedo was always on the lookout for consultancies for me in the United States and Europe. He introduced me to **Bryan Lefley,** a coach for the Italian Olympic Men's Hockey Team in the Lillehammer Olympics. Lefley played in the NHL with the New York Islanders during their glory years. I first met him in Switzerland. On several occasions, we met in Milan to discuss players and programs. On one trip to Milan, I finished the psychological profiling of the Italian team members. Lefley became enamored with living in Europe, and he was fortunate to have a family that also enjoyed the experience.

Switzerland was one of his favorite locales. From the quality of the Swiss health care system to the high quality of the Swiss schools, the experience was something Lefley was eager to discuss. All of this was made possible for me by Nedo. Once endorsed by him, all your doors open wider, and your life becomes enriched. I owe the introduction with Nedo to Nick Beverley. It is amazing to me how many people appear and reappear in the small world of hockey, a world I was fortunately part of for a significant part of my professional life. Nedo and I shared many personal conversations, as he was a delight to listen to. His insights and observations were important and uplifting. Thanks for the memories. Nedo, you have a special place in my life.

My time with the Kings organization had many star-studded experiences. Thanks, Nick and Roy, for letting it get off the ground and for nurturing it, and thanks to the lengthy list of players, coaches, GMs, trainers, equipment managers, members of the media, and office staff who made it **"a time to remember."**

COMMENTARY FROM CURT FRASER, COACH, ORLANDO SOLAR BEARS, IHL

Frank and I met in Orlando through John Weisbrod when I was coaching the Orlando Solar Bears. John and Frank had worked together, and he came with the highest recommendations. I wasn't sold on the "mental side" of the game, but Frank sold me on it. He came to Orlando one night, and I wasn't sure what to think. When I was a player, they had a psychologist come in. You had to hit a board with lights, and it was crazy. I wasn't sure. He was a nice gentleman. John said, "You have to meet Frank," and we sat down to chat.

It was interesting that he only wanted to meet with the players individually for a few minutes. After his quick meeting, he knew everything about everyone in five minutes. Plus, in that short period of time, he came back with a read on each one. I thought, if he could do that, he was good at reading someone. I asked, "Now what? Set up a plan?"

"No," he said, "If the guys need me, they'll find me."

Other psychologists would set up three hours with them in a conference room and test them, etc. Frank just sat in the locker room. Every player went over to him and said, "Hey Frank, I have this thing." It was like having your grandfather around. It comforted them and relaxed them. He guided them and helped the team. Frank could meet with a group of players and eliminate the distractions, and they focused on being a group. He could make everything go away around them, and they could reach their full potential of playing. He was very different from a regular sports psychologist and very effective. He loved coming to the rink. The guys loved him.

Frank helped me and some of the guys. He brought me to Little Italy in New York City. He was awesome at how he worked with the coaches and players, and he was an even better friend to me. I'd call him, and he was always available to chat and fix things. He handled people so well and was so friendly and social. He was a great friend and a gem; really special. Professionally, he was so different. He helped the players relax, play hockey, and focus on hockey rather than on family things and kids.

I knew Frank had high-profile people he was working with, including a figure skating client. One day, we were getting on the ice before practice. Frank was there to see the practice. He says to me, "Hi, let's go to lunch." The doors open at the end of the rink. Practice is about to end. Oksana [Baiul] comes skating on the ice, gives me a hug, and she says, "Hey, coach, can I show the guys some skating techniques?" Frank is laughing his ass off, and 25 players stood there with their mouths open. It loosened things up, and the guys talked about it for months. He was always looking for a way to help the team. It surprised everyone, and seeing Oksana was a great treat.

He liked to win, and he had a track record behind him, which proved he was a champ. Other guys were different; they were doctors. He was the best at getting the best out of everyone. Everyone wanted a piece of him to get better. Frank helped the young players who had no direction, even if they were in a slump financially or with their families.

I can't thank him enough. It wasn't by accident that the Solar Bears won the championship. He was a big part of it. I wish every sports psychologist could have learned from Frank. Players would come in and ask, "When is Doc going to be around?" Guys loved him and wanted him around.

COMMENTARY FROM MICHAEL SANTOS, AHL/NHL - NEW HAVEN NIGHTHAWKS/LA KINGS

I met Frank in fall 1989 while working for the New Haven Nighthawks. The hockey club was the minor league affiliate of the Los Angeles Kings. They had acquired Wayne Gretzky a year earlier and employed Frank, who was living in Connecticut at the time, as the sports psychologist for the entire organization. Though separated in age by four decades, we both had a fondness for an afternoon cocktail (only one), good food (of all kinds), and the Miami Dolphins.

While working for different organizations during the years that followed, we shared acquaintances, and our Orlando friendship grew, even withstanding a 2001 meeting between my Chicago Wolves and his Solar Bears in the 2001 Turner Cup Final. As was often the case, Frank walked away with another ring that year. After joining the Florida Panthers during the summer of 2010 I was able to coerce (with one cocktail and dinner at Café Martorano) Frank, who was then in his 80s and living in Palm Beach Gardens, to come to work for the team. A few weeks later, I assembled the team members in the theater of the practice facility to meet their new sports psychologist for the first time.

With everyone seated and curious, Frank entered the room. He was wearing a bright green blazer befitting the winner of the Masters Golf Tournament or the Grand Marshall of the New York City St. Patrick's Day Parade. He shuffled his feet like Mr. Tudball (a character played by Tim Conway in the popular 1970s TV show The Carol Burnett Show*) and slowly made his way across the room to the blackboard. He then found a writing instrument and carefully printed his name and contact information for the group. Once completed, he turned to greet the audience and introduced himself. "Hello, I'm Francis Lodato," he said. "You can call me Frank or Doc. I have put my contact information on the board for you. Call or email me any time. If I do not get right back to you, it's because I'm dead." The group of players were horrified. That was, until Frank flashed one of his patented smiles (the kind where the corners of his mouth seemed to meet the tips of his ears), and the relationship was formed. He always knew the right thing to say, even if it didn't seem so at the time. With Frank's help, that group of Panthers went on to make the playoffs for the first time in more than a decade and win the first division championship in the history of the franchise.*

COMMENTARY FROM ROBBIE FTOREK,
AHL/NHL - NEW HAVEN NIGHTHAWKS/LA KINGS

Doc Frank and I first met in 1985 when I was a player and assistant coach. I looked at him and saw a lot of scalp while sitting in the back and listening. Then the guys introduced me to him. He told me the things he would be doing and trying to do. During the season I talked with him. He was working with Nighthawks owner Joel Schiavone, who wouldn't hire anyone without a test.

Frank told me what it was and how it worked. He didn't take sides. He was a good person to bump things off of. He helped me out with my son. He tested him, and he was a little behind. He went to a prep school, which helped him. He talked with an individual player who ended up winning the Stanley Cup. It was interesting to see the interaction of the player and how he changed after talking with Doc. The guy had a great playoff, and the Devils won the Stanley Cup. I felt bad that Doc didn't get recognition for the work he did. I know he did a lot.

When I went to LA I talked with him. Doc worked consistently with Paul Fenton when he was in New Haven. He didn't tell me who he was working with, but one day he asked me, "I'm coming down the left wing, and what should I do to score?"

I told him about a few things like, "Maybe you should change the pace." Then Doc would translate that into English and work with Fenton on that. Fenton played well in LA. Then there were trades, and the new guys wouldn't pass to Fenton. I told them Fenton is going to be traded, and we moved him to Winnipeg. That was the only place he didn't want to go. I told him, "I'm doing this for you. If you don't do this, then who knows what. Go to Winnipeg and light it up like you can. You'll have a contract and your family will be ok." He swore at me, but I went ahead with it.

Rogie told me, "Fenton's going to Winnipeg." He ended up being their leading goal scorer. Great place to play hockey because it's so damn cold, and that's all they do. Fenton ended up having a great time there and it worked out.

COMMENTARY FROM PAUL FENTON,
NHL - NEW HAVEN NIGHTHAWKS/LA KINGS

I signed with the Rangers, and they had an affiliate with the LA Kings in New Haven. I was sent down to play there from 1986-87. Playing for Robbie, he assigned Frank to me, and we started to do a little work together that first year. I played in the minors for 4.5 years. Every time I was called up, I shrank myself and couldn't get over the mental hurdle to play in the majors. Over the summer he started teaching me deep breathing, a meditation-type exercise that calmed me down. It worked. I was called up, half a year in Hartford, 1984-85, and then played with the Rangers. I finally got my chance in LA after my first year in New Haven. I had a great start in New Haven with 11 goals, five assists in five games, and then I was called up. I never played another game in the minor leagues.

I continued the mental rehearsal. He told me, "You are as good as any of those guys." He gave me the tools to play at that level. He helped Glenn Healy and me, to prepare us to be mentally strong enough to play. I introduced him to people in golf. He'd help the golf pro when we'd play golf together. His demeanor and simple approach told us how to get over our mental struggles. That summer I did relaxation and visualization techniques. It's 20 minutes, and I told myself, "Just do this for 20 minutes." We had our first child, but I did it every day. I knew this was my last chance, and I couldn't fail.

Then after that summer, I was in the NHL for the next five years. Frank was such a wonderful influence. His teachings on deep breathing and visualization of what you thought you were going to encounter in the game—like tipping the puck, or retrieving a puck along the boards, or how you would attack a player with the puck or take it away, or shoot for a score—were incredibly game-changing. Then, in the game, I felt like I had already done it, already seen it because I had mentally prepared for it, and it was like it had already happened. Then I could stay calm in the moment. In a game, I scored a goal or tipped the puck, I would see the puck coming from the defensemen's stick and see it going in the net. It was almost freaky how it happened and the amount of clarity that was there. Frank's personality was so easygoing and you adapted and took to him. You had great trust in him.

COMMENTARY FROM GLENN HEALY,
NHL - LA KINGS

Frank had a massive impact on my career. I was not physically able because I hadn't put the effort in. I wasn't mentally ready either. The three sides of the triangle are: Talent–God gives some people talent; Knowledge–some people are given a lot of that too; and Intangibles–to me, that's like two kids playing hockey in the hallway of a hotel when we're at a tournament. If you want it more than me, you'll probably stick around more than me.

I was 5 feet 9 inches, and I didn't have a lot of talent. The talent side of the bucket wasn't full. You have to fill up the other two sides of the ledger. Frank really came in and helped me to become mentally tougher, to wipe away mistakes faster. He helped me with physical clues that prepared me, and to focus to visualize all those positives. I never would have made it to the NHL without him. He wasn't about to help with the physical, but mentally I was as prepared as anybody. I stayed for 16 years. The visualization was big. You get your mind in a state where all your thoughts are positive and making saves. Making yourself bigger in the net, feeling bigger, and feeling that every save is going to be made.

We had to take the time to get into a calm state. You build that positive energy off the ice, transfer that onto the ice. Face-offs give you clues to reset and focus. Or after a goal, I'd take my stick and swipe it in front of me (I wasn't cleaning the ice) to let it go, and it was most important for a goaltender. So I'd make the next save. You go into a game saying, "I get to make the first save, get through the first five minutes." Don't put the end result first.

I wasn't drafted, which made me question, should I be there? I wasn't big, should I be there? I wasn't talented, should I be there? Frank broke the game down into segments, and segments into segments. It all came together for me. I wasn't ready when I came on the team. I needed a little bit of seasoning and Frank provided that for me. During the relaxation and visualization sessions, as I went down the stairs, my arms felt heavy, and he helped to get my mind ready, and get ready for the positive. In hockey we spend a lot of time on skating coaches, goalie coaches, etc. But we aren't working on the mental part.

How does a guy in the Masters (golf) blow it? How does Gregg Newman blow it? How? It does happen. It's in your mind that you can't hit a fairway or make a putt. Athletes, we have to work on it. We don't work on the mental part enough to become elite athletes. The intangible side of the ledger led to many steps in my career and paid off. Frank was hugely responsible for my long career. Respect to him; he had no idea of the impact he had on me.

COMMENTARY FROM TIM BOTHWELL,
AHL/NHL - NEW HAVEN NIGHTHAWKS/LA KINGS

I started playing in New Haven, and that's where my playing career ended. It was a difficult year for the Nighthawks. We weren't a good team. Marcel Comeau was the coach. We had a bad team, a group of real characters, and I was on both sides of the fence as a player and assistant coach.

We had good people, but they were not very committed. Tough year. The fans were not very user friendly. If you're not winning, you're nobody's favorite, and they were tough on Marcel. Frank was invaluable that year. He would say, "Someday we're going to look back at this and laugh." Marcel would give him the evil eye. Frank was around a fair bit and the LA organization knew they had a lot to do in New Haven. Marcel had just come from the Western Junior League in Canada.

I was looking for a job, and I wasn't ready for a head coach job. I had an interview in Medicine Hat, and Marcel called the league head. I got an interview, and two years later I was in Phoenix with the Roadrunners, and Frank was there. In 1992-93 it was a young team and not a very good one. Frank was really helpful; that was the year LA went to the NHL finals with Gretzky.

I joined LA during the playoffs. I was two years at the Roadrunners, then University of Calgary Coach for seven years. Frank was with Wally at the Stampeders. At training camp, we'd get together for lunch; he was in Calgary for a couple of years. Then we came to know each other and know Pat too. My Mom's been in Calgary almost 70 years, and my uncle and cousin came to know Frank too.

In the late 1990s, he helped move furniture, and he earned his dinner! Ha! During 2013 Barb and I visited with Frank and Pat in Florida. We had an Airbnb, and the hosts left for the evening, so we had a lovely dinner at our Airbnb. As a player, I was familiar with relaxation and visualization from my years in St. Louis. I was a big proponent and wanted Frank around to offer these tools to the players who were interested. As a coach, I put a lot of value on these techniques.

The first year I met him was in 1989. He didn't try to jam stuff down my throat. He built a relationship first. This was unique in how Frank approached it from Day 1. I appreciated that as a player, and then as a coach. I knew this guy knew what to do and how to do it, and I gave him carte blanche. I had total confidence he'd do the right thing. The guys who are ready, will. The guys who are on the fence will ask questions and maybe take him up on it. Psychology in sports did not become mainstream until the 1980s. He was wise to take the approach he did. It paid benefits. The guys enjoyed him.

CHAPTER 11

NEW JERSEY DEVILS (NHL)

DOC FRANK'S LESSON
5 PRINCIPLES TO BUILD CONFIDENCE

At the opening of the Los Angeles Kings training camp in Hull, Canada, Robbie Ftorek, the head coach of the team, posed the following question to the draftees and free agents: Who has the most important position on this hockey team? Most of those who responded mentioned the goalie. Ftorek replied, "No, not the goalie. The equipment manager."

He then went on to explain that, once the team walked into the locker room and saw all of their equipment cleaned, in place, and ready to go, this gave them confidence. Everything was in order; now they could do their jobs. There may be doubters about this position, but there is both logic and experience that led Ftorek to embrace it. Looking good is one of the things that gives people confidence. Confident people never have to tell you how great they are. They demonstrate it to you. Some aspects of developing confidence in oneself follow:

1. Confidence is a prerequisite to success.
2. A truly confident person understands the dimensions of a task and what it takes to master it.
3. Confidence requires trust.
4. Confidence arises from a proper appraisal of the immediate situation.
5. Confidence is fleeting and fragile: nurture it.

PRINCIPLE ONE: CONFIDENCE IS A PREREQUISITE TO SUCCESS

What some people think is confidence is nothing more than bravado. The person who is always muttering how great he is actually tells the world that he is trying to convince himself of the truth of his statement. The truly confident demonstrate confidence through their accomplishments. Bragging is a sign of insecurity. It's also boring to hear. Dizzy Dean said it best: "It isn't bragging, if you can do it."

Confidence is giving yourself positive messages that tell you you can succeed. Standing over a putt, telling yourself that you can make it, is one of the steps to success. Where does self-confidence come from? Does it come from your parents, from your upbringing? Are some people born with it? Can you develop it? It doesn't matter. All that really matters is that, when you need confidence, it is present. You hit your seven wood with confidence. You overuse it because you are successful with it, often causing you to be short of the target because you needed a longer club. There are many differences between the weekend golfer and Mark O'Meara—the most important one being that no matter what club his caddy gives him, Mark knows he can hit with it and hit well. Except for the one iron that Lee Trevino joked not even God can hit, this is probably true of all professional and excellent amateur golfers.

Success in performing an activity helps build confidence. Nothing succeeds like success in building confidence. Someone who has learned something well has the confidence to communicate this to other people. Confidence is an inner feeling that enables and empowers one to perform at an optimum level to achieve success.

PRINCIPLE TWO: A TRULY CONFIDENT PERSON UNDERSTANDS THE DIMENSIONS OF A TASK AND WHAT IT TAKES TO MASTER IT

As we have already stated, success builds on confidence. Each success serves as motivation for future success. I know I can do it, and therefore all I must do is go out and do it. "Just do it" should be more than a slogan for a sneaker company. It should be so ingrained in the lives of each of us that success should be the desired result. It has often been said that the genius never fails—not because he is so talented, but because he knows his limits. He knows what to avoid.

During the 1972 undefeated season for the Miami Dolphins, Garo Yepremian was asked by Don Shula to kick an important field goal against Minnesota. The Dolphins were behind and their winning streak was in jeopardy. Garo, who had never kicked a field goal of this length, was at first apprehensive. Then he pulled himself together and thought, "The game and streak are important to all of us. If Don Shula thinks I can do it, and he has confidence in me, I guess I can do it." He went out and split the uprights with his kick. He even had some yards to spare. Later a forward pass to Jim Mandich in the end zone preserved the streak.

And so, in athletics or life, one must have the self-insight to know what one is capable of achieving. Not every avenue is open to everyone. A truly confident person understands the dimensions of a task and what it takes to master it.

PRINCIPLE THREE: CONFIDENCE REQUIRES TRUST

Often in the locker room of a winning team, one which has come back from a half-time deficit, one hears the comment, "I knew we were going to pull this one out."

Analyzing this comment, one sees its complexities. Surely the speaker doesn't think he is going to pull a victory out alone. What he means is that the unit, the team, had the necessary ingredients for success and that each member of the team had confidence in the other to produce a victory. Trust in oneself and in others leads to success. The team that feels it is adequately prepared for winning has the edge over the team with doubts. During one of the many glory years of the Calgary Stampeders under head coach Wally Buono, a perfect example of this transpired. The Ottawa Rough Riders had come out in the first half inspired and motivated to win. At the end of the half, they were leading the Calgary team. The second half was a different story. Calgary got back on track and pulled the game out of the fire. As the Stamps players came into the locker room, many were overheard to say, "I knew we were going to win this one."

Their trust in the game plan, the coaches themselves, and their teammates helped them on to victory. Confidence in leadership is essential for success. A leader who bungles and is disorganized and unfocused does not inspire confidence in those he leads. Tug McGraw instilled confidence in his teammates with the slogan "YOU GOTTA BELIEVE."

Coaches who inspire their players by saying, "The only way you will lose is if you beat yourselves," also push the right buttons. The first step to success is to be competitive. Once one realizes and trusts in the fact that one can compete, then one is on the road to success.

PRINCIPLE FOUR: CONFIDENCE ARISES FROM A PROPER APPRAISAL OF AN IMMEDIATE SITUATION

Knowing the reality of a situation can be a confidence builder. The man who detects an opponent's weakness will succeed. If he knows that the opponent has a weak backhand, the serve should be to the opponent's backhand. Good coaches do not often change their systems to beat an opponent. They expect the opponent to find a way to beat their system. In other words, my opponent must find a way to beat me. I've got enough confidence in my skills and preparation to know what I must do to beat him. One thing is sure—the better I execute, the more certain I am of victory. Bill Arnsparger was a great proponent of this philosophy. His message was, "I don't have to find a way to beat you. You have to find a way to beat me." The confidence Arnsparger had in his ability to put together a meaningful defensive scheme and in his players to execute it is a great example of confidence. Players' expectations must be realistic. They must have the mechanical knowledge and the ability to reach their goals. This breeds confidence.

Confidence also comes from facing the reality that one cannot undo an error. If I have made a mental error, I cannot undo that. However, I owe it to myself and my team not to dwell on it and compound the infraction by repeating it. Once I make an error, I must forget it, though I must try to analyze why it was made and make the proper adjustments.

PRINCIPLE FIVE: CONFIDENCE IS FLEETING AND FRAGILE: NURTURE IT

As mentioned earlier, confidence is fleeting. It may burst with enthusiasm one moment and be surrounded by the demon of insecurity the next. One prescription is to realize that you are where you are because someone noticed that you had the ability to perform the required task. Success may mean one thing to one person and another to others. A hockey player who plays a good overall game may feel that he did poorly because he did not score a goal. Still his contribution to the team was valuable. Performance evaluation must be objective. It cannot lead to self-pity. It must look for reasons, not for scapegoats.

Good players play through adversity. The dregs moan about it. Good players know their own mistakes. Poor players may try to build confidence by tearing down others. This process may work sometimes. But generally, it becomes an exercise in futility. One can never fully appraise his lack of confidence because he has developed a construct that will always serve his ego and never permit him to arrive at the truth. If one lacks ego strength, he may criticize another person so that he need not admit his own failure. This attitude destroys confidence. If a person's confidence begins to weaken, it can be weakened further by refusing to see one's responsibility in the failure.

Winners have confidence in all aspects of their endeavors. They trust, evaluate, and build on previous successes. They have enough ego resources to draw upon it in all competitive situations. If victory is in sight, they have the confidence to muster all of their knowledge, skills, and attitudes to attain success. They miss no opportunity. They leave no page unturned. A former LA assistant coach told me a story about Kobe Bryant. The coach and Kobe were competing with one another by shooting fouls. The coach shot first and did very well. As Kobe was approaching the end of his chances, he needed to sink all five of his remaining shots to win the match. Kobe paused, looked at the coach and said, "Coach, you realize this is all over." He then proceeded to sink all five shots and win the match. There was no doubt in Kobe's mind that he could achieve the desired goal. His confidence was a key factor in his success.

STEP 11
A "NO" MEANS A FUTURE "YES"

NEW JERSEY DEVILS

Time dims many memories. I do not recall whether I had contacted **Lou Lamoriello**, the New Jersey Devils' general manager, by phone or by mail. Regardless, I met with him in his New Jersey office. I appeared, outline in hand, on time, and uncertain as to what was before me. We exchanged some pleasantries and then I began my pitch. I had no idea as to whether he was a believer in, knowledgeable about, or seriously interested in hiring someone who works as a sports psychologist. He listened attentively to what I was presenting and even took some notes. When I finished, he seemed to have latched on to the comprehensive program for the team and the entire front office. We talked in detail about the way to initiate the program, its length of time, and the evaluation of it. After considerable time, we agreed that I would submit a program, and that we would meet again.

As I drove home, I was cautiously optimistic, but daunted by the amount of time I needed to put together a formidable proposal. About three days later, after spending long days and at least one sleepless night on it, I mailed the proposal. Days passed, and no reply. Was the time I had spent wasted? Would the proposal be implemented by someone else? Having some experience in the sports world, I knew anything was possible. Days later, I received an upbeat phone call from Lou telling me how I really understood the needs of the organization and that he was eager to implement it. Two things about this phone call were encouraging. The fact that it had been a follow-up call was an almost unique experience for me, and it offered hope. However, I never heard from Lamoriello again about the matter. No detailed discussion, no follow-up meeting, no nothing. Was this the way he operated? After a short time. I put the matter to rest.

Several years later, I received a phone call in my Hamilton Hotel room from Robbie Ftorek inviting me to breakfast the next morning. He wanted to discuss possibly consulting for the Devils' organization. I refused to become optimistic about it. Ftorek was coaching the AHL affiliate of the Devils in Utica, New York. I was traveling with the Calgary Stampeders at the time. We were due to play the Hamilton Tiger-Cats that Sunday. The coincidence of our both being in Hamilton, Ontario, on the same day was uncanny.

At breakfast Ftorek carefully, and in great detail, explained the plan. He had convinced Lamoriello, the Devils' GM, that I could help the overall operation.

Needless to say, the prospect of once again working with Ftorek and the opportunity to return to hockey were all-enticing. Once the presentation was completed, I thanked Robbie and told him I had been down that path with the Devils' organization, and my expectations of this plan becoming reality were slim to none. Ftorek insisted it was a done deal if I were to accept it. His word was good enough for me, but I was still leery of others in the organization who had a position to act on it. Again, Ftorek came through, and in 1993 I was the psychologist for the Utica Devils.

Ftorek followed renowned coaches, such as the ever-popular, gracious, and friendly Tom McVie and Herb Brooks who orchestrated the "Miracle on Ice." Our time in Utica was limited to one year; the team moved to Albany and became the River Rats. Many of the players moved to Albany with us. The roster of the Utica Devils was replete with future stalwarts in the Devils' organization. Players included: Jim Dowd, Ben Hankinson, David Emma (a 1991 Hobey Baker winner while playing for Boston College), Jarrod Skalde, Jaroslav Modry, Scott Pellerin, Dean Malkoc, Matt Ruchty, Bill Guerin (whose career seemed to be unending), Corey Schwab, and Marty Brodeur (who was the source of one of my most ridiculous predictions of my life—the prediction that made me steer away from any type of prognostication).

Ftorek, after practice one day, asked me what I thought of Brodeur's chances in the NHL. Without hesitation I answered, "I don't think he will make it." Sorry, Marty. Good thing you weren't listening. Years later at lunch, I relayed this story to Bill Torrey, president of the Florida Panthers, who graciously said, "If you are around this sport long enough, those things are bound to happen." Thanks, Bill.

As brief as the Utica experience was, some of the ties that were made there lasted a long time. One advantage from the Albany affiliation was that my trip was shortened by almost an hour and a half each way. The River Rats, with their enticing logo and with the spirit of being a new franchise, was a fun organization.

JOHN WEISBROD, GENERAL MANAGER, RIVER RATS

One memorable relationship that grew closer each year began the day I met the GM of the River Rats, 24-year-old Harvard grad **John Weisbrod**. He was one of many Harvard grads who made an impact in hockey. At first our relationship was distant. We exchanged pleasantries, made small talk, and that was it. One night several of us were showing off our putting skills, which was one of the only skills I possessed in golf. Weisbrod, an avid golfer, was impressed by my putting and thought I might be a formidable opponent for him. Little did he know that by the time I reached the green, any respectable score for a hole was out of sight. This opened the door to our relationship only slightly. The second incident occurred in Albany at the Metro Atlantic Athletic Conference (MAAC) championship. The Lady Jaspers of Manhattan College were about to put the final touches on winning the championship; the win brought with it an automatic bid to the NCAA Tournament. To Weisbrod's surprise I was on the Lady Jaspers' bench. He immediately went upstairs to Ftorek's office to inquire about my presence at the event. When he finished his exhaustive explanation, I had a new advocate for psychology and sports.

Weisbrod was instrumental in my obtaining many consultancies over the years. Through the many stages of my career, I have been viewed as a polarizing figure on one hand and as a unifying figure on the other hand. This dichotomy was caused by my bluntness, my somewhat confrontational style, and by my intolerance of those who pretend to be what, in fact, they are not. It was not surprising to me that, from the early days of our relationship, I found that Weisbrod was a person I felt I could trust, one whose friendship I could enjoy. In some ways, we were both cut from the same cloth. My behavior was modified by the passage of time. His was still in the early stages of formation. We could both be abrasive. In fact, I once said to him that he was "as subtle as a clenched fist." We both said what was on our minds, and we were sometimes guilty of putting our tongues in motion before our minds were engaged. The final judgment is still in the balance. His professional hockey playing career was cut short by injuries. John is intellectually gifted and perceptive. His ability to analyze situations and to draw logical conclusions was and is impressive.

As the years passed and we moved from Albany to Orlando, John and I became closer and appreciated each other more. We both knew that my knowledge of the technical side of hockey was limited, which caused me to rely on him for answers to questions that required knowledge of the game. I was fortunate, early on, that my tutors were Nick Beverley, Robbie Ftorek, Tim Bothwell, and Rick Dudley. John and I weathered storms together—the illnesses and death of his parents, his divorce, his parenting of his son CJ, and his choice to leave the Orlando Magic (a position that was both lucrative and pleasant) to return to his true love, hockey. Each crisis, each dilemma, brought us closer. John thanked me many times for my friendship and support of him. I, in turn, thank him for the job opportunities he offered me and for his loyalty and trust.

Conversations with John opened a new look into the hockey business. I never realized many hockey teams reported losses of millions of dollars each year. This astonished me beyond belief. I suppose, to some owners, an expensive investment like a hockey team was worth it. After all, it gave the new owners the opportunity to put their friends in sensitive positions despite the fact that these friends had no experience, training, or ability to carry out the demands of the job. The one thing some of these appointees were good at was reporting verbatim their conversations with staff to the owner—an experience I had the bad fortune of hearing.

Remember, pro sports is not good for your mental health. I left these conversations happy to have no involvement in the finances of a team and of all the machinations that went on behind closed doors. It struck me that teams were willing to go to great lengths to find money for players' salaries or for their pet projects. They seemed willing to go to the highly secured safe or to borrow money using their firstborn as collateral. As for staff salaries, the money seemed to come from a medium-sized piggy bank full of chump change. So be it. No one was forced to accept the offers or to take the jobs.

There were other changes occurring in hockey. Each year saw more American and European players entering the leagues in the US. Jim Paek was the first Korean in the NHL. His signing attested to the diversity in Hockey. Paek had a great impact on the NHL. Since he was the first player from Asia, he opened the doors to players from Sweden, Finland, and Russia. Not only was Paek the first Korean in the League, but, as a Pittsburgh Penguin, he was the first to have his name engraved on the Stanley Cup and the first Korean to have earned two Championship rings. Later he became director of Hockey Operations and head coach of the Korean national team. Jim and I worked together in Grand Rapids, Michigan.

When he was given the job with the Korean national team, he called me for advice. I sent him many pages of notes and observations for which he was grateful. The impact of this change from a league that was at first dominated by Canadian players was felt most by coaches who had to adapt themselves to players from other cultures, with different styles of play, values, and lifestyles. The transition worked. Not only did these players fit in well, they soon dominated play. At first it seemed to me that the resentment from Canadian players stemmed from the fact that Americans and others were taking away Canadian jobs. This was a similar experience to responses from white athletes in the states when black athletes joined the teams. On most teams that I had contact with, the change was working out well. Canadians and Europeans played on the same lines, shared defensive space, roomed together, joined each other in activities on the road, and sometimes became friends. No doubt, human nature being what it is, there are still some glitches. Nothing on this earth is perfect.

My time in Albany, plus the few assignments I had in New Jersey, was a blast. Ftorek and I had become even more comfortable working with each other. Some of the Jersey scouts became interested in what I was doing and suggested my name to management as being someone more valuable to the Devils' organization. One day, after a meeting in New Jersey, both Weisbrod and Devils goalie coach, Jacques Caron, shared that there were plans for me to become more involved with the Devils' organization and that I would have a role in the development camp the following summer. The plan, they said, "was approved by management."

My response to them was disappointing. Instead of enthusiasm for the plan, I told them it would never happen. They could not accept my reaction. Both privately asked me to explain my position. I had learned over my many years in academia that people in authority often acted in a strange but similar manner. If a contentious or unpopular issue came up, authority figures who could not defend their objections would agree in public to proceed, but then proceed in private to let it die. I was certain that my perception of the Jersey meeting was accurate. The passage of time, with no mention of or action on the proposal, proved to be right. The matter was never brought up again. Some behaviors are more obvious to observers than to those producing the behavior. Games people play soon become immediately apparent. In sports, as in many other walks of life, survival depended on learning how to protect your flank.

The year 1995 was a two-banner one for the New Jersey Devils franchise. Under the guidance of Lou Lamoriello, both the Devils and the River Rats became champions of their respective leagues. My time with the Devils was expanded only slightly. Two players were referred to me. One earlier by Herb Brooks, the second later by Lamoriello. The first objected and refused to see me. The second treated the referral as an opportunity not to be missed. We met regularly for two years. He proved to be an important cog in the wheel of success that the Jersey organization was experiencing.

As the season progressed in Albany, it was becoming obvious that we had a team capable of going all the way. Each game in Albany saw different players step up. One night it was outstanding goaltending from **Corey Schwab**; on other nights, it was a strong play by **Mike Vukonich, Bryan Helmer, or Cale Hulse**. Breakaways by **Steve Sullivan** were a common phenomenon. "The Sheriff," **Vadim Sharifijanov**, controlled the play many nights. **Matt Ruchty** had one of his finest years. **Pascal Rhéaume, Mike Dunham, Scott Pellerin,** and **Bobby House** each had their moment in the sun. **Bill Armstrong** helped lead the way. Their efforts were rewarded by a Calder Cup and a championship ring.

Meanwhile the team up top, New Jersey, was showing signs of its dominance. **Marty Brodeur** was reaching the pinnacle of his success. His goaltending was outstanding. Players like **Bill Guerin, Brian Ralston, Scott Stevens, Reid Simpson, Claude Lemieux, Stéphane Richer, John MacLean, Jaroslav**

Modry, Jim Dowd, Kevin Dean, and all the others made their presence felt. Together, with the coaching staff, all hands took off on a mission to bring the first Stanley Cup to New Jersey. The Devils dominated their rivals in their division, beating the Bruins 4-1; the Penguins by the same margin 4-1; and the Flyers 4-2. They did not lose again in those playoffs and swept the Red Wings 4-0.

Robbie arranged for me to attend Game Four in New Jersey. The experience was unbelievable. After the game, a sweltering June night in New Jersey, the line entering the Devils' locker room seemed to have no end. It also made princes and pawns equal. Next to me in line was New Jersey Governor Christine Todd Whitman, with whom I struck up a conversation. She was the most charming, accessible person I had ever met. My only regret was I did not live in New Jersey and could not share in the many things she did for the citizens of her state. She made the long wait tolerable.

By the time I entered the locker room, fully drenched from the heat of the night, I was ready to take a deep breath and to enjoy the festivities. My friend, Cory Schwab, was standing above me and immediately emptied a full bottle of champagne on my head and clothing. The mingling of my sweat with the beverage made for a sticky rest of the evening. My first thought was of my impending drive home to Newtown, Connecticut. Suppose, for some reason, I were to be stopped by the police. How could I satisfactorily explain the state I was in?

I did not permit those thoughts to inhibit me in any way. The evening was outstanding. The players greeted me, even offering me the Stanley Cup to sip from. After making the rounds I headed home. My car smelled like a saturated bar rag. After removing my jacket and tie, I realized the liquid Schwab had poured on me had penetrated right to my skin. My dilemma was whether I would drive home slowly or simply at the regular speed. I arrived in Newtown unscathed. The remaining problem was the persistent odor in my car for many days. Every moment from that night was five-star.

I thought it could never be equaled. It was, however, and surpassed by other moments in my NHL career. My remaining years with the Devils found me working with head coach **John Cunniff.** Our working relationship was fine. He was fun to be around and open to what I was selling. One day he came to me and said I should consider not coming around anymore. He was unable to get a commitment from Devils' management about my continued work. Mercifully and bluntly, he told me I was no longer being paid. I have never been formally released. All in all, my time with the Devils was positive. Being checked by Gordie Howe in the doorway that led to Ftorek's office was only one of many memorable moments. I was lucky to have had the experience.

COMMENTARY FROM PETER HORACHEK, NEW JERSEY DEVILS / FLORIDA PANTHERS

I met Frank through John Weisbrod in Orlando when we won the championship there. I had worked with different sports psychologists, but he was the only one I trusted. Frank allowed players to feel comfortable, and you could talk with him as if he was a coach. He talked about how to make the players better. He had a knack for finding the right thing that the players needed. He loved the routine part. Players need a routine to keep them focused. Most players I dealt with took it home. If you're upset, and you're going to take it home, then you need to learn to shut it down. And turn it back on for game day.

Frank's perspective was that they turned on the light switch when they came in the back door to the stadium. He helped them focus. That's what a sports psych is supposed to do: teach them how to be a better version of themselves and help them focus. He helped me understand the players and how to get the best out of them. He kept the players' secrets. He would say, the player will respond better with X rather than Y–for example, hard coaching versus more encouragement.

I have his picture and the whole staff from the Orlando Solar Bears in my office. That is the most prominent picture. We needed all the pieces in there to win. It took all the pieces to win, including Doc Frank. He was part of the group and part of the family. Other psychologists were more interested in their books than in the team and how to make each player a better version of themselves.

He was part of me; I didn't feel threatened. He advised me how to work with the players. He was able to disarm, make everyone comfortable, and have a few words to prompt us to make a change or think about things differently. His idea was your idea. He would compliment me about things I did not expect him to compliment me on, and it lifted me up. He brought out the best in the players. He helped them focus. "Turn it off when you leave the rink, and then turn it back on when you come back to the rink," he often said. It helped the players show up in a positive and energetic way and to be the best version of themselves. He also showed them how to get there. The best teams are those that practice well, and he helped the players do so. He never asked for any credit or a pat on the back. It was always, "We did it." It made me feel good about myself. I also did visualization and breathing exercises, which helped me with my sleeping.

He saw things I didn't see, he relayed them to me, and then it was up to me to act on them or not. Then I would talk to the players one to one. I never lied to them, but helped them understand why; also that it's not about you, it's about team. With that approach, they were responsive.

CHAPTER 12

BOSTON BRUINS (NHL)

DOC FRANK'S LESSON
7 PRINCIPLES ON THE IMPORTANCE OF COACHABILITY

Each year, leaders of industry and education spend millions of dollars wining and dining motivational speakers, many of whom are athletic coaches. The purpose of these encounters, at least ostensibly, is to pep up the workers, increase production, and make the environment a better, more efficient place. Few, if any, of these things happen over the long term. There may be some immediate show of enthusiasm, but this is generally short-lived. The underlying reason for bringing in motivational speakers is the hope that the audience will at least listen and that one message may help a person improve their attitude and morale. The people in charge hope that each person attending the lecture or seminar will be coachable. However, many employees are not.

The following principles will help people become more coachable:

1. Coachability requires recognition of the need for change.
2. The more accurately a person's learning style is assessed, the more coachable a person will be.
3. Effective coachability involves understanding the effect previous learning has on the person.
4. The greater the readiness, the more coachable the learner.
5. Motivation to succeed influences coachability.
6. Faith in leadership makes players more coachable.
7. Certain coaching and management styles may impede learning.

PRINCIPLE ONE: COACHABILITY REQUIRES RECOGNITION OF THE NEED FOR CHANGE

Hockey teams, basketball franchises, and baseball organizations spend considerable funds preparing a draft list each year. The one thing that gets a prospect's name on the draft list is the hope that, once drafted, the individual will be capable of listening to coaches so that he can refine his talents and contribute substantially to the club that is investing megabucks in him. Since players are drafted at a young age in professional hockey, the draft has been called "the world's most expensive crapshoot." Many who succeed in high school athletics never succeed in college athletics. Success on one level of athletics may indicate success at the next level, but does not guarantee it. Perhaps, and this is only an educated guess, one reason for the lack of success is the inability of the player to absorb what coaches offer at the next level. Players may have become satisfied with what they have accomplished and may not feel the need for improvement.

One who is teachable must constantly remain curious about learning. He or she must want to advance to the next level. These people see the need for change and are willing to explore the pathways open to them, whether that pathway is instruction from the golf channel or reading numerous how-to books. This is further evidenced by the increasing number of players who spend hours viewing videos of their games in the hope of gaining new insights into their performance.

PRINCIPLE TWO: THE MORE ACCURATELY A PERSON'S LEARNING STYLE IS ASSESSED, THE MORE COACHABLE A PERSON WILL BE

To learn in any field, one must develop the ability to absorb what is being taught. Most people must develop their listening skills. Others must observe what is being done and copy it. Still others must execute a task after they have had the task demonstrated to them. Basically, being coachable depends on tapping the learning style of the individual learner. Lecturing to a group of people in a room may seem effective, but the odds are against significant change occurring.

Productivity doesn't just change overnight. The most important principle in all of educational psychology is that individuals differ. Most educational psychologists fail to realize this in their classrooms, treating all students the same and testing them with a common exam. Since all people are unique, winners are also unique. Winners' physiques come in all sizes and shapes, their intelligence varies and their backgrounds differ. It is only reasonable that their learning styles vary as well, running the gamut from auditory to tactile learners. Their desire to change ranges from a high of 10 to a low of 1 on any scale valid to measure such change.

Dave Dickenson, a former quarterback for the British Columbia Lions, was on his way to establishing the passing record for the Canadian Football League, a record long held by Matt Dunigan. Through a quarter of a game against the Ottawa Renegades, Dave was pulled from the game. His coach, Wally Buono, approached him after the game and explained why he had substituted him. Dave's reply was, "The record doesn't mean anything to me; I'm glad you made the change. I want to be around at the end of the season."

PRINCIPLE THREE: EFFECTIVE COACHABILITY INVOLVES UNDERSTANDING THE EFFECT PREVIOUS LEARNING HAS ON THE PERSON

A serious problem may arise from the fact that a person's previous knowledge of an area may impede learning. Simply put, what a person has previously learned may interfere with learning new material, particularly if the new material is similar to the old. This may also be referred to as a type of fossilization. In learning languages, for example, a problem may arise from the fact that a person has had previous experience with that language. A child may have learned at home from parents, grandparents, and siblings. Grammar may have been employed incorrectly.

Pronunciation may have reflected a region that uses a dialect. Taking a formal language course that tends to be pure in pronunciation and more precise in grammar may prove confusing to the person studying the language. This barrier of the old interfering with the new must be recognized and accounted for.

A person may have taught himself a golf swing, which is at best, poor. Others may have learned hockey, soccer, or baseball incorrectly. Instructions are required to change. In addition, muscle memory may complicate new learning. A young golf pro I worked with many years ago taught himself a golf swing prior to having any knowledge of the mechanics of the swing. After many years of lessons and practice, he was able to abandon the old swing most of the time. However, when he wasn't fully focused or if he was fatigued, the old swing would show in his game.

Adapting to the change required in learning a new skill may meet resistance from the learner, rendering him less coachable. If a person has learned something early in life, this pattern may be especially difficult to change. There are times when an athlete's attachment to a previous coach is so strong that it causes the athlete to unconsciously reject what the current coach is presenting. The person who can analyze the problem and develop logical solutions that can enhance learning has the best chance of seeing progress through coaching.

PRINCIPLE FOUR: THE GREATER THE READINESS, THE MORE COACHABLE THE LEARNER

Readiness to learn is an aspect overlooked by education and especially by parents. Doting parents too often push young children to learn. Teachers assume that a child who reaches a particular age is ready to learn the curriculum prescribed for that age. Coaches must be able to assume that a player, either drafted or in some other way assigned to a team, is ready to learn.

This assumption, in the ideal, is valid. But in the real world it may be less so. Many things make a person ready to learn a particular skill or bit of knowledge. A woman may desire to learn how to play golf so that she may accompany her husband on the golf course. A teenager may want to learn to dance so that he may become popular in social settings. A person may desire to master a foreign language simply for his own edification. The *why* is not as important as the *when*. If one begins to dispose oneself to learning whatever is at his maximum curiosity or intellectual arousal for the task, the learning will be richer and more quickly internalized than at other times. If the learner is not ready to change, learning may defy coaching or teaching skills. Without readiness, learning is difficult, if not impossible.

During the time I helped with the New York Giants, an assistant coach, Allan Webb, was trying to coach a newly drafted running back who was having difficulty learning new plays. Alan and I worked out a plan that, at lunchtime each day, Allan would spend that hour with the running back and review the tape of the previous practice. The conclusion of this story was that Allan had done such a good job that the running back ran for over 700 yards that season. Two components were present here: (1) the running back was willing to listen, and (2) the coach was able to assess the player's needs.

PRINCIPLE FIVE: MOTIVATION TO SUCCEED INFLUENCES COACHABILITY

Coachability also involves motivation. How many times have free agents who have signed on with a new team failed to produce? Fans and people not earning astronomical salaries assume that the money alone is enough of a motivator. That assumption is obviously not true. Whatever conditions are present on a particular team that serve as distractions to these players reduce the motivation to achieve, or interfere with the means to achieve. Consider:

- Why was Shaquille O'Neal a more complete player under Coach Phil Jackson than he was under previous coaches?
- Was Jackson able to provide the spark that motivated the big center?
- Did O'Neal merely mature?
- Was the environment more conducive to winning, therefore providing greater motivation?

Any of these reasons may explain the phenomenon. Other reasons yet to be uncovered may contain the answer.

PRINCIPLE SIX: FAITH IN THE LEADERSHIP MAKES PLAYERS MORE COACHABLE

Many times the "star effect" helps a team succeed during the first years under the tenure of a highly publicized coach. If a superstar among coaches is brought to a team, the team may have enough confidence, at least initially, to exceed the previous year's production. This confidence may stem simply from the fact that the coach's reputation preceded him and that the players believe he is capable of the leadership that produces success. The methods employed by the coach who has taken on the mantle of franchise savior may work initially.

But often they wear thin. Was Rick Pitino a victim of this in Boston? Was Pat Riley's magic wand losing its potency in Miami? Was Mike Keenan the prime example of this? Was Phil Jackson the exception to the rule? Sometimes coaches whose reputations precede them, who are expected to change a team's destiny immediately, lose their aura. They must either make an immediate impact or they run the risk of their act running dry. Players expect success from these coaches immediately; if it does not happen the players may be reluctant to follow.

Sports enterprises tend to recycle coaches, and sometimes the results are outstanding. Casey Stengel with the New York Yankees was one example. Still, the recycled ones who failed are too numerous to mention. These coaches did not lose the smarts they had in their respective sports. Perhaps they lost their credibility, at least insofar as getting the most out of their charges.

PRINCIPLE SEVEN: CERTAIN COACHING AND MANAGEMENT STYLES MAY IMPEDE LEARNING

Certainly players who relate well to coaches and their styles succeed. In these cases, personality conflicts are held to a minimum, and mutual respect is attained. As soon as a player (or a worker, for that matter) questions the motivation of a leader, trouble develops. Young coaches or supervisors face an additional hurdle. If a young person is seen as ambitious and willing to step on and over people to succeed, he will quickly fail.

Management styles that belittle others in order to elevate the manager may gain results that will put out a brush fire, but will not be able to combat a major flare up. Head football coaches who demean or belittle their assistants in front of players exemplify this behavior. It is essential for those in authority to look into themselves. Many do not realize the image they reflect toward those who work for them. Many educators, supervisors, or coaches feel that they are above the need to evaluate themselves. These are not the great leaders. The winners among the great ones are constantly looking at their leadership styles, searching for ways to improve. The great ones look at their leadership styles so that they may improve communication techniques, productivity, and harmony. Professional development is the continual renewal of skills.

Nevertheless, a coach's style may be so grating or so annoying that it overwhelms the players' coping mechanisms and produces failure. The field of education has always been concerned with training leaders. Too little attention has been given to the training of followers. Still, the majority of people are followers. Only the select and, in a very specific way, the gifted are leaders.

Sometimes people, like students in school, are not coachable/teachable because real leadership is lacking. Other times the fault may lie in the one being coached. Good leaders know how to tell the difference. This knowledge may be the reason why they are successful. The first to be fired is a coach, but often this is an unjust move. The implication is that the team or some of its members have not progressed; in other words, they have not been coached properly. Perhaps the principles previously enunciated have been ignored or overlooked.

STEP 12
CHAMPIONS MUST BE COACHABLE

BOSTON BRUINS

The year 1990 was one of change and challenge for me. The 1990s contained many new paths. After many hours of deliberation and prayer, in the late winter of 1990 I decided to retire from teaching. The two years prior to my retirement had been torture. I lost my enthusiasm and the fire in the belly had gone out, leaving only embers. I was in an administrative and teaching job. The job was created by the provost, Walter Emge, who sensed the signs of my impending burnout. At first I looked forward to the bell that would herald the start of class. It freed me from the minutiae of administration, cajoling discontented faculty members, preparing course offerings, and working with the admissions office to find ways to keep our ship afloat. Later on, when I heard the bell sound, I wanted to run away instead of toward the comfort of the classroom. Clearly, it had become time to go. It wasn't going to be difficult, I assured myself. I had many roads untraveled and others yet to be explored.

Two of my part-time interests were still available to me: my involvement with sports that began in the late 1950s, and the counseling I was doing with seminarians. Add to that the unfinished writings, the bucket list of trips, the golf outings, and the increased opportunities to visit with our children, and it all made my decision enticing. I had no second thoughts, no looking back, and no regrets. I made one request of the administration: that they continue my health insurance. They did, but at my expense. The provost had encouraged me to ask for it and had approved my petition only to be overruled. It was not the appreciation shown for my years of dedication to a job that I had expected. Amazing, isn't it, how similar work settings can be?

For the first time in over 40 years of my work life, I was not tied to a school calendar. I had some time to myself, which turned out to be a troublesome thing. It gave me time to think about issues I had denied for many years. The most important of these issues was self-imposed. Being busy, spending many hours commuting, served as a good means of escape. While our children were growing up, I never permitted myself to have thoughts of them becoming adults and leaving home. The only thought I allowed into my consciousness was that they would marry a local boy or girl and live close by. We would babysit their children, and the whole family would spend many Sundays at dinner with my wife and me. After all, isn't that the way life was to be lived?

My wife and I never lived, for an extended period of time, more than two hours away from our parents. That scenario never played out for us. The pain of my children leaving home became even greater after my retirement. I missed them at meals. I missed watching football on Sundays. I missed pizza from Lavelles in Brookfield. I missed the sound of their laughter, drying their tears after disappointments, and driving with them through the foothills of the Berkshires in the fall, when the leaves were resplendent in announcing their farewell. My solitary moments often ended in tears. Passing their empty rooms was a cruel reminder of their absence. I had never expected this to happen. But, no matter what, life goes on. The sadness of their departure has never left me.

Fortunately for me, the self-torture I put myself through could be lessened by work. Each of my two part-time interests took on a life of their own, helping me to absorb the pain. With retirement, new issues came to the surface.

In 1992 we bought a house in Palm Beach Gardens, motivated in part by the close proximity of our house to the dwelling of my father-in-law. The first year we spent only one week there. Though my income, including my retirement monies, far exceeded past incomes, money was not a consideration. The Newtown house was beginning to show its age—the roof needed to be replaced, the siding had served us well but had to go. "Sell" or "move" became a frequent topic of conversation.

Another topic, which I preferred to ignore, was how much longer I could hold on to the two new careers I was juggling. It was clear, in my mind, that the first to go would be the work at the various seminaries. The question was "When?" The solution to my problem began to unravel itself. The arthritis in my foot was beginning to become a problem. Driving long distances was becoming painful. In 1992 I retired from seminary work. As easy as it was to leave Manhattan College, leaving the seminaries was another matter. I loved the work, respected its importance, and enjoyed the company of the people I worked with. But life goes on. The decision to leave the work that I loved made moving to Florida a viable option. My second career had ended. Now I could give my third career more time and attention.

My NHL involvement lessened while my CFL work expanded. I had enough to keep me going. With my advancing age and limited mobility, travel became challenging. Trips to see the children, grandchildren, and Europe were becoming even more precious. Major decisions in one's life should never be made frivolously. Neither should they be mulled over ad infinitum. The move to Florida was in the offing.

On October 4, 2003, we moved from Newtown, drove to the house of our daughter, Denise, in Newark, Delaware, and continued on to our new address. The move was more traumatic than anticipated. I began to miss our Connecticut house and the opportunities it offered. The space the house in Newtown provided, the variety of amenities, and its proximity to New York City and Boston all became matters that required adjustments. Perhaps if we had not become so familiar with the environment around Palm Beach Gardens, the awe of an unfamiliar place could have served us better in our adjustment.

On Sundays, we missed taking impromptu rides through the foothills of the Berkshires or trips by train into Manhattan. My golf outings were becoming more limited, due mostly to the lack of playing companions. We took solace in travel. I became more entrenched in my sports work. Writing was also beginning to take up some of my time. Our social life, though limited in Connecticut, was nonexistent in Florida, except for the occasional visitor from up North. These visits dwindled with each passing year. My wife had some family members who lived not too far away. Otherwise, it was zilch.

Fortunately for my sanity, and because of the good graces of John Weisbrod, I had consultancies in Orlando—first with the IHL team, the Solar Bears, and then for two separate stints with the Magic. Trips to Orlando were about a three-hour drive from Palm Beach Gardens. My adjustment to Florida was slowly coming around. The climate was the first selling point, the convenience of our home to churches, stores, outlets, and restaurants the second. The ease of living became an additional attraction. Though not as much of a paradise as advertised, Florida's advantages were coming to the fore. No overcoats, no snow shoveling, no black ice on the roads all added to the plus list.

One day out of the blue, I received a telephone call from **Peter Chiarelli**, the GM of the Boston Bruins. "This is Peter Chiarelli. I'd like to speak with Dr. Lodato," was how a phone call began that changed my life for the next 10 years. First and foremost, I didn't know who this person was. Then I couldn't believe the content of the conversation. Peter was looking for someone to lead a workshop on leadership for the Boston Bruins. It was unclear how he came upon my name. The irony of this call was that I had considered my work with the NHL a closed book. I was 80 years old and not hotly sought after.

After a lengthy conversation, Chiarelli promised to call again in a few days. After a week had passed and I had not heard from Peter, I thought the issue had become moot. To my surprise, the following week the call came. We were still on the burner phones. We talked for a long time, discussed many issues, seemed to agree on all of them, and still neither of us committed.

Again, I received a phone call in a short time. This call came while I was visiting the Truman House on Key West and lasted for a long time, causing my travel companions much agitation. I was insensitive to all my surroundings. This was an opportunity of a lifetime and I was not going to let it get away. All details were ironed out, dates were set, venue secured. The employment agreement would be at my home upon my return. The meeting was arranged. Five Boston Bruins players were assigned to meet with me.

BOSTON BRUINS LEADERSHIP WORKSHOP, LONGBOAT KEY, FLORIDA

The players, **Zdeno Chára, Marc Savard, Patrice Bergeron, Glen Murray** and **Marco Sturm** comprised the leadership group. Disbelief about this opportunity was the only word that describes my reaction. I had misgivings about doing the job since I had been away from the experience. My confidence level was pretty low. So I asked for more time and a more detailed explanation of the expectations. After much time and many phone calls, I was ready to do the job. My preparation for it could not have been more thorough. Countless hours were spent on reading the plethora of books on leadership. Giuliani, Powell, and Summitt became household words. All was put in place. Dates were chosen. I rarely felt prepared to present a workshop; however, ironically this time, I was satisfied with my preparation. My confidence level had been restored.

The only thing to do now was to be confident that the delivery equaled the preparation. It did. The first Bruins' player I met on Longboat Key, prior to our seminar, was Patrice Bergeron, who arrived earlier than the other players. Each was to contact me and attend a pre-workshop introduction. I was surprised at the diversity that existed among the players. The group consisted of a player from Germany, Marco Strum; Zdeno Chára from Slovakia; three players from Canada; Patrice Bergeron from the province of Quebec; Marc Savard from the province of Ontario; and Glen Murray from the Canadian Maritimes. Each was at a different stage of his career. They all were serious and curious. Obviously, they didn't know me.

I was familiar with one of the names, Marc Savard. He had played in Atlanta under my friend Curt Fraser who commented to me that Marc had an exceptionally good pair of hands and that he had bought Curt's house. The players involved in the seminar proved to make up one of the best groups I had ever worked with. Their questions, enthusiasm, and warmth added to the success of the sessions. It was not only a rewarding professional experience, it was fun and revealed the high caliber of the players who existed in hockey. After a week together, we parted ways, never expecting to see one another again.

CURT FRASER

Nicer guys might exist, but they come about rarely, if at all. **Curt Fraser**, in my book, is one of the few gems one comes across in the journey through life. Standing over six feet tall, he had a full head of black hair and an infectious smile, which indicated he was fun-loving and capable of being a prankster. Curt became one of my most valuable friends. A phone call to or from him was sprinkled with joy and laughter, and lifted my spirits. Sincerity, loyalty, and good flowed from all of his pores. He was, as a player, one of those workers who quietly achieves great things but who might fall through the cracks and go unnoticed.

In addition to being a better-than-average player, he was one of the toughest players of his time. In the WHL with the Victoria Cougars, he scored over 40 goals in a season twice. He possesses a Bronze Medal, which he earned with Team Canada in the 1978 World Junior Championships. He was rewarded for all of these achievements by being drafted 22nd overall by the Vancouver Canucks. Curt immediately made an impact on his new team. He scored 35 points in the 1978-79 season and followed that by scoring 42 points the following season while improving his plus-minus rating by 14 points. He continued to flourish after he was traded to the Chicago Blackhawks, where he scored 94 goals in five seasons.

After his trade from Chicago to Minnesota, he retired during the 1989-90 season. His first coaching job was as an assistant for the Milwaukee Admirals, and he became the head coach in 1992. Later he led the Orlando Solar Bears to The Turner Cup Finals. From there he became the first head coach of the expansion team, the Atlanta Thrashers, which was the first of his many jobs in the NHL.

A stint in New York with the Islanders was followed by a turn in St. Louis with the Blues. He then returned to the AHL as head coach of the Grand Rapid Griffins, a job he held for four seasons. In 2012 he joined the coaching staff of the Dallas Stars. But hockey was not his only passion. In addition to enjoying fine food, particularly a grouper sandwich, he had an insatiable passion for boating. I can attest to this from firsthand experience.

One day during the first of the recent NHL lockouts, I received a call from him. I was living in Florida, and he was going to be in my area that day. The phone call went something like this:

"Bombay, what are you doing today?" (When we first worked together in Orlando he decided to call me "Dr. Bombay," a name that stuck with him and Weisbrod, our general manager at the time.) I replied to his question that I was doing nothing that day, inquiring what he had in mind. "I am shopping for a yacht near your home. Would you like to join me?"

"Sure thing," I said. "I am free, and my kids call us every night. I usually have nothing to tell them. Tonight I can say I went shopping for a yacht today. Tell me what time you want to go."

We decided on 11:00 a.m.

The next few hours were an eye-opener for me. The vessel he was focusing on was an enormous boat in my rowboat life. It had four bedrooms, TVs in each room, was radar equipped, seaworthy, and could right itself. Fueling it cost, at that time, tens of thousands of dollars. Dock fees were enormous, insurance out of sight, and the cost was well over a million dollars. This day had turned into a lark until he sounded serious. I will never know how serious he was then, but he started talking about selling his homes and boat. Considering the fact that, when the lockout was over he would be headed to St. Louis, I began to share some concerns. He did not take to them and counterpunched with arguments as to why he should buy this boat. After much more discussion with the salesman, we left and began looking for a place for lunch. Luckily, the place we found had grouper sandwiches on the menu. The fish sandwich was like an elixir. His mood softened. His good humor returned. To this day I have no idea whether or not he blames me for not purchasing the vessel. It has never come up again.

Whenever his team is close by, he calls and we have dinner together. His call is anticipated, and the joy of his company gives me something to look forward to each hockey season.

BOSTON BRUINS: THE FOUR-YEAR JOURNEY TO "THE CUP"

Unbeknownst to me, the Bruins had a vacancy for the position of team psychologist. The drug and alcohol educator, Dr. Max Offenberger, was already on staff. I suspect he and Weisbrod, who was a Boston scout, were responsible for my being chosen to lead the workshop. Perhaps they were also instrumental in bringing about phase two: my being offered the Bruins job. Without a moment of pause, I accepted the offer. I was one piece in the five-year puzzle intended to bring the Stanley Cup to Boston. The goal was accomplished in four years. In 2011 the Stanley Cup, after a long absence, returned to Beantown.

I never met the GM of the Boston Bruins, **Peter Chiarelli.** All our conversations were over the phone lines. It started this way. The success of the seminar and the subsequent offer to join the Bruins ranked high on my list of satisfactions. It also helped to restore my lack of self-confidence. Many factors made this an outstanding experience.

The graciousness of the team's president, **Charlie Jacobs,** and his many interactions with me were both enjoyable and significant. Jacobs, an accomplished equestrian, introduced me to the world of horses. The quality of most players that he had assembled made the work day pleasant and profitable.

Claude Julien's warmth and friendship, as well as the cooperation of the assistant coaches, was important and helpful.

The interaction with staff made for pleasant memories: **Dale Hamilton-Powers, Karen Ondu, Don DelNegro** the trainer, **Eric Tosi, John Bucyk, Cam Neely**, **Matt Chmura,** and so many others.

But the person who helped make the experience special was Peter Chiarelli. An interesting aside was that Peter was the captain of the Harvard hockey team on which Weisbrod played. My relationship with Chiarelli was at first distant. As the years went on he began to trust me and confide in me. I learned to appreciate his many talents and understand the pressures that his position as GM put him under. It was his decision to be certain that I was not overlooked in any team matters—reminiscent of my days in New Haven when Mlakar and Beverley made my entry into the hockey world a memorable adventure. My opinion on matters concerning players was solicited by Chiarelli. Our interactions became more relaxed and productive over time. And in 2011, with Chiarelli's approval and initiative, I hosted the Stanley Cup for a day.

If Chiarelli had searched the internet for me when I was hired by the Bruins, the important detail of my age would have come to his attention. People in the office told me after I had been hired that Peter was dumbfounded when he learned of my age. I teased him about it many times, threatening to file charges against him over age discrimination if I were to be fired. I also pleaded with him when the time came to fire me to not cite the meaningless bromide used by so many general managers: "We are going in another direction." Come on guys, use your creativity or have your owners hire someone to come up with something original. Give us a break!

As I have said many times before, all in this life is temporary—the tenure of GMs and coaches even more so. Chiarelli was not rehired by the Bruins. Soon after his release, he was hired in the same capacity by the Edmonton Oilers. Hockey became a better place with his return.

My experience in sports was reaching close to 50 years; still, my Bruins' experience was similar to one dying and going to heaven. I loved the Bruins' organization.

A word about some of the people who became memorable on my journey through a career in sports: They are not only the millionaire athletes or the superstars, but others who contributed, to a greater or lesser degree, to the smooth operation of a franchise. They are trainers, equipment people, media people, physicians, dentists, and office people. And they are not, even though the sports world is still a male-dominated environment, all males.

One such person in my travels was **Dale Hamilton-Powers**. On my first visit to the Boston Bruins' office on Legends Way, I was led down a long corridor by Karen Ondu to the office of then-GM Peter Chiarelli. Seated behind a desk was this diminutive, pleasant, smiling woman who welcomed me to the organization. As I awaited the return of her boss to the office, we engaged in a long conversation. I knew immediately this was a person I could trust and learn from, and one I would come to like and admire. I was right on all counts.

Dale was the administrative assistant to the GM, a job that seemed to have no description. She handled anything and everything that came up efficiently and promptly, on a daily basis. In the meantime she worked on passports, answered numerous phone calls while making each caller feel important to the Bruins' organization, and greeted impromptu visitors who had an affiliation with the Bruins. She cajoled complainers, tried to mediate the problems that follow office politics, controlled tickets to the press box, and performed countless other duties of which I have no knowledge. I am a notorious klutz when it comes to getting expenses in on time. Each time I presented my expenses, she organized them for me and ensured I was reimbursed as quickly as possible.

She was also protective of me. On one occasion I invited someone I knew from the Boston area to a game. Not knowing anything about Bruins' politics, I put my foot into it. The next day, as I made my visit to the office before going to practice in Wilmington, she told me in whispered tones, but with authority, that my guest was not a welcome visitor to the Bruins' organization. I thanked her and resolved to clear my guests before I could wear out my welcome.

Another incident annoyed me concerning tickets. I generally gave my tickets for home games to the people who ran the valet parking service at the Liberty Hotel. The men and women staffing the parking lot were very solicitous of me, and they were not, despite the fact that they were lifelong Bruins fans, in a position to afford tickets. After the Bruins won the Stanley Cup, the tickets became scarcer. I had heard from another person in the office that a comment was made that "my tickets were only given to the hotel staff, therefore they should become available." The comment was not made by an administrator of the Bruins. I mentioned my snit to Dale, who merely shrugged it off, saying, "In a large organization, these things happen."

Among my fondest memories of Dale and her husband, John, were the times we would go out to dinner in Boston. Dale, who was well connected, would call her contact, ensuring we would get a prime table anywhere. After 48 years in the Bruins' office as a greeter to ex-players and coaches, a passionate and loyal Bruins' fan, a walking encyclopedia of Bruins history and trivia, and generally the straw that stirred the drink, Dale Hamilton-Powers retired. She had reduced the commitment time to care for her ailing husband, who died soon after her retirement. I know no one is irreplaceable and that we are all relegated to the role of "I will never forget what's-his-name." However, with that retirement, the office staff of the Bruins was, despite the many fine people there, never the same. So be it.

SOMMER CHRISTIE, SPORTS PSYCHOLOGIST

During the summer of 2011, after the Boston Bruins defeated the Vancouver Canucks to win the Stanley Cup, Chiarelli celebrated his Stanley Cup Day with family and friends at the University of Ottawa. While there, he met Sommer Christie, a sports performance psychologist. They engaged in a brief conversation, which was significant enough for him to consider her as a candidate for the job in Boston after I retired. Women had served as psychologists in the NHL before, and Chiarelli was shrewd enough to recognize that women were as capable and as able to contribute to the success of a sports team as were their male counterparts. Since hockey is a small world, entry into it and acceptance by it is by no means a given. Having a sponsor is an ace up one's sleeve. Having a sponsor such as Peter Chiarelli is akin to holding on to a royal flush in a high stakes poker game. Christie had her foot in the door, and she needed someone to open it further so she could gain entry.

At training camp the following season, Chiarelli introduced Christie's name into our conversation. The years were rapidly catching up to me, and since he and I had become closer to one another in our professional and personal relationships, taboo topics were freely discussed. I was old when I first took the Bruins job. I was now older, and my mobility was being challenged. The conversation about my replacement was both fitting and proper.

Peter asked me whether the prospect of meeting and evaluating Sommer Christie as a candidate was of any interest to me. The thought was intriguing. I agreed, and took her contact information. As fate would have it, I would be in Toronto with the BC Lions the same time as Christie was in that city. We arranged to meet at the Skydome Hotel before our game against the Toronto Argonauts, and had an extended coffee hour. Once we solved all the ills of the psychological world in particular, and the rest of the world's ills in general, we watched the BC Lions add another win to their long streak of successes.

Interestingly enough, this young woman was excited to meet me. In fact she was counseled by her father to listen carefully to what I had to say and to take copious notes. This amused and flattered me. I mentioned to her that I saw my first task as one of trying to be relevant to the organization. But my longevity in the league, my assortment of championship rings, and the fact that my name was recognized in several sports gave me an aura I neither understood nor felt I deserved. Nevertheless she asked questions, and I tried to answer them as honestly and as directly as I could. The more we talked, the more I began to realize that this young woman was accomplished in her own right. She was a successful and gifted athlete who had access to many sports organizations. Her humility clouded her many feats.

As we parted ways she appeared happy to have met me, and I was left impressed as to where she was professionally. We promised to stay in touch, and that we did. Seven years later our contacts became more frequent; her success with Canadian Olympic athletes was an expected occurrence. She has been an advocate on my behalf, nominating me for several awards. She at one time visited my wife and me in Florida where we outlined many projects we would like to do together. However, she became serious about completing her doctorate. Our projects were put on the back burner in hopes of getting to them later. A project I was particularly hopeful we could complete together is one I call "The Anatomy of Winning." Over the years, I compiled a list of qualities that winners embody. I am hopeful it will one day become a book. I would be honored to see my name associated with hers on its publication.

DAVE PASKEVICH, SPORTS PSYCHOLOGIST

When Dave Paskevich was not traveling the world helping Canadian Olympic hopefuls reach new heights, and when he had some precious moments to spare, he arranged his schedule for our phone call, which lasted until his next meeting or class. I never put the phone down without having learned something new or without having heard an interesting story about his many experiences working to enhance an athlete's performance. If ever I was in need of a name to suggest for a consultancy in sports psychology, the first name to come to my mind would be **Dave Paskevich**. I know he will tap into the potential of each athlete and give it his best shot. When I read of his accomplishments, I was awed by them. He teaches, he researches, he administers, he reads, he counsels athletes, he lectures, and the list goes on and on. At the time I wrote this section, he had just returned from the Olympics in Pyeongchang, South Korea.

One season when I was consulting to the Boston Bruins, I encountered Dave in Boston. At that time, he was consulting with the Calgary Flames. We had the opportunity to compare notes, tell war stories, and lament the fact that the prestige of sports psychology, though considerably improved from the time we started (I started in the 1950s), was not where we hoped it would be. Sure, most teams have some connection to a "sports shrink." Connection does not mean conviction. In our experiences we found that, at times when we could have been of assistance, we were not consulted. I told him of an experience I had. One day the then-head coach of the NHL team I was consulting invited me and the two assistant coaches into his office to view a video. He was awed by the presenter. He wanted to immediately invite the person to make a presentation to our team. When I told the coach I had trained the presenter, he asked, "Why didn't you tell me?" The fact that he had little or no time for me was completely overlooked. Unfortunately, Dave had similar experiences. For a brief moment, we felt downtrodden.

We hoped the sports scene had become more sensitive to what psychologists can bring to sports. We agreed it had, and that we would continue to promote our profession. Considering the number of times psychological intervention is mentioned by TV commentators during the Olympics and other sporting events, the profession has come a long way. This is due to the efforts of people like Dave Paskevich, who inspire their students and spread the word that the relationship of psychology to sports is worth exploring. In my mind, I think, "They ain't seen nothing yet. The future is getting brighter." Programs such as the one at the University of Calgary deserve a pat on the academic back. No wonder heights previously unachievable have been exceeded.

In the future, I hope the contributions and achievements of sports psychologists expands in great magnitude. A harmonious working relationship between a head coach and a psychologist is an essential ingredient for success.

CLAUDE JULIEN, HEAD COACH, BOSTON BRUINS

A new head coach at the Bruins' helm began to give me pause. Rumor had it that one or more previous experiences in working with psychologists had negatively colored **Claude Julien**'s picture of them. To me, this was understandable. Coaching styles and psychologists' styles do not always coalesce. I wondered how this was destined to be played out. After some cautious encounters, we began to become more comfortable with one another; I assured him that even though the rules were unwritten, I knew them. The head coach was not only your coworker; he was, in fact, your boss. Following his wishes was fine with me. I was not going to test the limits. After all, most coaches, because of their daily interactions with the players, had a better read about the chemistry of a team than did some hotshot practitioner who made monthly visits. If there were negative thoughts, they were well hidden.

Julien was generous with his time for me, and he listened attentively as we talked. Within weeks of our first meeting I became comfortable. Soon he began to update me from visit to visit. He encouraged my work with the leadership group, which was becoming more solid with each passing visit. Coach Julien and I established a routine: After each home game I attended I completed my postgame chores with the players and waited for Claude to finish his. Then he drove me to the hotel I stayed at during that visit. Those short trips did wonders in cementing a relationship with the coach, which endured beyond our days of working together.

ZDENO CHÁRA, DEFENSEMAN, BOSTON BRUINS

Zdeno Chára was a gem to work with. He kept me informed and sought my counsel, which led to strengthening the bond that saw the light of day in Longboat Key. Over the years, my relationship with Chára flourished. At times he invited me to attend player-only meetings. Never was I questioned by management about the goings-on in those meetings, which underscored the class of the people in the organization. The leadership group invited different players to some meetings, which expanded the importance and influence of the group. Group membership changed, and each change brought new ideas, new blood. The core of the leadership group remained: Chára, Bergeron, and Sturm. Their continued interest and ingenuity paid off, and the group was working out better than most expected.

The players who attended the seminar bought into what I presented. Each of them contributed in their own way. Chára and Bergeron, two team leaders, showed enthusiasm, which became infectious. Many factors make relationships between players and other employees of major sports organizations difficult. Not only does the disparity between players' earnings and the rest of the franchise hinder camaraderie, but the players' lifestyles, ages, and backgrounds help to confuse the issue.

My situation was slightly different. Consultants are hired to address a specific problem. Once the problem is addressed, the consultant moves on. In most organizations players treat consultants in a friendly manner and make the working environment pleasant and productive. This was my experience with the Boston Bruins, and it was due, in part, to the welcoming I received from the leadership group led by Chára. He is an example of the high caliber of most of the Bruins players during my time with the team.

Chára is a physical specimen; standing at six feet nine inches, imposing enough simply for his size, his body was a well-tuned machine. His daily workouts, dietary restrictions, work ethic, and determination accounted for his dominance on the ice. His hockey instincts added to the other traits that accounted for his success on the ice. Off the ice, Chára is a pensive, studious, sensitive, and spiritual family man. While I was employed by the Bruins, I occasionally ran into him as he rode his bicycle through the streets of Boston.

Sometimes he was headed to the Catholic Church to pay a brief visit. Each time, he asked me if I needed anything, or if there was anything he could do for me. One example of his generosity was the year my identity was stolen. All the people on my contact list were contacted. They were told that I was in Spain, and that I lost my wallet and needed immediate financial help. To my knowledge, Chára was the only one of my contacts to respond. He exchanged emails with the thief but became suspicious of the fellow. Chára then asked him where our leadership seminar was held. The lowlife ceased contact. Another example of Chára's concern for people occurred when my wife had a second hip operation. He was one of the first people to respond. He asked if I needed any type of financial aid because there was a players' fund, and he would have gladly designated it to be used if I were in need. It demonstrates the type of spirit that lives inside of Chára.

When I was with the Bruins team, Zee and I met several times. When I was not with the team, emails were the order of the day. My meetings with him were always informative and productive. I would suggest readings to him and he quickly ordered them. After he read them, we discussed the ways in which the material could be applied to the Bruins' organization. The manner in which Chára led the players during the 2010-11 championship season had a great impact on the team's success. He provided a great example to his teammates, including during the rigors of spring training. He was disciplined and cognizant that going the extra mile showed cooperation with the "powers that be" (front office management).

Chára competed for Slovakia in the Winter Olympics in 2006, 2010, and 2014. He recorded the hardest shot at the 2012 All Star Game Hardest Shot skill competition. The shot was recorded as 108.8 mph, a record difficult to match. His many concerns and kindnesses to me are one of many memories I cherished over the 10 years I spent with the Bruins. Fortunately for me, Chára and I remained in contact.

PATRICE BERGERON, FORWARD, BOSTON BRUINS

Another stalwart member of the Boston Bruins during my time there was **Patrice Bergeron**. Since he was the first Bruins' player I met on Longboat Key prior to our seminar, he holds a special place of honor. Bergeron was a talented forward who won the Selke Trophy for being the Best Two-Way Player in the NHL. He won the Selke four times and was a finalist for eight straight years; plus, he has many other feathers in his hockey cap. Each year after the ceremonies when Bergeron was awarded the Selke, I teased him by saying, "You and Stefanie need to build an extra room on your house just to display that trophy." But the Selke is only one accomplishment. He also owns Olympic Championship trophies from when he represented Canada in the World Junior Championships, and a Stanley Cup ring from his time with the Bruins in 2011.

A future Hall of Famer, he is also popular among Bruins players. His opponents marvel at his many and varied talents. He made the jump from Junior Hockey to the NHL in 2003 and in his entire career he demonstrated grit and determination by playing after severe injuries. His presence alone served as motivation for his teammates. He joined many other Bruins players who played either while battling or immediately after serious injuries—players like Zdeno Chára and **Gregory Campbell**. When **Brad Marchand** joined Bergeron on the first line, the team seemed to be on fire. The two men meshed and have a high regard for each other. The line continued to sizzle with the addition of David Pastrnak.

Chuck Kobasew was introduced to me by Patrice. Chuck, a steady, reliable forward, spent four seasons with the Bruins after the Calgary Flames. It was a sorry day when Chuck was traded from the Bruins to the Minnesota Wild. He spent three more years in the NHL, and he finished out his career in the Swiss A League. His character, integrity, and loyalty make him unforgettable. One summer he drove many miles from his home to visit me at the Lions' training camp.

In addition to Kobasew, Adam McQuaid, Torey Krug, and Kevan Miller played with grit and determination. McQuaid and Miller were both quick to answer the bell in defense of their teammates. Krug was always willing to stand his ground to protect his side of the ice and was an excellent penalty killer. I remained in touch with McQuaid, who was traded to the New York Rangers, then to the Columbus Blue Jackets where he suffered a major concussion, causing him to miss a large chunk of the 2018 season.

As the years went on, my enthusiasm for the Bruins' organization never waned. Our GM was skilled in finding the right player to rent for a year to fill a gap. The most notable was the signing of **Mark Recchi**, who played a great and important role in helping bring the 2011 Stanley Cup to Boston. Some of these player rentals worked out better than others. When right wing Jaromir Jagr was brought in, the expected change never occurred. He did not adjust to his line mates, nor they to him. Jagr's style of dangling the puck around the net seemed to affect Marchand, whose style was to take off for the net. It did not add up to another Cup.

GREGORY CAMPBELL, CENTER, BOSTON BRUINS

The men who suited up for the Bruins for the Stanley Cup finals consisted mostly of players whose great seasons never went that far into June. The roster Chiarelli and the scouts had amassed was a force to be reckoned with. The addition of **Gregory Campbell**, a dedicated, committed player, was an awesome step forward. He played 47 seconds with a broken leg that was caused by a shot from **Evgeni Malkin** during a Pittsburgh power play. Barely able to move, Campbell continued on the ice. His heroics that night earned praise from his coach, Claude Julien, and exemplified the Bruins' attitude during that season. "The way I look at it, and it might sound naïve of me, I was just trying to do whatever I could to kill the penalty," Campbell said to reporters afterward. His injury made him a household name because of his tenacity and grit.

Was it a symbol of what the Boston team was made of as they fought their way to the Stanley Cup Finals? To many people the answer is a resounding, "Yes!" Whatever it was, it exemplified the character of the man I came to know and admire. When I first met Campbell he was riding an exercise bike after a Bruins' home game. He was quiet and focused on the task at hand. I spoke with him very briefly as he eyed me with caution. As we came to know one another, we joked about being each other's idol. I wasn't joking—he was really one of mine. I saw in this man a depth and sincerity that led to his high level of determination. I imagined him attacking each task in his life the same way, giving all that he had to offer. Campbell was as fierce a competitor as I had seen in all my years working in sports. His contributions to the Bruins' success on the fourth line with Shawn Thornton and Dan Paille were repeatedly mentioned in the media.

In addition to meeting expectations with his play, he did not shy away from dropping the gloves when he felt that action was called for. In sports, the stats only show one part of the picture. A player's contribution to the team on and off the ice, along with his spirit, his energy, and his overall demeanor, all help complete the profile. Perhaps the picture of the man can best be seen in the following comments spoken by his teammates:

> "The fact that he took that shot and he couldn't even move and he was still trying to play and get in the lane. He did a great job, and we really wanted to play for him. It just shows his character. He's always battling. He's always doing whatever he has to do, and he's been huge for us in these playoffs so far."

> *—Brad Marchand*

"That's the kind of player he is. He's a real dedicated individual to his work and to his game, from off the ice, to on the ice to taking care of himself, demeanor, everything else. What he did surprised a lot of people, but it didn't surprise us because that's just who he is."

–Claude Julien
(recalling the drama produced by Campbell's block the previous night)

"I'm not sure if I've ever played with anyone who spends that much time at the rink. He loves it. He grew up with it. I'm sure he's a little down in the dumps, but he's around the guys and we will help him out any way we can. He's still a big part of this team whether he skates or not."

–Two-Time Stanley Cup Winner Shawn Thornton
(Campbell's line mate on the Merlot line)

To know such a man is a privilege not to be taken lightly. It is one of the joys of working in sports. To see someone work so hard to achieve his goals, no matter what the field is, must be a motivating factor in the lives of those who know that person.

Dennis Seidenberg helped to shore up the defense, as did the presence of **Johnny Boychuk** and the young **Adam McQuaid**. This unit, led by Zdeno Chára, knew how to protect a lead and, at pivotal times, help add to it. The steady play of **Andrew Ference** was much appreciated. On offense, the Bruins were a unit to be desired. Bergeron was proving his value with each shift. **David Krejci** had become a reliable player in the faceoff circle. His scoring touch and his playmaking ability were attracting attention in every NHL city. The addition of **Chris Kelly** and **Rich Peverley** proved to be invaluable. The willingness of the ever-agreeable **Shawn Thornton**, to put his body on the line either to protect his teammates or to make a statement, went a long way in ensuring success. Thornton, much to the disapproval of some of his teammates, had taken it upon himself to greet me with the words, "Glad to see you made it. Happy you are still alive." This made me feel accepted. I appreciated his warmth and humor. I too was happy to have made it another day.

Nathan Horton, with his aggressive style of play, was pivotal in our team's success. The rookie, **Tyler Seguin**, was proving the Boston scouts right in their assessment of his talents. The services of **Michael Ryder,** whose play seemed to elevate itself during the playoffs, was an added bonus. The "Little Ball of Hate," the antagonist, the overall pest, **Brad Marchand,** had arrived—his moment had come. He took advantage of it. **Mark Recchi's** play, **Daniel Paille's** speed, and

Milan Lucic's physical presence ensured the Bruins' success. The spectacular goal tending of **Tim Thomas** cannot be overlooked. Thomas, one of the mentally toughest athletes I had ever been around, almost defied opposing players to score against him. Despite his unorthodox style of play, his stellar regular season was punctuated by his being named MVP.

Luckily for the Bruins, their backup goalie, **Tuukka Rask,** was more than equal to the task when called upon, and even more stellar when he became the starting goalie. It is in the building of a lineup that the effectiveness and creativity of coaches shines brightly. Julien and his staff put together a fourth line that was the envy of the league. He placed on it Gregory Campbell at center, Shawn Thornton, who added talent and grit to the line, and the speedy Dan Paille. It is hard to be certain as to how many of the games' outcomes were affected by these men. But one thing is certain—their contributions helped in a big way to bring the Cup to the Boston Fans.

NHL playoffs are always grueling, following long and tedious seasons, which brought about player fatigue. Knowing that each player was playing in some degree of pain made the playoffs a physical and mental challenge. It was confirmed when the Bruins played three seven-game series before securing the Cup. Traveling with the team taught me a great lesson—the players, the coaches, the trainers, the equipment guys, and just about everyone was almost totally spent. The long-distance trips between Boston and Vancouver in the final series only added to the stress and strain. But the Bruins, heroically and without fanfare, survived.

The puck was dropped and game seven started. With sweaty palms and dry throats, we watched with anxiety and anticipation. The box was full of Bruins VIPS, some of us pacing, offering support to whomever crossed our paths. I wouldn't be surprised if some prayers were directed heavenward. Sometimes games seem to be played out in twice the allotted time. This was one of those games. During the third period I walked past John Weisbrod who announced to me, "This game is over." The words comforted me, but since there was still time on the clock, I couldn't relax. After what seemed like an eternity—finally—the game ended and Boston prevailed!

This was my third experience with a team that had reached the NHL finals. I was up to that time 1-1, a loss with the LA Kings and a win with the New Jersey Devils. This one, with Boston, was the sweetest. Chiarelli's five-year plan was completed a year sooner than anticipated. It confirmed for all of us involved that all the ingredients that made for victory had been mixed well.

The behavior of the Vancouver fans made a distinct impression on me. Despite their disappointment and the totally unacceptable behavior of some who were rioting downtown, these fans in the stands watched the trophy handed out by the commissioner—the trophy they had hoped to have been theirs. They applauded the Bruins' victory and Tim Thomas' acceptance of the MVP award. I was standing by the players bench as Zee Chára skated over to me, smiled, hugged me, said a muffled thank you, and went on with his celebration.

After the picture taking, the players met with family, and the team ambled down to the locker room. In the trainers' room, I was carrying on a conversation with Zee. Suddenly, he stood up, said he couldn't walk, and began to throw up. Other players joined him, sharing their own discomfort. Each of them received an IV for rehydration. Dehydration had done to them what opposing teams could not accomplish.

In the locker room, corks were beginning to pop; the ritual was beginning, only to be abruptly interrupted by a policeman who announced to the "powers that be" that if we wanted an escort to the airport we had to leave immediately, since the unit was needed to help contain the meaningless riots.

The trip to the airport was joyous but otherwise uneventful. We passed close enough to see the flames produced by the rioters, but not close enough to be in any danger. At the airport, I left the team. I was due back at the training camp of the BC Lions who were embarking on their season, one that would see a Grey Cup victory for the Lions.

Celebrating a Stanley Cup win is not a one-day affair. It begins the moment the final buzzer sounds and lasts right up to and, for some of us, beyond the opening of the next season. During the summer of 2011 I was astounded when I received a phone call from the NHL office informing me that I would have my own day with the Stanley Cup. At first I thought the call was a hoax. But it was not. Of all the sports fantasies I'd had, this one never was indulged. After some changes of dates and venues, the Cup was delivered to the home of our daughter, Denise, on October 12, 2011. The decision was made to go to Delaware, since we had few friends in Florida and none who cared the least about hockey. The party was attended by relatives, neighbors, and friends of Denise. All the guests were encouraged to have a picture taken wearing my Stanley Cup ring. None refused. The rings were presented at a posh gala before the start of the 2011-12 season.

On January 23, 2012, the last formal celebration that the Bruins organization was to participate in was a meeting at the White House with President Barack Obama. That day in Washington, tens of thousands of pro-life advocates descended on Washington to voice their displeasure with the Roe vs. Wade decision of the Supreme Court. It was also the day Obama was to deliver the State of the Union address. Other than that function, there were no other agenda items scheduled for the president that day. After getting through many levels of security, we were given a tour of some rooms in the White House (not open to the public), and we waited. It was a long wait until the president arrived.

After spending some time with select members of the Bruins staff, the function began before a large audience. Massachusetts was represented by its two senators and the members of the House of Representatives. Politicians of all stripes filled the room. Senator John Kerry went the extra mile to mingle with members of the Bruins' organization. His charm and wit made for an enjoyable encounter. After the president delivered his prepared speech, he remained for a while talking to the other politicos. A White House staffer made it clear that our visit was over by thanking us for our presence and showing us toward the exit. This was an opportunity not to be missed. All of these experiences were, to say the least, beyond words. Thanks to the Boston Brass for making these events happen and for permitting me to be a part of them.

In no way was the road to a dynasty in Boston over. Creating consecutive championship runs has always been difficult. It had become even more difficult with the introduction of free agency and the salary cap. Teams who were at or near the cap had little wiggle room to negotiate when it came to signing free agents. Other teams were left hanging, not knowing in which direction their free agents would go.

The summer recess that began for players around the middle of June was seen by many to be another bump in the road. Summer rest and rehabilitation was shortened. Winning two or three championships in a row was never a slam dunk. It was now a half-court shot, blindfolded. Each year the present championship team had a bullseye on the back of each returning player. An upset win by a weak team would make their season. In addition, current rules in the NHL made a return to glory even more difficult. The salary cap imposed on the league makes it difficult to keep a team intact and, at the same time, try to build for the future. It is almost an impossibility to reward stellar performances and to sign up-and-coming players. The cap is so structured to prevent inequities in team spending for talents. But hold on—these Bruins had one more chance before hope for a budding dynasty faded.

The chance to win two Stanley Cups (2011 and 2013) in three seasons was not to be sneered at. They made the best of that chance only to fall short in game six with a 3-2 loss to the Chicago Blackhawks, who were also trying to create their own dynasty. The first game of that final series saw the Blackhawks winners of a three-overtime game, and building momentum from that game on. Boston won the next two. The two teams went into game 6 down 3 games to 2. The game was at home. Our bags were packed for the trip to Chicago. Our optimism was high. The team was confident. With two minutes left in the game, the Bruins held a one-goal lead only to see it evaporate and to turn into a 3-2 Chicago victory.

Holding on to a lead in this series had become an albatross for the Bruins. The addition of Jagr did not bring the magic signing Recchi did in 2011. Regardless, Chicago won. The dreams of Boston becoming a dynasty were put on hold. The loss, and the timing of it, was devastating. Was it time to rebuild? Had the team run out of rabbits to pull out of the hat?

In 2013-14 the Bruins lost in round two. In 2014-15 and 2015-16 they were out of the playoffs. The waters around Boston were becoming rough for both the GM and head coach. When a team starts a losing trend, rather than trying to right the ship, most teams opt for change. The shoe had fallen, and Peter Chiarelli was the first to go.

Over the years, when I was in Boston for home games, I waited until all the mundane, postgame chores a head coach has to endure were completed. Then Claude and I would have something to eat and review the status quo. After the departure of Chiarelli, insecurity set in. Julien and others began to wait for the other shoe to fall. It did. It was the shoe of Claude Julien. Firings are always difficult. They affect not only the person fired and their family, friends, and coworkers, but also an entire organization. My mobility was making it more difficult for me to travel as I once did. It was time for me to go, but my loyalty and love for the Bruins was sanguine as ever. I did not want to leave, at least not completely.

Don Sweeney, the new GM, listened carefully and sympathetically to my proposed options. They were rather simple and direct. Option one was that an announcement would be made that I would not be returning to the Bruins. The logic behind this was to assure other clubs that were interested in my services that I was under no obligation to the Bruins. The other was that I would be retained at a lower fee in some type of emeritus capacity.

Neither of these options were carried out. Though I was at first angry, and then disappointed, my time with the Bruins was so memorable that my loyalty never waned. I had hoped to retire from the NHL as a Bruin. It was not to happen. Instead, it was decided that since I could not travel with the team, I had become expendable. No fanfare. This was the end.

COMMENTARY FROM ZDENO (ZEE) CHÁRA, BOSTON BRUINS

I met Frank in Sarasota, Florida, in 2007, when he was hired by the Boston Bruins and we had our leadership group. We flew to Sarasota, and it was recommended that we should attend this leadership seminar. Frank was recommended by Peter Chiarelli. The leadership seminar lasted two to three days. Frank didn't know much about hockey. We had to guide him a little bit on hockey fundamentals. He welcomed the conversations about hockey and how things worked around the locker room and management. He listened and explained about football. Then he talked about the importance of leadership and working together and being on the same page. And how to "plant the seeds" with the team. He was very impressive. At first we were surprised by his age, and then we realized that he was active, which made him younger inside.

Frank led us with exercises on trust and communication. Then I invited everyone over to my place in Florida. We had a big dinner and barbecue. We talked a little about the seminar, and then we talked about family, schools, kids, and everything. We came to know more about each other and about Frank and his big family. He came on road trips, and he helped some players. We kept in touch.

Frank was very important later on when navigating situations with the Bruins. He taught us a lot about life, how to communicate, and how to respect each other more. He was such a good human being. It is a privilege to have good friends. In Chicago I met his family in his hotel room, and it was great. He was a tremendous friend and so helpful to us. We loved Frank and it was such an honor. He taught us a lot about sports, leadership, and about life.

CONCLUSION

SAYING GOODBYE

IT WAS ONE HELLUVA RIDE

Nothing is forever. Accepting that reality is, at times, far more difficult than one might have anticipated. Ever since I was a child I never liked saying "Goodbye." When visitors or family members left our home, I was sad. I retired from my first career, college teaching and administration, after 44 years with no regrets, no looking back. My second career was counseling men who were preparing for the priesthood in the Catholic Church. This career included working for three dioceses, three religious orders—one based in Rome, Italy. I was able to leave it with some regret, but no real angst.

Leaving the sports world was a devastating experience, one from which I have never fully recovered. The timing for my retirement was long past. I was in my 90s when it came crashing down. My health had deteriorated; my mobility was compromised. Plane travel was becoming next to impossible. My consultancies in Boston and Vancouver were too far from my home in south Florida.

The curtain had fallen on a world in which I had struggled to gain entrance, one that I found challenging, rewarding, and fun. Even in my most rational moments I knew it was time to say goodbye, but still did so with great reluctance. Circumstances surrounding my departure from the BC Lions after 15 years and the Boston Bruins after 10 years left a bitter taste in my mouth.

In Vancouver I found it difficult to get a statement concerning my retirement. One reason that was given was that I was not a paid employee, and therefore there was no evidence that I had ever consulted for the team. This was despite the fact that I was awarded two Grey Cup rings. I realized later that I was partially to blame. Had I gone directly to Wally Buono, it would have been handled differently. One should always respect the politics of sports.

The departure from the Boston Bruins had its own sour moments. From the start of my employment with the Bruins I developed strong feelings toward ownership, management, office personnel, players, and coaches. The years prior to winning the Stanley Cup were full of anticipation. Everyone was motivated to succeed. In some inexplicable way, I felt closer to the Bruins than I did any of my other consultancies. Perhaps I should have left them earlier, more graciously.

When it became obvious that it was over, everywhere but in my mind, I suggested either one of two options: make a formal announcement of my retirement or, as I hoped, provide me with an honorary title like emeritus so that I could be a Bruin for life. Neither option was granted. The third and final blow came from the CFL. When Wally Buono first suggested to me that I be nominated to the Canadian Football League Hall of Fame in the "Builder Category," I was opposed to the idea. I said to him, "I don't have a chance." But the nomination went through. I mentioned the nomination to Peter Dalla Riva, a retired Montreal player and a Hall of Famer himself, and he was supportive of the idea. The more people I spoke with, the greater the fire in my stomach grew. I was now hoping that I would be named. I was not.

Apparently, over 30 years of pro bono services to the Canadian Football League, worth many thousands of dollars per year, was not enough. Despite the episodes at the end of it all, it was one helluva ride—one I was fortunate to have taken part in, one that I would repeat over and over again.

A LETTER FROM
DR. FRANK LODATO'S DAUGHTER,
JANICE LODATO

My dad, Francis J. Lodato, Ph.D., was a sports psychologist, a trailblazer, and a loving and devoted father. Growing up, my dad presented me with many unique opportunities, including attending hundreds of minor league hockey games during my high school years. It's where I learned a lot about hockey, had a blast cheering for our team, and waited patiently, long after the game was over, for my dad to finish working with the players and coaches, often after he had already worked another job. I'm sure having a second set of eyes on the long drive home at night on country roads was helpful for him too. I also traveled many times to Montreal for Canadian Football League (CFL) games and to cities like Hershey, Pennsylvania, and Sherbrooke, Quebec, for American Hockey League (AHL) games. It was a great adventure, as he followed his dream to apply the practice of hypnosis to sports.

Hypnosis was a tool that my dad used with us at home too. At one point in her life, my mother was so adept at using self-hypnosis that she did not require Novocain for a dental procedure. When I was in high school and experiencing a series of migraines, my dad hypnotized me on our living room sofa. I can still remember the texture of the sofa and the pressure of his thumb on my third eye and the instant pain relief I experienced. Later on, he taught me the self-hypnosis techniques that I have utilized in many situations throughout my life.

My dad had a dream that he would write a book with each of his three kids. He realized this dream before he died, with my brother, Ray, (*But We Were 17 and 0*) in 1986, and with my sister, Denise, (*Eboli to Brooklyn–One Way*) in 2017. However, this book that he and I collaborated on was not done when he passed away in 2021. Finally, I'm fulfilling his wish to publish a book together.

In this memoir, he emphasizes many aspects of being a successful sports psychologist. Honestly, these are the qualities that made him successful in his numerous jobs and endeared him to so many people:

- **Relationships.** He always put relationships first, and when you spoke with him, he made you think there was no one as important as you in the whole world.
- **Dedication and drive.** When he decided to do something, he was 100 percent dedicated to it and unswerving in his focus and drive.

- **Work ethic.** For most of his adult life, he worked multiple jobs at once to provide for his family and to advance his career.
- **Humility.** He could disarm you with his humility and his genuine curiosity. He could set aside his ego and get to know anyone—from the wait staff in a restaurant to a gold-medal Olympian.
- **Trust.** People trusted him and for good reason. He kept all the secrets shared with him. We never knew any details about his clients' lives. No gossip, ever. You trusted him, and for good reason.
- **Winning.** He always wanted to win. He wanted to win the consultancy that he was pitching but he also wanted his athletes and teams to win. He was all about winning. For the athletes and coaches, he knew that sports was their profession, and he was completely committed to making sure they succeeded.

In reading this memoir, one thing that may not be immediately apparent is that my dad's role as a team psychologist evolved over the years. Initially, he was doing a lot of learning style analysis, which helped coaches know the most effective way to present information to their teams. Over the years, the combination of task analysis, visualization, and self-hypnosis became the cornerstone of his practice as a sports psychologist and the winning ticket that athletes sought him out for.

He was always available for his athletes and coaches. Though his role was not primarily one of a counselor, he did that whenever it was needed. He accepted calls from players before and after games, regardless of the time zone difference, to give encouragement or a task review, and hear any other updates they wanted to share.

There are many athletes my dad worked with who are not included in this memoir. Mostly those are individual athletes: figure skaters, golfers, equestrians, martial arts experts, soccer players, and track and field athletes. They, too, were all valuable in the development of his practice and his career; any omissions were made to maintain the structure of the book around teams. (I am responsible for any omissions in regard to testimonials or interviews.) He cherished working with all of you.

Long before Nike adopted this slogan, my dad would often say to us:

"Just do it."

To honor him and his legacy, please go for your dreams: Just do it.

—Janice E. Lodato, M.A.

APPENDICES

CANADIAN FOOTBALL HALL OF FAME NOMINATION LETTERS

Mark DeNobile
c/o Canadian Football Hall of Fame
Executive Director
Hamilton, Ontario

Dear Mark,

It is my absolute pleasure to recommend Dr. Frank Lodato to be inducted into the Canadian Football Hall of Fame as a Builder.

Dr. Frank and I have had a working relationship since 1990, when I joined Wally Buono's coaching staff as an Offensive Coordinator and Dr. Frank was our Sports Psychologist. I thoroughly enjoyed my time working with Dr. Frank, and came to realize him as a truly valuable asset to our football teams. His undeniable skills and talents in the sport psychology world helped numerous players and coaches reach greater heights on the field. Dr. Frank Lodato, in his capacity, was a difference maker. Dr. Frank has worked for many professional leagues (CFL, NFL, NHL) and with many Olympians. He is honest, dependable, generous, and extremely hardworking.

I would like to cite some examples of how he made a difference:

1. During training camp with the Calgary Stampeders in 1994 we had a running back, Tony Stewart, who joined the club late in the 1993 season. Tony was a talented player, but was having trouble with his assignments during training camp and the preseason games. I was perplexed because Tony would correctly answer my questions in the

meeting room. I presented this problem to Dr. Frank who then had a session with Tony. Dr. Frank advised me that Tony was a visual learner. I altered my coaching technique to include visual learning in my meetings with Tony, and he went on to have a great year. Tony ended the season with 1120 yards rushing, 586 yards receiving, and scored 19 touchdowns.

2. Another example of Dr. Frank's great work is Allen Pitts. Now Allen was a great player, but during the 1994 training camp, Allen was inconsistent in catching the ball. Allen was coming off an injury he sustained in the 1993 season and his concentration in completing the catch was not consistent. Dr. Frank suggested I make a clip of 10 plays of Allen successfully making a catch, and a clip of 10 plays where he failed to complete the catch and show the clips to Allen in slow-motion so he could see the difference with his eye concentration and his head movement. I believe this aided Allen tremendously as he continued on with his great career. Allen finished the 1994 season with 126 catches for 2,036 yards and 21 touchdowns.

3. Dr. Frank is currently working with our field goal kicker, René Parades. They chat during the week and then right before the game starts throughout René's career with the Stampeders. René has established a new CFL record for most consecutive field goals (FG) at 39 and a new CFL record for FG efficiency at 94.7 percent. When the game is on the line, René is clutch.

I know he has helped several coaches over his 34 years associated with the CFL and mostly on a volunteer basis; that speaks volumes about the man. Through his friendships and relationships over the years, and his generosity to help people and organizations, Dr. Frank has made all of us better coaches, better players, and therefore a better league.

I want to thank all of you for your consideration in allowing Dr. Frank Lodato to be inducted into the Canadian Hall of Fame.

Sincerely,
John Hufnagel

JOHN HUFNAGEL, PRESIDENT AND GENERAL MANAGER
CALGARY STAMPEDERS FOOTBALL CLUB

From: Geroy Simon
Subject: Quote

"Dr Frank has been an instrumental part in my career and everyday life. We had an intense connection from our very first session. His teachings and exercises on visualization have been a tool that helped my career soar into a stratosphere I'd never imagined. It is also integral in my daily life now. Dr Frank is a lifelong friend and mentor that I've cherished for many years."

Geroy Simon, Wide Receiver, BC Lions

CFL HALL OF FAME SELECTION COMMITTEE ATTN: MARK DENOBLE

December 8, 2017
Re: Francis Lodato Induction as a Builder

Dr. Frank is a coach and strength trainer. He helps build strength in the most important area for an athlete and team: mental strength.

I can't speak to his lengthy tenure throughout the league, volunteering with priceless help for players on every team except Toronto and Winnipeg since 1982. I can speak to his time with the BC Lions from 2003-2008.

During that span our team won 74 regular season games and lost just 34. We finished 1st in the league for 4 straight seasons and had 2 Grey Cup appearances, 1 Grey Cup Championship, and numerous player awards.

We were strong physically, but so was every other team in the league. Our ace in the hole was Dr. Frank Lodato.

Frank helped many players overcome anxiety, mental blocks, and perceived physical obstacles that allowed us to trust ourselves and our teammates and play fearless football, even when returning from injury.

Please accept this letter as an endorsement from one player as a reflection of a small piece of a large legacy left by Dr. Frank throughout the CFL.

Sincerely,
Jason Clermont, Slotback, BC Lions

To whom it may concern,

I wanted to become a professional football player since I can remember. In having fulfilled my dream I am left looking back at how in the world I was ever able to accomplish such a feat. The glaring reality is that I was extremely fortunate and lucky to have been surrounded by so many great people every step of the way. In 2003 I was at a real crossroads in my professional career. I was entering my third season and barely holding on. My confidence at that point in my career was shaky at best. Then I met Doctor Frank Lodato.

He came along with the new coaching regime at the time. At that point in my career, I had little belief in the impact sports psychology could have on not only the performance of a player, but the development of a person. I was hesitant to buy in. The amazing thing was, though, Frank was never selling anything. He was just there if you needed him. The amazing thing was, the second you chatted with him for five minutes, you immediately found your-self wanting more. Frank brought value to absolutely every player that cared to give him their time. It wasn't just his knowledge or techniques either, but rather the way he was able to message them. He had an unbelievable ability to connect with everyone and to make you feel that he really understood you. The greatest gift any coach can ever possess is the ability to instill the belief in their players that they really care about them as people. I have never seen someone as gifted at that talent as Doc.

I played on some great teams, playing in five straight Western Finals at one stretch, winning two Grey Cups. We had lots of talent and great coaches, but so did everyone else. At the highest level of sports, it's always the "other" things you have or do that end up being the difference. For us, that was Doctor Frank. He was our magic bullet that enabled each of us to always maximize what we had and to work through any issues as efficiently as possible.

His visits were always a highlight of our season. He is loved and respected by every player and coach that he has ever dealt with. A true master of his craft and one of the most generous and kind people I have ever known.

I couldn't even begin to guess at the vast number of athletes Frank has not only helped on their field of play, but their life overall. I am eternally grateful for my fortunate relationship with Doc. I'm not confident my career would have made it as far as it eventually did.

Frank Lodato is not only a Hall of Famer, but a true pioneer, bringing the world of psychology to sports before anyone. He's an amazing man that I am not only grateful to know, but very proud to call my friend.

Angus Reid, Offensive Lineman, CFL player – 2001-2013
Two-time Grey Cup Champ – 2006, 2011

From: "Iannuzzi, Marco"
Subject: HOF nomination for Dr. Frank Lodato

To whom it may concern:

I, Marco Iannuzzi, Harvard graduate, 6-year BC Lions veteran and current active player, would like to nominate the one and only Dr. Francis Lodato— or as I like to call him "Ol' Frankie-boy"—to the CFHOF.

I will briefly skim over the things I believe you already know, that is: he has offered his skills throughout the CFL for the last 34 years at no charge! He was, by my research and by the account of many, the forefather of sports psychology, a standard in today's sport. Aside from these two absolutely un-paralleled facts, I would like to share my personal experience with Doc.

In 2011 I arrived in Kamloops, BC, for BC Lions training camp, with what I felt was a very good grasp on life; Harvard- and MIT-educated, mar-ried for two years, one daughter and one on the way, 1st round draft pick, starting my new business at RBC, life was good, but the balance of things was quite delicate to say the least. From the very first moment that he addressed the team, he was the most captivating presence of a guest standing in front of an audience that I had ever experienced, even more than the HOF'er Wally Buono, and I would even venture to say greater than Barack Obama, whom I had the pleasure of witnessing speak in a room of 200 on his campaign trail in 2006. There was a very strong sense that you could feel in the room, as if you could reach out and grab it in the air. It was a certain feeling of respect for his knowledge, for his experience, goosebumps on arms, hair standing up on neck sort of thing. I remember staring at the rings under his eyes, the rings under his ears, the rings under his neck, thinking that this man had lived four of my lifetimes and that he had been helping athletes like all of us in that room for at least three of my lifetimes. As he shared his stories of teams he had helped, the undefeated Miami Dolphins, the all-time Boston Bruins, the Stampeders of the '90s with Wally (teams I watched growing up in Calgary), the championship rings, it was like he was simply reading a list of the all-time greatest teams ever in history, and yet he was a part of all of them!

My first one-on-one conversation with Doc was over lunch and it was as though we were lifelong buds of 20 years! The following day, our next conversation over lunch, he revealed that he had spent the evening reading up about me online—which for the then 87-year-old, was quite impressive.

While I am on the topic of technology, would you believe that of every person that I have met in my entire football life and beyond—coaches, professors, teammates, friends, even my very own brothers—there are only two people that still message me before or after every game: my father and Ol' Frankie-boy!

Over the years, there was one specific time when the gravity of life was really weighing on me. Now my personal makeup is one that does not seek external conversation to work through issues, but on that day for some reason while I was driving, something in my head said, "Call Doc Frank." The man helped me dearly that day, dearly.

Listen, I could go on for another 500 words, 1,000 words, but what I really want to get across is this: I have had the great pleasure in my life to be around and befriend all-time great coaches, all-time great players, national leaders, world leaders, business leaders, academics, and without a shred of doubt I know that every single one of them could learn something from Doc Frank. If they were fortunate enough to get a moment of his generous time, they would certainly give the same glowing report that reads: this man knows, this man cares, this man will tell you he is no more special than any man/woman in the room, but that is only because he brought every man/woman in that room up to a special level.

I wrote this nomination without the standard recommendation letter structure, but rather in free verse because I wanted to genuinely portray the depth of the impact that this man has had on my life and the lives of those around me. I sincerely hope you will consider Doctor Francis Lodato as a future inductee to the CFHOF. Thank you for your time.

Regards,
Marco Iannuzzi

APPENDIX 2:

REFLECTIONS FROM ATHLETE CLIENTS OUTSIDE OF FOOTBALL AND HOCKEY

COMMENTARY FROM MICHELE SHARP, HEAD COACH, MANHATTAN COLLEGE

I had just gotten a coaching job at Manhattan College. Doc had just retired from Manhattan. He had gone to the men's office and they had shooed him off. They offered him to me. "Will it cost?"

He said, "It's free."

I said, "Yes."

He dove in 100% with the kids. I met him in 1992 and mental imagery was just taking form. I was very open to it. We had Gina Soma and she was our best player. He made an effort to get her on board. She tried it and her free throw percentage went from 60% to 85% from working with him.

He was so persistent with the team. Scheduled time with the players. Time in the practices. He did whatever he did. He walked them through the relaxation stuff and visualization. He was hard to say no to. He made a personal connection with them and then would say, "Give it a try." They saw results. He wasn't aggressive. Fatherly persistence. "I'm trying to help you. If it doesn't work let's try it together." He was always about the team.

He taught me how to do the relaxation and visualization techniques so I could do it with the players.

They saw it was working and wanted more time with him. And would ask for him.

He had made a bet with me. "If I win a ring (championship with Manhattan), I'll get you a Coach purse."

He was like a Dad to me. He was so supportive. He followed me to Kean University and he worked with me there. They all bought in. They were open to it.

He worked with my son, Michael. Frank was the only guy Michael would talk to.

He was always in my corner and wrote me a beautiful recommendation letter that I still have.

He always remembered my birthday. He would call me back whenever I called. He would say, "You're slacking." He said what I needed to hear and not necessarily what I wanted to hear.

COMMENTARY FROM ASHLEY BUEGE, SOFTBALL, NORTHWOOD UNIVERSITY

I was a student in college, 3,350 miles from home, playing on my school's softball team. I had been struggling with the "yips" since high school.

I remember going into Rollie Massimino's office, in tears and telling him how I just couldn't throw the ball from *here* to *there*. He told me he had the perfect person I could speak with, who had been helping his basketball team. I contacted Dr. Frank and made an appointment to meet with him.

I borrowed my roommate's pink Neon and drove to Dr. Frank's home. After knocking on the door I was greeted with a big smile and a warm *"Hello."* He asked me where I was from—I told him Vancouver. He said he knew it well and had just finished reading *The Sun* and *The Province* (the local newspapers).

Truthfully, I can't remember specifics in our sessions—though I do remember they helped. I remember the visualization helped and I was able to use what he taught me to control my throws. But what I remember most is Dr. Frank coming to watch my home games. Seeing him in the bleachers meant so much to me.

We built a 16-year friendship. We had many visits in Vancouver when he worked for the Lions. We went to football training camp, watched hockey games, and shared many meals. When I got married, we ended up moving a mile from his home. He got to know my family, and most special to me, my son, Shea, was lucky enough to meet him.

The last time I saw Dr. Frank, he gave me a BC Lions cap to give to my son, Shea, which now hangs on his bedroom wall.

Dr. Frank was a special man who touched the lives of many in a very positive way, including mine. His kindness, his genuineness, and friendship meant the world to me, and he will be someone I will carry with me for the rest of my life.

APPENDIX 3:

SELF-HYPNOSIS EXERCISE FROM DOC FRANK

INSTRUCTIONS FOR SELF-HYPNOSIS SESSION

Deep breathing is done with a breath that goes into the belly/abdomen. Try for a breath that is an inhale for four counts and an exhale for eight counts. A longer exhale tells the nervous system to relax.

Prior to doing the self-hypnosis exercise, complete the task analysis and be able to visualize it in your mind. The task is always visualized and executed perfectly.

During the session, if other thoughts arise or if you feel anxious, acknowledge the thoughts and feelings, thank them, and return to the breath and the visualization.

Ideally, the self-hypnosis is repeated daily. Set aside about 15-20 minutes for each session.

1. Sit or lie down in a comfortable position. Feel the chair or the support beneath you. Notice the temperature of the room. Observe your breath: inhale and exhale. No need to change it.
2. Close your eyes.
3. Pause.
4. Now deepen your breathing into the belly. (Inhale for four counts. Exhale for eight counts.)
5. Feel your body sinking down, completely relaxed.
6. The mind focuses on the inhale and exhale.
7. Enjoy the relaxation.
8. Inhale and exhale.

9. Now visualize a beautiful staircase with a handrail. There are 20 steps and with each step you'll take a single deep breath in and out.

10. Gently holding the handrail, step down, 20, breathe in, breathe out. Then step down, 19, breathe in, breathe out. Then step down, 18, breathe in, breathe out, etc.

11. When you're at the bottom of the stairs you're even more relaxed.

12. Pause: feel the deep relaxation. Breathe in and out.

13. Now gently erase the image of the staircase.

14. Visualize a large black curtain on a wall. In front of the curtain there is a white puffy feather floating left and right, right and left.

15. Follow the feather back and forth about 5-10 times.

16. Pause: feel the deep relaxation. Breathe in, breathe out.

17. Now gently erase the image of the curtain and the feather.

18. See yourself doing the task you have practiced.

     a. Each step is perfectly executed.
     b. Envision your success.
     c. Smile at all steps being completed perfectly.
     d. Breathe in and breathe out.
     e. Repeat the task five times.

19. If you feel any resistance or anxiety, focus again on the breath and then return to step 18.

20. After visualizing the task five times, see the staircase again. This time, go up the stairs. Step up, one, breathe in, breathe out; Step up, two, breathe in, breathe out, etc.

21. At 20, notice how relaxed you still are. Breathe in, breathe out.

22. Now you are ready to come back into the room.

23. Breathe in and breathe out.

24. Slowly and gently open your eyes.

APPENDIX 4:

MENTAL EXERCISE FOR THE JACKSONVILLE ICEMEN (ECHL)

ONE

Either seat yourself in a comfortable chair or lie down on a comfortable couch or bed. Close your eyes and take a very deep breath, releasing that breath slowly. Repeat this breathing exercise until you become physically relaxed. Feel the heaviness in your extremities and find yourself in a state of relaxation. Concentrate only on inhaling and exhaling. Do not permit any extraneous thoughts to enter into your mind. If you are seated, as you exhale, feel yourself sinking into your chair while your pelvic area is slowly pulling the rest of your body downward. If you are lying down, feel yourself free-falling through space. Once you have achieved this state, you are ready for the next step.

TWO

Enjoy the state of relaxation for a few moments and then visualize yourself standing at the top of a very deep staircase. Descend the staircase, one step at a time; with each step take a deep breath and exhale it slowly. When you have reached the bottom of the staircase (20 steps) you will be even more relaxed. Pause for a few seconds and then proceed to the next exercise.

THREE

Erase the image of the staircase and replace it with the image of a large black curtain. In front of this curtain, visualize a large, white, puffy feather floating slowly from left to right and from right to left. Repeat this 5 to 10 times until you are completely relaxed. Pause for a few seconds.

FOUR

Erase the image of the feather and curtain and replace them with the image of you perfectly executing each step in your task analysis. Repeat this five times.

When you are ready to step out on the ice, take a series of deep breaths, exhale slowly, and execute the steps in your task analysis.

APPENDIX 5:

THE LIFE OF FRANCIS J. LODATO, PH.D.
MAY 27, 1926 TO OCTOBER 8, 2021

Francis Joseph Lodato died at home on October 8, 2021. He was 95 years old and lived in Palm Beach Gardens, Fla.

Born in Brooklyn, N.Y., in 1926 to Gennaro and Marietta (Adami), he had six siblings, all of whom had immigrated from Italy. Frank attended Nativity Elementary School, LaSalle Academy, and graduated from St. John's University with Bachelor's, Master's, and Ph.D. degrees. He also earned a Master's Degree from Fordham University. The youngest in his family, he became the first to attend college. During his teens, he worked at A & L Manufacturing, a company founded by his brothers that remained in his family until 1970.

Dr. Lodato taught at Manhattan College from 1968 to 1990. Prior to Manhattan, he also taught at St. John's University, Seton Hall University, and the College of Mount St. Vincent. During sabbatical leaves and summer sessions, he taught at Biscayne College (now St. Thomas University), Our Lady of the Lake University, and Barry University. At Manhattan, he served as a Professor of Education and was at one time Director of the Evening Division and Summer School. He contributed articles to the *American Journal of Clinical Hypnosis* under editor Milton Erickson. For 28 years, he was a consulting psychologist for the Diocese of Brooklyn at Cathedral College of the Immaculate Conception in Douglaston, Queens, and in a similar capacity for the Archdiocese of New York at St. John Neumann Residence. In recognition of his service to the Church, Frank was honored to be a Knight Grand Cross of the Order of the Holy Sepulchre. He also consulted at Lincoln Hall Boys

Haven for 10 years and was school psychologist for the Bedford Public Schools in the early 1960s.

Through his training in counseling psychology, "Dr Frank" single-handedly developed an expertise in sports psychology, working with athletes in the NFL, CFL, NBA, NHL and AHL, as well as several Olympians. He worked with the New York Giants, Philadelphia Eagles, Montreal Alouettes, Calgary Stampeders, British Columbia Lions, Orlando Magic, Los Angeles Kings, New Jersey Devils, Boston Bruins, New Haven Nighthawks, Orlando Solar Bears, Detroit Vipers, Albany River Rats, and numerous athletes on an individual basis. He was an integral part of 10 championships with professional teams, including Stanley Cup titles with the Devils (1995) and Bruins (2011) as well as three Grey Cups with the Stampeders and two with the Lions. He is part of an elite group of people who earned championships in both the CFL and NHL, and the only one to achieve it in the same year.

He was a curious and thoughtful person, and one of his passions was writing. Frank co-authored two books — *Creating Your Christian Engagement* and *Growing Up Loved*, both with John Barry Ryan; *But We Were 17 and 0*, with his son Raymond; *Eboli to Brooklyn, One Way*, with his daughter Denise; and an upcoming memoir with his daughter Janice. He was the author of both scholarly articles and frequent columns in *The New York Times*, *Fairfield County Catholic*, *The Newtown Bee*, *New Haven Register*, and other publications. He hosted a radio show on sports psychology on WLAD entitled "From the Sports Couch."

He first visited Italy in 1986 when he was 60 years old, and enjoyed connecting with relatives whom he had not known until this time of his life. Their warmth and hospitality provided a source of happiness. He was an avid believer in phone contact as a primary form of communication and would speak to those closest to him daily.

Frank was married to Patricia (Casey) for 64 years and they raised three children — Denise, Raymond (Bronwyn), and Janice (Christopher), and doted on their four grandchildren. They lived in New York, Connecticut, and Florida during their marriage.

BIBLIOGRAPHY

Ackles, Bob, and Ian Mulgrew. 2010. *The Water Boy: From the Sidelines to the Owner's Box: Inside the CFL, the XFL and the NFL*. Wiley.

Carson, Harry. 2011. *Captain for Life: My Story as a Hall of Fame Linebacker*. St. Martin's Press.

Carson, Harry. 1987. *Point of Attack: The Defense Strikes Back*. McGraw-Hill.

Giuliani, Rudolph. 2002. *Leadership*. Hyperion.

Lodato, Francis, J., and Denise T. Lodato. 2018. *Eboli to Brooklyn–One Way*.

Lodato, Francis, J., and Janice E. Lodato. "An Ethical Model for Sport Psychologists." *Interamerican Journal of Psychology* (*Revista interamericana de psicología*). 1992.

Lodato, Francis, J., and Raymond M. Lodato. 1986. *But We Were 17 and 0*. IQ Publications.

Mack, Gary. 2022. *Mind Gym: An Athlete's Guide to Inner Excellence*. McGraw Hill.

Mallozzi, Vincent M., "Basketball: Far Above and Beyond the Call of Coaching." *The New York Times*. March 19, 1995.

Powell, Colin, and Tony Koltz. 2012. *It Worked for Me: In Life and Leadership*. Harper.

Reid, Angus. 2018. *Thank You Coach: Learning How to Live by Being Taught How to Play*. ABR Media.

Saunders, Tom. 2005. *Golf: Lower Your Score with Mental Training*. Crown House Publishing Ltd.

Saunders, Tom. 1997. *Golf: The Mind-Body Connection: How to Lower your Score with Mental Training*, Mind-Body Golf, Ltd.

Summitt, Pat. 1999. *Reach for the Summit: The Definite Dozen System for Succeeding at Whatever You Do*. Crown Currency.

Tart, Charles, T. 1972. *Altered States of Consciousness*. Anchor Books.

REVIEW INQUIRY

Hey, it's Janice here.

I hope you've enjoyed the book, finding it both useful and fun. I have a favor to ask you.

Would you consider giving it a rating wherever you bought the book? Online book stores are more likely to promote a book when they feel good about its content, and reader reviews are a great barometer for a book's quality.

So please go to the website of wherever you bought the book, search for my name and the book title, and leave a review. If able, perhaps consider adding a picture of you holding the book. That increases the likelihood your review will be accepted!

Many thanks in advance,
Janice Lodato

WILL YOU SHARE THE LOVE?

GET THIS BOOK FOR A FRIEND, ASSOCIATE, OR FAMILY MEMBER!

If you have found this book valuable and know others who would find it useful, consider buying them a copy as a gift. Special bulk discounts are available if you would like your whole team or organization to benefit from reading this. Just contact email: info@janicelodato.com or visit http://www.janicelodato.com.

ABOUT THE AUTHORS

Francis J. Lodato, Ph.D., graduated from St. John's University with bachelor's, master's, and Ph.D. degrees, and earned a second master's from Fordham University. Dr. Lodato taught at Manhattan College in New York from 1968 to 1990. Prior to Manhattan, he taught at St. John's University, Seton Hall University, and the College of Mount St. Vincent. During sabbatical leaves and summer sessions, he taught at Biscayne College (now  St. Thomas University), Our Lady of the Lake University, and Barry University. At Manhattan, he served as a professor of education and was, at one time, director of the evening division and summer school. He contributed articles to the *American Journal of Clinical Hypnosis* under editor Milton Erickson. For 28 years, he was a consulting psychologist for the Diocese of Brooklyn at Cathedral College of the Immaculate Conception in Douglaston, Queens, and in a similar capacity for the Archdiocese of New York at St. John Neumann Residence.

Through his training in counseling psychology and clinical hypnosis, "Dr. Frank" developed an expertise in sports psychology, working with athletes in the NFL, CFL, NBA, NHL, and AHL, as well as several Olympians. He worked with the New York Giants, Philadelphia Eagles, Montreal Alouettes, Calgary Stampeders, British Columbia Lions, Orlando Magic, Los Angeles Kings, New Jersey Devils, Boston Bruins, New Haven Nighthawks, Orlando Solar Bears, Detroit Vipers, Albany River Rats, and numerous athletes on an individual basis. He was an integral part of 10 championships with professional teams, including Stanley Cup titles with the Devils (1995) and Bruins (2011), as well as three Grey Cups with the Stampeders and two with the Lions. He is part of an elite group of people who earned championships in both the CFL and NHL, and the only one to achieve it in the same year.

Dr. Lodato coauthored books—*Creating Your Christian Engagement* and *Growing Up Loved: A Guide for the Family*, both with John Barry Ryan; *But We Were 17 and 0*, with his son, Raymond; and *Eboli to Brooklyn—One Way*, with his daughter, Denise. He was the author of scholarly articles and frequent columns in the *New York Times*, *Fairfield County Catholic*, *Newtown Bee*, *New Haven Register*, and other publications. He hosted a radio show on sports psychology on WLAD titled *From the Sports Couch*.

Dr. Lodato passed away in October 2021.

Janice E. Lodato, M.A., coauthored with her father, Frank Lodato, "An Ethical Model for Sport Psychology" in the *Interamerican Journal of Psychology*. A graduate of Bowling Green State University with a master's degree in philosophy and a bachelor's degree in philosophy and communications from Trinity University (San Antonio, Texas), Janice is currently a project manager working with software development teams. Janice is also a Reiki teacher and a certified yoga teacher. Previously, she taught philosophy at Albuquerque Technical-Vocational Institute (medical ethics and business ethics) and was a teaching assistant at Bowling Green State University (Intro to Philosophy and Philosophy of Death and Dying). She also taught photography at Delaware College of Art and Design (digital and film), Wilmington; Oasis Lifelong Learning Center, Tucson; and Newark Arts Alliance, Delaware.

You can reach Janice at: www.janicelodato.com